CULTURE, CREA
AND ENVIRON

Nature, Culture and Literature
05

General Editors:

Hubert van den Berg (University of Groningen)
Axel Goodbody (University of Bath)
Marcel Wissenburg (University of Nijmegen)

Advisory Board:

Jonathan Bate (University of Warwick)
Hartmut Böhme (Humboldt University, Berlin)
Heinrich Detering (University of Kiel)
Andrew Dobson (Keele University)
Marius de Geus (Leiden University)
Terry Gifford (University of Leeds)
Demetri Kantarelis (Assumption College, Worcester MA)
Richard Kerridge (Bath Spa University College)
Michiel Korthals (Wageningen University)
Svend Erik Larsen (University of Aarhus)
Patrick Murphy (University of Central Florida)
Kate Rigby (Monash University)
Avner de-Shalit (Hebrew University Jerusalem)
Piers Stephens (Michigan State University)
Nina Witoszek (University of Oslo)

CULTURE, CREATIVITY AND ENVIRONMENT

NEW ENVIRONMENTALIST CRITICISM

Edited by

Fiona Becket and Terry Gifford

Rodopi

Amsterdam - New York, NY 2007

Cover Design: Erick de Jong

The paper on which this book is printed meets the requirements of "ISO
9706:1994, Information and documentation - Paper for documents -
Requirements for permanence".

ISBN-13: 978-90-420-2250-8
©Editions Rodopi B.V., Amsterdam - New York, NY 2007
Printed in the Netherlands

Contents

Introduction

Fiona Becket & Terry Gifford

Culture, Creativity and Environment: new environmentalist criticism is a collection of new work which examines the intersection between philosophy, literature, visual art, film and the environment at a time of environmental crisis. Ecocriticism, described nearly a decade ago by critic Richard Kerridge as "the new environmentalist cultural criticism", calls for a poetics derived from the interface of imagination and ethics, but predominantly informed by modern environmentalism (Kerridge 1998: 5). In this light, the current volume is a work of ecocriticism, although not all the contributors would wish to define themselves first and foremost as ecocritics. In part, the struggle to escape such narrow designations is demonstrated by the diversity of ideas in the book, and by the range of cultural media that have stimulated these ideas.

If it is the human imagination in its diverse technological modes that might offer some practical solutions to the environmental crisis that our species has produced, the political will to implement new greener technologies will only come, it could be argued, from a popular shift in ways of thinking about our relationship with our home planet. As we re-imagine what that relationship might be, and also re-examine what we value in the relationship, we need to bear in mind that what we represent in our words and images is a material world which much discourse in the humanities over the last two decades, at least, has dismissed or side-lined from discussion.

Literature of the 'wilderness' and the pastoral ideal have been extensively treated in ecocritical studies, in the main from North America. We need not start, however, by conflating 'nature' and 'wilderness', as the current book demonstrates. New work is needed which responds to the recent resurgence of interest within the humanities regarding the intersection of ethics and aesthetics, particularly in response to environmental crisis. This volume of essays represents the thought of a range of individuals from differing intellectual and cultural backgrounds and acknowledges the necessity for, and importance of, environmental political critique in the field of literary and cultural studies. As a collection it has its origins in a conference organised by the Association for the Study of Literature and the Environment (ASLE) which took place at the Bretton Hall campus of the University of Leeds in 2002. Not all of the essays printed here, it must be said, were presented at the conference, and those that were have undergone radical revision in the intervening time. The book, however, like the conference, attempts to juxtapose critical and creative work in the context of a project which is only too aware of ethical imperatives. This book is unusual, then, in the way in which the 'imaginative', 'creative', element is privileged, notwithstanding the creativity of rigorous cultural criticism. Genuinely interdisciplinary, this book aims to be inclusive in its discussions of diverse cultural media (different literary genres, art forms and film for instance), which offer thoughtful and thought-provoking critiques of our relationships with the environment. The essay by Val Plumwood is a challenge to dominant philosophical discourse at the levels of content and language. Judith Tucker, an artist and an academic, examines the contours of her painting in the context of a meditation on place, experience, and the activity of painting as a mode of 'dislocation'. Judith Rugg recalls conversations with artist Anya Gallaccio in her dissertation on living sculpture.

Other essays collected in this volume offer original interpretations of a range of texts which are perceived to identify, in diverse ways, a heightened consciousness (in the artist, writer and thinker) of the materiality and, often, the limits, of the world (as the place of our dwelling). These essays develop further some of the debates that currently characterise ecocriticism, including the status and character of ecocriticism itself. They attempt, sometimes implicitly, sometimes explicitly, to decentre the human subject from certain kinds of intellectual investigation. Some deal with representation, some with discourse, and others deal with 'world'. There is also speculation about the future agendas for ecocriticism, aware as the contributors are of the limited reach of current debates. All together the essays demonstrate the opportunities ahead for the emerging field of ecocriticism in its heterogeneity, within and beyond the academy.

While this volume was inspired by individuals working independently within what could broadly be termed the new environmentalist criticism, it does not seek to define or delimit 'new environmentalism', seeing itself, rather, as a contribution to green cultural critique with an emphasis on writing, film and the visual arts and philosophy. Within the humanities separate discourses have developed that inhibit dialogue between critical analysis, creative writing and the performing and visual arts, for example. Such separations increase when one considers the discourses within which these imaginative activities continue to be critically debated. Ecology provides a model from the sciences for bringing diverse specialisms into productive dialogue, and the urgency of the cultural debate about environmental crisis has provided the trigger for the increase in recent years of an environmental cultural criticism.

So while the earlier volume in this series, *Nature in Literary and Cultural Studies: Transatlantic Conversations on Ecocriticism*, edited by Catrin Gersdorf and Sylvia Mayer (2006), deals with the theoretical, national and ethical implications of the representation of nature in everyday culture, the present volume evaluates the aesthetic and ethical issues thrown into relief by imaginative engagements with environment. As Val Plumwood points out, our ability to transcend the ethical and aesthetic categories and discourses that have contributed to our alienation from our environment is dependant upon an enlargement of our imaginative capacities. In one sense this book recognises the attempts of creative artists, in a range of media and from a range of cultures, to prompt and probe that imaginative enlargement. At the same time, meeting the challenges offered by the deep connections envisioned by creative artists requires imaginative and linguistic expansion from critical commentators. In a modest way this book might contribute to what Ted Hughes, speaking of the imagination of each new child, described as "nature's chance to correct culture's error" (Hughes 1994: 149). It is hoped and expected, then, that the essays collected here will promote and provoke discussion about the task of environmental cultural analysis, but the volume also acknowledges the futility of keeping such debates within the 'ivory tower' – ultimately 'new environmentalism' as discourse intersects with a desire for action at micro and macro levels.

The book opens with a *tour de force* in the form of Val Plumwood's highly original investigation into the nature of stone, "reclaiming", as she says, "agency and intentionality for matter". In part a continuation of aspects of her previous work, 'Journey to the Heart of Stone' presents us with a challenge to the values of what Plumwood calls the scientific reductionism of instrumental culture. It is a chapter which attempts to synthesise ecological rationality with "radical-romantic openness" in approaching the material world – "re-enspiriting matter". As she has argued, most extensively in *Environmental Culture: the Ecological Crisis of Reason* (2002), the dominant forms of rationality are inadequate to the task set itself by green cultural critique, and 'Journey to the Heart of Stone' embodies a forceful response. And crucially, this retort, for such it is, reveals the extent to which writing acts to disrupt the power of "human-centred reductionism" and to disturb its authority in our instrumental culture. How fitting, then, that Plumwood's original and persuasive dissertation should begin this volume of essays which take as their themes literature, painting, sculpture, film and philosophy within a context of critical green writing and new environmentalist thought.

John Parham's essay on John Stuart Mill asks "what is (ecological) nature?" in an ecological reading of the *Principles of Political Economy*. Beginning with an account of the extent to which Romanticism informed Mill's thought on social questions, Parham investigates the close and logical connections between Mill's political economy, his view in 'On the Definition of Political Economy' that physical and mental laws act in concurrence with one and other, and produce Mill's emphasis on a conception of "quality of life" that is recognisable in current social ecology. Mill's political economy depends on an understanding of questions of sustainability that engage us now: the shortage of "natural agents" that accompanies industrial and agricultural 'advancement'. As Parham argues, "Mill's socialism broadly corresponds to the emphasis on sustainable, decentralised governance in contemporary ecological social philosophy" seen ultimately in terms of the "stationary state" and its fusion of political economy and ideals gleaned from romanticism. Given that Mill's emphasis on nature remains dominated by a sense of its resource value (problematic for some environmentalists), Parham proceeds to examine Mill's interrogation of the meaning of nature in the essay 'Nature' (1874), and concludes that his arguments constitute "a broadly ecological conception of nature", one that ultimately acknowledges the interdependence of humanity and the physical world. This, suggests Parham, reveals Mill's legacy to have been "an ontological understanding of the human place in nature as an essential prerequisite to defining green political economy".

Judith Rugg's essay examines the self-conscious disruption of received ideas about women and nature embodied in three 'garden' works by the sculptor and land artist Anya Gallaccio that used plants and flowers as their principal media. The garden, as "intimate domestic space" and "refuge" and "extension of female domestic labour", is subject to a critique by works which themselves dismantle the dominant sense of gardens as "cultural enclaves against fenceless anarchic nature". Informed by the writing of Julia Kristeva, in particular the essay 'Women's Time', Rugg considers how Gallaccio's works play with different concepts of time within a gendered debate, and how they allow a concentration on diverse cultural constructions of the feminine. Growth and degeneration are central to these works which use 'live' nature in their composition and which, hence, "blur the boundaries of culture and nature".

Keeping house, "defining and sustaining a meaningful relation to our natural environment" is Hannes Bergthaller's theme in his ecocritical reading of Marilynne Robinson's novel *Housekeeping*. Having first established the traditions that underpin Emersonian environmentalism, in Robinson's novel, suggests Bergthaller, "the experience of wholeness and stability is available only in the domain of art." In contrast, "the phenomenal world is a quicksand of deception, disappointment, decay, and inevitable loss". This essay questions the assumptions of the environmental movement in the United States to the extent that they are perceived to be "built on the conceptual heritage of New England Transcendentalism".

Where Emerson stresses the need for a language in which to express and understand nature, William Langland, writing in a much earlier tradition of course, develops the notion in *Piers Plowman* of "the world as a book". In her essay Gillian Rudd examines Langland's use of this literary topos and the complex condition of viewing humanity as both (detached) 'reader' of nature, and included within (human) nature. Rudd skilfully permits us to think about the impetus in Langland's world to 'Do well' (embodied using allegory in the poem) in terms which raise questions about (in today's terms) environmental responsibility. Langland both deploys the topos of world-as-book in *Piers Plowman*, and offers a critique (via his dreamer, Wil, often in dialogue with Reson who replaces the more benign Kynde), of the implications of that perspective.

In his essay Greg Garrard examines the relationship between eco*criticism* and *eco*criticism in the context of an analysis of the environmental dimension of Ibsen's *An Enemy of the People* and shows to what extent the theme of pollution – actual as well as spiritual – informs the central aesthetic of the play. Garrard begins his critique with a discussion of the deep ecology of Joseph Meeker, drawing on Meeker's 'The Comic Mode' (the "analogy between comic survival and evolutionary adaptation"), and examines the assumptions of this position in relation to the values of Ibsen's Dr Stockmann. Ibsen's concentration, via Stockmann's stated values, on eugenics is juxtaposed with Meeker's development of the notion of survival in comedy in a discussion of the human animal, and that bizarre and discomforting formula, 'eugenic comedy'.

Axel Goodbody examines the notion of the wild animal developed in the fiction of Otto Alscher, with a particular emphasis on the role of the hunter in German culture. Goodbody provides a succinct survey of the implications and resonances of the hunt, including its socio-political dimension. However, his principal area of interest is "the [...] complex relationship with wild animals and nature exemplified by hunters" which concerns itself with questions of exploitation, 'stewardship', even conservation, and power alongside a related debate on what constitutes 'natural' behaviour, with reference to the writing of Ortega y Gasset and Erich Fromm. Alscher, the 'hunter-writer', is then established in historical and geographical contexts, prior to an examination of the representation of the animal in his writing in an essay that explores the paradox of the hunter and nature lover.

Also in an engagement with literary texts, in particular Yann Martel's *Life of Pi* and Barbara Gowdy's *The White Bone*, Graham Huggan combines an analysis of the representation of the animal with an examination of the interconnectedness of postcolonial and ecocritical discourses. Huggan shares with Garrard an interest in the limits and possibilities of ecocriticism, and with Goodbody an interest in questions of wildness, animality and representation. The two novels at the heart of this analysis can be understood as "attempts to decolonise the beast fable" with abstracted animal figures transformed into "ecological subjects", and leads into a discussion about the constructedness of animals and the dualities of "animal-endorsing" and "animal-sceptical" texts. Huggan concludes by stressing the urgency of forms of "active exchange between the critical projects of postcolonialism and ecocriticism", and finalises his essay with a look at the future of English Studies and the tensions between 'pan' and 'post-humanist' approaches to research in the field.

Matthew Jarvis examines the environmental aesthetics of two sequences in Barry MacSweeney's *The Book of Demons*, 'Pearl' and 'The Book of Demons', and the poetic use of urban environments ("the generic locus of suffering") in one, and the moorland environment (the Allen Valley, "the organic world", "non-colonised") in the other. In his critique of MacSweeney's representation of 1950's rural England Jarvis draws on Frederic Jameson's discussion of postmodern nostalgia but argues that 'Pearl' does not "recall" stylistic iconography or resort to a benign "retrospective simulation" that "eclipses the present (and all of its problems)". For the poet the Allen Valley is potentially a locus of personal salvation, rather "the place in and through which salvation may be found" (reinforced by reference to MacSweeney's medieval intertext, the alliterative poem *Pearl*).

Judith Tucker is a painter whose essay, 'Painting Landscape: Mediating Dislocation', is a meditation on place and painting, the writing of which is a "texted equivalent" to the artist's studio practice: "an interweaving of [the artist's] activities with considerations of related issues and references both visual and literary". It becomes a "genealogy" of her "thinking/practice". The essay title is inspired by a passage from Marion Milner's *On Not Being Able to Paint* on what Tucker calls "the illusion of connectedness" with a landscape at the moment of painting. Then, in a reflection on her origins, Tucker examines the relation between a felt rootlessness and the painting of landscape as a form of mediating absence and longing. Finally, attention is turned to actual and notional ruptures in the work itself, in its form and composition, the breaks which are implicit in the work – between the landscape and studio, maker and viewer, viewer and painting.

The visual theme is pursued in a different medium and context in Guinevere Narraway's essay on Luis Trenker's film *Der verlorene Sohn* (1934), of interest in part because of its form – a hybrid of the *Bergfilm* and the *Heimatfilm*, "two genres which specifically foreground the relationship between the human community of the *Heimat* and the natural environment". Narraway examines critical analyses of the blood and soil ideology of the film and argues that "the reactionary and racialist discourses in this film are not a result of anything immanent in nature itself." She concludes, "[r]ather, they are a product of the consumption and mechanical reproduction of nature". This thesis is examined in the remainder of the essay with reference latterly to the work of Arnold Fanck, an influence on Trenker.

Just as the volume begins with a philosophical investigation into the limits of philosophy, so it concludes with Louise Westling's essay on 'Heidegger and Merleau-Ponty: Ecopoetics and the Problem of Humanism'. Westling discusses Heidegger's "reactionary Humanism" and his hierarchical notion of the human subject, human dwelling and *Dasein* in contrast to Merleau-Ponty's "embodied phenomenology" and "genuinely ecological view of the human situation and poetry's function". In the course of the discussion Westling re-examines the relevance of Heidegger and Merleau-Ponty for ecocriticism, with particular reference to Heidegger's essay 'Building, Dwelling, Thinking' and Merleau-Ponty's *Phenomenology of Perception*. For both, the issue of language, in particular poetic language, is central. Hence, Westling brings together, at the end of the volume, and in a robust but dispassionate way, the elements of criticism and creativity which have been taken on diverse journeys in the course of these wide-ranging chapters.

The editors of *Culture, Creativity and Environment: new environmentalist criticism* would like to thank the Series Editors and all those at Rodopi who assisted in the publication of this book. Axel Goodbody was especially generous with his offers of advice, help and practical assistance regarding the formatting of the volume.

Bibliography

Hughes, Ted. 1994. *Winter Pollen*. London: Faber and Faber.
Richard Kerridge. 1998. 'Introduction', in Kerridge, Richard and Neil Sammells (eds). 1998. *Writing the Environment: Ecocriticism and Literature* London and New York: Zed Books Ltd. 1-9.

Journey to the Heart of Stone

Val Plumwood

Abstract

Can environmental writing help break down the wall of human/nature dualism that has long separated western culture from the larger-than-human-world? Critical thought can help by tackling concepts like anthropomorphism and sentimentality whose main function is to delegitimate boundary breakdown between the human and non-human. But creative writing can also play an important part by making visible new possibilities for radically open and non-reductive ways to experience the world. Western philosophy, with its obsessive focus on human consciousness, has only with difficulty extended respect and consideration beyond the human to the human-like – animals and living things, excluding items like rivers or stones.

In western culture and philosophy, stones have not been given an honoured place, and mind is seen as the pinnacle of existence, a pinnacle our species and ours alone, has climbed. For we moderns, stones are insignificant and anonymous, often in our way, but sometimes useful for our projects when torn from their place and history, crushed to pave roads and paths. Stone is dead matter, a mere resource or pure enabler – its character uninteresting, expressive of nothing but meaningless coincidence. Yet even the smallest stone represents an amazing conjunction of earth forces whose complexity puts to shame the puny puzzlings of humankind. If stone is the skeleton of our planet, and the dirt its flesh, humanity is an insignificant piece of the biota, a microscopic flea in the jungle of flora and fauna that lives upon its body. The culture that refuses honour to stones refuses honour also to the great earth forces that have shaped and placed them. The eviction of spirit and honour from stones and from the earth is one of the greatest crimes of modernity.

This is an account of how we can see stones differently, as individuals, as makers of meaning, as prophets, teachers and tellers of tales, and of how Plumwood found all this and more in the Heartstone, an unusual stone with impressive powers of metaphor.

The cultural tasks for a critical green ecological writing are many, but should include opening readers to ways of challenging the experiential framework of dead and silent matter entrenched by the sado-dispassionate rationality of scientific reductionism. Instrumental culture makes of its objects of attention a terra nullius, a prior vacancy, the better to inscribe its own ends. The Romantic movement often represented a partial and limited challenge to dominant reductionist frameworks of experience and rationality, and we must take care that its dismissal is not used to delegitimate writing which gives us other ways of seeing.

Romantic rejectionism, rather than dismissing the entire endeavour, is better directed against certain dematerialising and backward tendencies in Romanticism, and its failure to adequately challenge dualisms that separate use and respect, reason and emotion. Perhaps eco-writing can help heal this rift and show us routes to a new synthesis of ecological rationality with radical-romantic openness in writing about the world of experience. This would be rational and ecological in the sense I explicated in my last book, as developing countervailing forms of rationality to the sado-dispassionate scientism in current vogue – for example, forms in which you approach the world with the aspirations and expectations of the lover, for exchange of mutual nourishment with a lively and respected partner.

Part of this project is the re-enchantment or re-enspiriting of the realm designated material (which includes reclaiming agency and intentionality for matter). There are several caveats here, needed to ensure that romantic mistakes are not repeated, that the challenge it represents to instrumental culture is not subverted by dominant agendas and concepts. A corresponding critical task is discrediting bullying concepts and jargon, such as anthropomorphism, that have helped delegitimate richly intentional ways of understanding the world. We, in the dominant culture, need to find new critical and experiential bases that enable us to transcend this impoverishing ideology and self-confirming reductionist practice (see Weston 1996).

Caveats: it has to be emphasised that the project of re-enspiriting matter can only be in good faith if it is accompanied by, even led by, the re-materialisation of spirit as speaking matter. Instrumental culture has prepared an exceptional place for speaking matter, (which romanticism did not sufficiently disrupt), as the exceptional context of the fairy-tale, or the irrational space of the eerie and haunted. But if it is the space of everyday wonder and quotidian enchantment (and why aim for less?) that is in need of reclamation and recovery, ethical and philosophical theories that legitimate a rich intentionality for as wide as possible a range of non-human actors and descriptors will probably prove most useful (see Plumwood 1993). This would bring such a writing project into a convergent course with that recent radical tendency in environmental philosophy that has stressed that respect and attention must go 'all the way down' and need have no boundary or limitation (see Plumwood 2002; Weston 2003; Birch 1993). As Deborah Rose puts it, "nothing is nothing" (Rose 1996: 31).

A radically intentionalising anti-reductionist writing of the world might make visible whole new interspecies dialogues, dramas and projects previously unimaginable, that can re-open the door to the world of wonder. It might dispel the sado-dispassionate 'imaginary' (Brennan 1996) that has supported and naturalised the post-enlightenment illusion of human monopoly of the mindful, cultural, intentional elements in the world, of science as a searchlight piercing a dark formless universe – thus freeing us to re-write the earth as sacred, earth exploration as pilgrimage, earth knowledge as revelation. To be honest and solid, such a writing must be grounded in corresponding cultural practices that can re-materialise spirit as everyday wonder and material, bodily labour.

Traditional western thought has identified, as a major plank of its rationality, closely limiting objects of constraint and concern, often confining concepts of agency to humanised 'subjects' that extend the marks of a human consciousness. As I argued in *Environmental Culture: the Ecological Crisis of Reason* (2002), it is no coincidence that such reductionisms minimise the space allowed the Other, and maximise the extent of the 'empire of mere things' over which Enlightenment Man claims mastery, and hence available (as terra nullius) to the colonising, instrumentalising and self-maximising rationality of the market and commodity culture. But a radical writing project should encourage us to think beyond these boundaries, to reinvest with speech, agency and meaning the silenced ones, including the earth and its very stones, cast as the most lifeless and inconsiderable members of the earth community.

How can we re-present experience in ways that honour the agency and creativity of the more-than-human world? This big work of cultural change is, above all, a task for writing. Much of the power human-centred reductionism has over us is gained by using concepts like 'anthropomorphism' to enforce segregated and polarised vocabularies that rob the non-human world of agency and the possibility of speech, with departures from reductionist standards declared irrational or superstitious. Writing is an important place to disrupt this power. Again, the marks of human-centredness include denying and minimising the agency of those others on whom we depend, and this plays a big role in our inability to understand our ecological plight. A decentring program could not only give us a more modest sense of our human role, one that cultivates more self-reflection and gratitude for the support and bounty the non-human world provides for us, but also lead to a widening of our sensibilities beyond the conventional boundaries of the human-like, towards inhuman elements of the world.

1. Stone Sagas

Such a project would not be one that based respect on a classed-up, distant admiration for the unusually large and impressive – the grand cliff or gorge – but could recover a sense of wonder for the quotidian earth and the least of its children. For even the smallest stone represents an amazing conjunction of earth forces whose complexity puts to shame the puny puzzlings of humankind. In Chinese philosophy, stones have spirit and narrative, or energetic power and identity (chi). The Japanese honour stone enough to make gardens of it. Yet in western culture, stones have not been given an honoured place, and mind is seen as the pinnacle of existence, a pinnacle our species, and ours alone, has climbed. For we moderns, stones are insignificant and anonymous, often in our way, but occasionally useful for our projects when torn from their place and history, crushed to pave roads and paths. Stone is dead matter – a mere resource or pure enabler – its character unremarkable, expressive of nothing but meaningless coincidence. Yet if stone is the skeleton of our planet, and the dirt his flesh, humanity is an insignificant piece of the biota, a microscopic flea in the jungle of flora and fauna that lives upon her body.

There are dissidents, of course, to the dominant culture's devaluation of stones. Even among Anglos there are odd 'stone-freaks' – stone students, stone builders and stone venturers among them. But not many, even among western dissidents, would come to think along the lines of American Indian philosopher Vine Deloria. Deloria tells us that for his people the universe is experienced as

> alive and not as dead or inert. Thus Indians knew that stones were the most perfect beings because they were self-contained entities that had resolved their social relationships and possessed great knowledge about how every other entity should live. (Deloria 1999: 34).

Stones as the most perfect beings, not restless, like beings with unresolved social conflicts – this sort of understanding would never occur to us in the modern west. First, because we would automatically rank humans as the most perfect beings. Second, because we have forgotten how to reverence stones as teachers and travellers from worlds beyond our time, ancestral creators who made the character of their place. The culture that refuses honour to stones, refuses honour also to the great earth forces that have shaped and placed them. The eviction of spirit and honour from stones and from the earth's body is one of the great crimes of modernity.

In Western philosophy stones are nothing. Stones are at the bottom of the pile in moral consideration according to most versions of environmental ethics, not even registering zero on the scale of ethical attention – unless they are lucky enough to get into the category of cultural objects by being inscribed by humans or somehow attracting their cultural attention, when they might be held to have 'aesthetic value' or 'heritage value'. (These rankings reveal a certain narrowness and human-centredness to the discipline.) Unsurprisingly, given this bias, we seldom encounter stones as individuals, as makers of meaning and metaphor, as prophets, teachers and tellers of tales, in the way of the peoples from whose experience Deloria writes.

Lacking western reductionism and insensitivity, Deloria's culture could imaginatively leap the gulf between limited animal horizons and the vast time-scale of stone. From a human-centred and animal-centred perspective, stone appears as lack – lack of mind, lack of life, and lack of mobility. But to a more self-reflective culture, stone is not lack; stones do have powers of mobility, as Deloria tells us, although they do not need to use them. It is we humans who lack balance, moderation and calm, we humans who have an excess of mobility. This excess (in which, among all animals, modern humans are most excessive) has practical consequences: it means we seldom get to develop relationships with particular local stones, or glimpse the immense forces that have formed them. So we have less sense of our place in the universe, of our significance in the scheme of things, and this fosters delusions of human grandeur that can be as impoverishing as they are dangerous.

1.1 Using Stone

One place to start expanding our sensitivity to stone is with the sort of radical openness to the Other we tend to associate with the unreality of magic, together with the naivety and primitiveness of childhood story, where stones speak and give advice. That we confine this wonder to fairy stories speaks volumes about the instrumental reductionism we have normalised as adult life. It is a common mistake to assume that projects providing for the needs of daily life require the instrumental mode. No project needs to be undertaken in a mean, arrogant spirit of closure to the potential and agency of the material, of praising only the sides of materials that will further some fixed, predetermined end of ours, and ridding the world of whatever goes against it.

Stone students and venturers admire and learn from stones by climbing on and physically encountering them. In the conventional recreational model, such people make use of stones instrumentally, as a means to their own improvement and enjoyment, changing them to fit whatever concrete form is desired. For this instrumental model, no constraints or demands are imposed by the stone Other's existence or maintenance, and the result is liberty to use others for whatever purpose strikes your fancy. Even at this level, the monological freedom of instrumentalism is self-centred, and attended by irresponsibility, emptiness and the loss of meaning.

The psychological distance of instrumentalism means you can change the stone Other without risk of mutuality – being changed in turn by that other. But the real stone lover takes stones seriously as ends in themselves, attending to them as beings in their own right and key constituents of their place. Both pleasure and significance may be the more intense for climbers who can see themselves not as primarily using stones but as being in conversation with them, physical intimacy being a way to bring over the stone's own remarkable features and formations. Such people can talk of stones in the dialogical terms of encounter.

Great stone formations are impressive and can be admired from a respectful distance, in the mode of majesty. Although it goes against the dominant instrumental grain, we can relate to less majestic stones in a respectful way even while using them for a human end, like building a small stone shelter. This calls for some struggle both with stone devaluation and with the dominant commodity culture that strives to hyper-separate use and respect, nature and culture, user and used. The 'foundstone' worker must be sensitive both to the individuality of stones, in shape, for example, and to their membership of a kind, to differences in parent material indicating strength and malleability. A stone-using project is best undertaken in a spirit of openness to what stones have to teach, and of attending carefully to each stone, its individuality and genre. Through such disciplines of moral epistemology, we become both better wall builders, and better at recognising stones as prophets and honoured teachers that can make metaphors that guide us on our personal journeys through life, love and death.

It was in such a spirit that I began the project of building my house from found stone. The location and shape of foundstones, individual stones as found in the landscape, express powerfully the agency of the world, both as chance and as metaphor, as creatrix and earth mother, as planetary and interplanetary force. This is what we like to call 'coincidence', declining to investigate further its meaningless jumble. Were we more appreciative of the creativity of the more-than-human world, we might find both wit and wonder in the insights and metaphors these creator beings throw our way, especially in their shaping and placing of stones. Some call these metaphors of placement mystery or magic, some synchronicity, but stingy human- or god-centred rationality dismisses them as coincidence or chance.

We dislike chance, as an element which cannot be controlled, and seek to belittle and reduce it – 'mere', we call it. "That (mere) stone came to be there through (mere) chance", we say. But what we call 'chance' is usually the intersection of multiple narratives far too intricate and complex for us humans ever to know – for example, the narratives of pre-history and geology that could explain how a certain stone came to be in the place where it lies. Those who have learnt the power of nature as agent know there is nothing 'mere' about chance. Chance is an important expression of the agency of the more-than-human world: chance is for us to delight in and decipher, not deplore and diminish.

Losing contact with both stones and chance as teachers and metaphor-makers, we lose an important source of wit, wisdom and wonder in our lives, for stones can speak to us of the 'big themes', of life and death, time and transience. As a bush child, I was struck by the mysteries hiding in the big stone outcrops around our farm, but my culture gave them no mind or meaning, except for their potential to harbour suspicious characters. In the city, life seemed to be lacking something. As a city teenager, I encountered few free, unmodified stones, and got poor results in the spatial shapes section of the intelligence test.

In early mid-life I moved back to the bush, to a small clearing in tall forest, and built a stone house, favouring stone because it was abundant on site and gave protection from fire. Fortunately, my poor spatial test results didn't stop my adult self from making a solid house of carefully fitted foundstones, and some fair drystone walls. For my house walls, I found sandstone from the nearby forest, levering out and collecting exposed, or partly exposed, stones that called to me from the forest floor. The forest yielded a good supply of fine flat stones that fitted well into the wall, needing only a little light shaping. As I shaped individual stones and placed them in the wall, I came to get an eye for a good fit, and to lust after particularly shapely stones I knew were lying out there in the forest.

My practical and political inspiration for stone building lay in the work of Helen and Scott Nearing (1979), and philosophically, in the project of rematerialising spirit implicit in the thought of the romantic radicals who believed that in the labour regime of commodities the instrumental rationality of modernity has split apart use and respect. The split between spirit and matter, use and respect, reason and emotion, mind labour and body labour that lies at the heart of modern dematerialisation, of the instrumental mode and the industrial revolution, was challenged by radical romantics like Thoreau, Morris and Karl Polanyi, and more recently by bioregionalists like Gary Snyder, who strive to re-unite the heart and head, the place of attachment with the place of production.

The work of providing for basic needs (or 'bread labour' in the terms of Gandhi, Kropotkin and Nearing), the vocation of equality, has been split off from the more highly regarded mental labour and assigned to an inferiorised caste of 'body people', or 'hired hands', substitute-energy workers.[1] It has been individualised, managerialised and stripped of wholeness, gratitude and responsiveness to place. Restoring honour and meaning to physical labour is part of the project of reclaiming speaking matter. A good form of life would rematerialise the 'ghostly occupations' of modernity, and could be recovered partially at the level of the household by combining intellectual labour with 'bread' labour, growing food and building shelter from local materials in healthy ways respectful of the earth, of other lives and elements. These elements include both bodily labour and the labour of nature, which could be blended harmoniously so as to nourish and honour the material, ecological body of the earth. So I thought, with the fervour of youth, and mostly still think.

1.2 Prophetic stones

While working on the house stones, I thought about the insights one of my American Indian students had related in a philosophy class I had taught in Montana the previous year. Her people, the Blackfoot tribe of the Northwest, were known both as fearsome raiders and also as a tribe that understood and honoured stones. She told us how her grandmother, walking hand in hand with her own great-grandmother, had been reproved for the careless kicking of a stone. Stones, said the old Indian lady, had their reasons for being where they were, and were not to be moved lightly, as if those reasons did not count. And some stones – not every stone, mind you, but certainly some stones – were stones of power, could teach and foretell the future. Since it could not be known in advance of a deeper acquaintance which ones these were, all stones should be honoured, and treated as if they were, potentially, such prophetic stones.

Building in foundstone is a metaphor for many things, including building relationships. I linger over this idea as I reach for a stone to fit an awkward space in the wall: will this key-shaped stone be the one

---

[1] This is part of the dynamic that has created the energy crisis.

to link my wall stones together? I am always optimistic, but often wrong. You never know until you actually pick it up and try it in place to test whether it fits or not. Stone wall-building, like love and friendship, is an adventurous and experimental art. There is great satisfaction in getting in a stone that fits well, but always there is an element of making do. Nothing fits perfectly. The test is: does it stay there, and add beauty and strength? According to indigenous wisdom, being able to make something out of whatever life throws in your way is an important skill for living well. Working with foundstone certainly exercises and tests this skill.

The stones I collected made a good, solid house, cool in summer, like a cave, and cool in winter too. If they did not make for a solid love, they at least made good metaphors for love. The cordolith, or Heartstone, I found was almost buried in the earth, with only a little of its top showing. There followed a slow excavation, as of the nature of the beloved. So the potentiality of those we are drawn to is hidden at the beginning, and is uncovered bit by bit, sometimes with difficulty and pain, or with growing excitement and pleasure as unsuspected treasures are revealed.

1.3 Discovery of the Heartstone

It was during a brief flush of the foolish happiness of new love in late summer that I first noticed the top of the Heartstone protruding a few inches from the soil under the grove of Sassafras trees up towards the tank. It was in an area I had traversed quite often, but I had never remarked this stone before, except as something to avoid tripping over. I had certainly never before desired it. Although at this stage I could not know the remarkable shape that would eventually be uncovered, the little piece showing above the ground began to exert an inexplicably powerful attraction. A brief inspection suggested the exciting possibility of a large stone with two perfectly flat parallel surfaces, a stone that could be useful for paving a bare patch that had developed outside my door, where the tender grass had too often been trodden down.

Like a new love, a buried stone is always a gamble. You never know just what digging will reveal, whether it will repay your time, emotional effort and likely injuries. A highly desirable profile above the soil might be matched by a highly undesirable one beneath the ground. For that reason I do not put much effort usually into buried stones – but this time it was different. I had fixed my desire strongly on a stone whose contours were largely hidden. I made a preliminary investigation, digging around it with a spade, and attempted to move it with a steel post. This excavation suggested exciting potential but difficult access, and left the overall shape of the stone as much a mystery as ever. The two parallel major surfaces continued, perfectly flat, well down past any easy excavation. Try as I might, I was unable to feel even the slightest movement when I levered against the sides. The stone was either very large, or was somehow wedged under other stones or grasped by tree roots. Eventually my levering efforts were repulsed. The steel post I was using began to bend, and finally glanced off the stone's surface and hit a finger, causing much pain and swelling. I set the task of acquiring the stone aside temporarily.

It was clear that to free the stone I would need better technology to increase my mechanical advantage, namely, a lightweight crowbar. I had lost the last crowbar, leaving it where it lay after weary days of work collecting house stones, and the forest had swallowed it. The new crowbar I now acquired was of great assistance. At last I could feel the stone shift! It was like feeling a child move in the womb, and gave me confidence that I could birth this stone into the light of day. I had still to move a number of other stones above it, cut through a web of enclosing roots, and find a way to lever up the object of my desire by pivoting and pushing other smaller stones under it, the patient work of hours.

Working physically like this on moving one relatively smallish stone out of the millions in the surrounding area gave me a yard-stick of energy that made more concrete and graspable the immense work of the earth in slowly forming and shaping this piece of its body. The sandstone layer the Heartstone came from must have been laid down gradually and imperceptibly, (not unlike love) until a convulsive gesture of the earth lifted it up, exposing it to the cracking, weathering action that shattered its primeval unity and scattered the divorced fragments.

I recalled the Blackfoot grandmother's advice about not moving stones lightly from their place. But the Heartstone was clasped so tightly by the earth, there was no way I could be accused of moving it lightly or casually. Clearly this stone had called me, I reasoned, and anyway, I was only moving it a short distance away from its place to a more honourable and visible one. I laboured on at my task until finally, with a hearty heave on the crowbar, I got one end of the stone out of the large hole I had excavated. Now one corner was up above the ground, and I was able to push the whole thing out. This was the moment of full revelation the true stone lover hopes and works for, when the stone lies fully exposed at your feet, and at last you can take in its shape. With heartfelt satisfaction, I saw that the form was an almost perfect heart, about 30 inches long and 8 inches thick, and beautifully flat on both sides! I marvelled at the symmetry, the parallel sides, the fine grain, and the perfectly smooth, unblemished surface of the Heartstone.

As I levered the Heartstone into the wheelbarrow, careful not to stress it, its considerable weight fell fully onto my already injured finger, making it doubly painful. A large blood-blister formed, and it looked as if I might lose the nail. The dominant culture, which resigns us to disabling injury as the inevitable fruit of love for any active heart, draws confirmation and cynical satisfaction from such events. As it turned out, the injury, like much that was associated with the Heartstone, was highly prophetic of the injuries of the love relationship associated with it.

I set the stone in the ground near my door. But when the Heartstone became moist, a long, fine crack could be seen running from the centre of the heart lobes down to the lower right hand side. Here again, the cordolith provided solid guidance in the form of metaphor. True, the human love represented by its broken surface layer did not flourish, but this break is superficial. The stone, and the gift of love it represents, remains reliable in shape, firm and stable to tread on, and shows no sign of growing smaller. I have noticed that Birubi the Drum, wombat of my heart, likes to stand on the Heartstone of an evening to graze the grass around it, which is exceptionally vigorous, bright and green.[2] Here perhaps is a further teaching of the cordolith: the loss of human love does not mean a ruined or useless life – on the contrary, a broken heart may be a creative resource, and love is not limited by species.

---

[2] A wombat is a small marsupial bear that lives in a burrow.

1.4 Journey into the Heart of Stone: the Stone Country of Arnhem Land

After these first steps into the heart of stone, it came to seem far from 'romantic', in the common meaning of impractical, absurd or irrational, to think of stones as potential prophets, teachers and powers or agents in our lives. The next, and perhaps most crucial, step in my awakening to the heart of stone was a mysterious glimpse, through sheets of blinding rain, of a great balanced rock, which seemed a warning from the land, just before I was taken and almost killed by a saltwater crocodile along the East Alligator River in Arnhem Land in Australia's tropical north. The balanced rock is a symbol of vulnerability and danger, but also represents survival, being the maximum in stone resistance to the processes of decay, the original sandstone sheet distilled down to the smallest vertical unit of endurance, already struggling in the river of time.

A decade later, to give thanks for an unlikely survival in that river,[3] I undertook a stone pilgrimage in the same area, a journey (up Baroalba Creek) into the stone country of the Arnhem Land Plateau, among some of the oldest stone formations on earth. This is a land where stone is the main actor, and knowledge of stone is the meaning of a journey, a land of stone sculpted by time. In this region, strangely humanoid figures of shrouded gods and finely balanced sandstone heads gaze out over country formed by two thousand million years of vigorous marital struggle between mother earth and father sky, between the sandstone and the hyperactive tropical atmosphere. Along the skyline, great weathered stone figures, the most worn and tested of their children, still bear their forms, prescient of dissolution, into the future.

From a poolside camp above the escarpment as our base location, my companion Mark and I set out to walk up the creek into the arid interior of this piece of the stone country. We journey through a mighty landscape of silent, solemn ruins; the intricate detail of their

---

[3] Also in the East Alligator River. See Plumwood 1996.

great wrecked ramparts seems imbued with the heightened significance of dreamscape. Before us, forming the northern walls of our shallow valley, rise battered towers of stone the size and complexity of cathedrals, toppled and leaning at precarious angles, fantastic pieces in some game of giants strewn carelessly across the floor of this rocky world. Every turn of the creek brings new tilted columns, crazy stacks or shady temples into view, new disclosures of the unimaginably infinite variety of the earth narrative that is weathered stone. Each formation is a revelation to be encountered on its own terms and in its own time, rather than commanded to fit some pre-established schema by a supreme, impatient, all-knowing eye. We are truly in the presence of the Old Ones.

It is hard to follow the map, so confusing is the intricate detail of the ruined ranges and so vast the scale of this enigmatic country. Like the vegetation, we cling precariously to the creek, holding our senses open for the call of an important Aboriginal art site. We have been told there are some binitj art galleries here that we balanda may visit without offence, but have been given little more than a vague indication of where they might be.[4] The country will tell us where they were, if we are meant to know. For this culture, the land is an active presence; it grows you up, teaches you, misses you, and calls to you (see Neidjie 1986 and Rose 2004). Even de-sensitised balanda travelling in this country find it hard to escape a sense of the land as a realm of powerful and intentional beings, ultimately the land of the Old Ones, the creator beings. To those of us from reductionist balanda culture, who have in our conceptual frameworks systematically denied the power of the Old Ones – of ancestral processes, of stones – experiencing that power can evoke the kind of fear we associate with the eerie.

In baking heat, we walk up the creek into the higher parts of the stone plateau. As we leave behind the shady canyons, pools and the creek-side rainforest groves of umbilik , the heat of yegge (early dry) is visibly reflected in heatwaves rising from a region of much harsher country, great stone expanses where most of the vegetation in sight edges the creek or clings to the sides of distant ranges. The wattles,

---

[4] Some Aboriginal people of Arnhem Land use the terms *binitj* for Aboriginal people and *balanda* for non-indigenous people.

previously growing mainly up in the higher and drier parts, now move down onto the creek margins, and sparse spinifex occupies the broken country stretching away from the creek. It will be six months before more rain falls, and most mobile life in this fierce land depends on the small flow of water now trickling away down the exposed rocky ledges.

The creek itself soon disappears underground into deep fissures, and when we pick it up again gratefully we stop to wet our shirts and hats to keep cool. Mid-afternoon, almost as we are ready to turn back, we see from the creek bed a long low line of collapsed rock that suggests the outline of a cave. The etiquette is to call to make contact, establish our presence, ask permission to approach. (My own ringing "cooee" call is well practiced, since I have spent much of the previous summer walking in grizzly bear country in the northern Rockies, where you must call constantly to warn the grizzlies of your presence and avoid dangerous surprises. "That silly Cooee call again! Another loud-mouthed, tasteless Australian!" I imagine the bears yawning.)

From the creekbed I hail the stone ramparts: "Cooee! It's Val and Mark. Can we come up?" Immediately the cliff-cave replies, its voice strong and clear, "Come up!" Before entering a special or sacred area, binitj may call to let country and ancestors know they are present and to seek permission to enter. What could be the point of such a practice of seeking permission for balanda? They are many: to acknowledge power in the land; to respect and acknowledge the place, other agents and prior presences, whatever these may be; and to express a dialogical understanding of relationship to the earth as communicative partner. Also to register respect for binitj culture, its creations and customs, for any artefacts that might be present, and to be open to and respectful of Aboriginal narratives of the land.

The cave is cool and dim, and the magnificent art gallery on the cave walls is well guarded by ranks of great stone blocks fallen from the roof. Upon the walls of the ochre-whitened passages running beneath the shattered roof we recognise figures associated with several prominent themes in binitj culture – the double rainbow serpent entwines itself, recycling turtles and fish, kangaroos and humans, ocean, rain and creekwater. We admire the powerful realisation, close observation of the paintings, wondering at their meaning. Then, round the corner, we gasp and clutch each other in amazement. Upon the wall, outlined clearly in red ochre, is the life-sized profile of an animal that has been extinct upon mainland Australia for perhaps 5,000 years, the Thylacine, or marsupial wolf. The person who made this painting was familiar with the Thylacine, beyond all doubt. The animal in this painting bears its broad-based tail, not as an afterthought or optional extra, like a dog, but as a powerful and crucial continuation of its body, like a kangeroo.

Then we see something else. Directly underneath the painting lie a set of large, white doglike droppings. Perhaps these are from the Thylacine's canine rival, the dingo, credited with thylacine extinction. I prefer to think that they have been left by the Great Thylacine itself, as a token of its unseen presence, and that of the Old Ones, the ancestors. It is appropriate that stone holds the traces of this being, the Thylacine, for the endurance of stone is a counterpoint to the transience of individual and species life, and for indigenous philosophy, provides a layer of continuity that grounds identity. Most balanda think the Thylacine, a recent victim of instrumental culture, is gone forever, except for some few traces like these. But that is not the message of this place.

1.5 Coming back to Bedrock: Breaking the Silence of Stone

Is this, as reductionist culture suggests, a special, eerie, haunted place that I write of here, one visited by ghosts and goblins, spirit inhabitants of an extra, supernatural 'shadow' dimension that lies mysteriously behind the illusions of everyday life – the realm of superstition, the anti-rational? Or is it rather the kind of account that results when we take the land and other non-human actors seriously as mindful, intentional subjects and real agents, daring to employ some of the same intentionally-charged language we would use for ourselves? If the latter, would this not be the sin of anthropomorphism? As I argued in my last book (Plumwood 2002), the charge of anthropomorphism – of invalidly attributing human-like characteristics to the non-human – completely begs the reductionist question in assuming that intentional language can be applied only to the human sphere. The instrumentalist framework on which the reductionist impulse and its charge of anthropomorphism relies, involves, of course, a Faustian bargain, for it offers power over the world at the price of draining it of life and the possibility of revelation. If anthropomorphism means writing an active, intentional, ecological world, and expanding our range of sensitivity to non-human actors and elements, it would be highly rational, especially in the current dire ecological situation, to have more of it!

But did the balanced rock really give a warning, the cave really call back, the Heartstone really predict? Surely this can all be explained away – the call was just an echo of the human voice, the Heartstone's crack, like the dropping under the thylacine painting, a sheer coincidence. Plainly these redescriptions are calculated to deprecate non-human agency and confine any active intentionality to human actors, leaving nature 'lifeless' and trading consumability for wonder. The Stone Country evokes wonder. But this is tinged with paradox, for it is a revelation of the extraordinary character of what the western framework of reduction renders trite and invisible as 'sheer coincidence' – treats as boringly familiar and unimportant background – that is foregrounded and communicated so powerfully in the extraordinary formations that surround the traveler: the struggle of stone against time and atmosphere.

On the matter of 'coincidence', places like the Stone Country confront us sharply with the difficult knowledge of our limitations, for in the complex and intricate narrative that explains the emergence of the correspondingly complex and intricate forms we see around us, we can, as human observers, never know the full story that matches the intricacy we observe. We can discern only a few of its broader outlines: that all this has evolved through the ancestral processes of sea, rain and wind that have sculpted it through deep tides of time. To save face, our instrumental culture conveniently dismisses the rest under the rubric of coincidence, contingency, accident, or formless chaos, belittling all complexities it cannot know or control. So we silence stone and trivialise its story.

The question is: can we write stone teaching, stone acting, stone speaking, stone guiding, without being trapped in the familiar 'New Age' or gothic-romantic repertoire of the dualistic, the irrational and the romantic discourses that instrumental culture has set aside for us - the permitted realm of exceptionality and intentionality allocated for superstition, the haunted, or the supernatural, the eerily inexplicable? Can we write stone as much from SCIENCE as from ART, from philosophy as from poetry, from reason as from emotion? Can we write nature as active, responsive partner for everyday stone and daily experience, not just for the occasional impressive or exceptional place? For it is the former we will need if we are to change our everyday lives, to have a sense of how the earth supports us and how we take it for granted – a sense of the sacred in the earthly life around us. I believe we can, but it will be easier if we can see through concepts like anthropomorphism and romanticism that are precisely designed to keep in check any greater openness to the speaking and acting stone that is all around us.

Active stone: Flocks of migrating honeyeaters are flying up my valley, pausing every few hundred yards to collect stragglers and reassure youngsters. They come from near and far, in this ancient autumn movement, individual parties of small, striving birds, tiny Silvereyes and excited Yellow-faces, usually less than fifty, but sometimes larger or smaller flocks, some of a single and some of mixed species, voices calling as they come. Some fly thousands of miles from as far away as Tasmania after a crossing of the wild Bass Strait, streaming up valleys and along major ridges, a current of birds flowing northward to the great winter nectar grounds of the Sydney Sandstone.

In a wonderful example of the intricacy and mutuality of co-evolution, the great sandstone plateau has evolved a nectar-rich flora of heaths and swamps fertilised by brush-tongued, avian nectar–eaters. Because sandstone dries out, this is also a flora that expends much of its flowering energy over the winter, when moisture is maximised. Since at this time nectar is scarce for the honeyeaters in surrounding regions, there are willing legions of migrant reproductive workers from neighbouring places. So the sandstone country sustains the honeyeater form, and allows more birds and more flowers to flourish elsewhere in the region. Stone ties itself into the larger ecological economy, to the enrichment of all, and lies at the base of everything that lives around it.

Speaking stone: my house walls are made from a special kind of sandstone, a conglomerated sandstone into which are kneaded occasional small round river stones, like raisins in bread. This local stone is lightly conglomerated compared to the coarse, soft conglomerate of the mountains to my north, a wild, complicated landscape of hidden caves and valleys adventurous walkers love to wander. These coarse conglomerates tell a story that refutes our illusion of stone as silent and static, a complicated, amazing, but quite readable story of the weathering of a hard bedrock into rounded river stones, later compressed with finer weathered materials as sand beneath an ocean, then lifted up and exposed as soft conglomerate. Conglomerate, like so much else, is built up from those who went before, those we count for nothing.

Many small, attractively rounded river stones from the original bedrock have now weathered out of this stratum for a second time, and lie scattered around these parts. At first, I just accepted them. Who knew why stones were where they were? After a long time, and much local exploration, I began to sense a mystery, because there is nothing like them to be seen in any of the exposed cliffs or rock outcrops around here. Where had they come from? There was indeed a mystery here, but the secondary mystery was: why was I incurious for so long? Why did it take me so long to search out the story of these twice-weathered stones, written in the walls and in these mountains? This extraordinary story was right there before my eyes for half my life, but it took another journey, another pilgrimage to other stone country to frame the puzzle and more local walking to supply its missing pieces, as a final encounter with the original bedrock, the ultimate Old One from which these stones and ultimately much else around here (including the cordolith) were made.

That is another story of speaking stone I do not have space to tell here. The point is though, that this awakening to the heart of stone required also a different kind of journey, a conceptual journey that moved stone from the background of consciousness to the foreground, from silent to speaking, from mindless vacancy to intentional actor, from the ordinary to the extraordinary, the wonderful, even the sacred. Perhaps this is a journey those honouring and writing stone could show our jaded instrumental culture how to make. Must we write the worlds of wonder off as extinct, like the vanished Thylacine, or can we learn through practices like these to let them live again?

Val Plumwood

Bibliography

Birch, Tom. 1993. 'Moral Considerability and Universal Consideration' in *Environmental Ethics* 15: 313-332.

Brennan, Teresa. 1996. *History After Lacan*. London: Routledge.

Deloria, Vine. 1999. *Spirit and Reason: the Vine Deloria Reader*. Colorado: Fulcrum.

Nearing, Helen and Scott. 1979. *The Good Life*. New York: Schocken.

Neidjie, Bill. 1986. *Kakadu Man*. Canberra: Mybrood.

Plumwood, Val. 1996. 'Being Prey' in *Terra Nova* 1(3): 32-44. Reprinted in David Rothenberg, and Marta Ulvaeus (eds) 1999. *The New Earth Reader: The Best of Terra Nova*. Cambridge: MIT Press. 76-92.

— 1993. *Feminism and the Mastery of Nature*. London: Routledge.

— 2002. *Environmental Culture: the Ecological Crisis of Reason*. London: Routledge.

Rose, Deborah Bird. 1996. *Nourishing Terrains: Australian Aboriginal Views of Landscape and Wilderness*. Canberra: Australian Heritage Commission.

— 2004. *Reports from a Wild Country*. Sydney: UNSW Press.

Weston, Anthony. 1996. 'Self-Validating Reduction: Toward a Theory of Environmental Devaluation' in *Environmental Ethics* 18: 115-132.

— 1998. 'Universal Consideration as an Originary Practice' in *Environmental Ethics* 20: 279-289.

What is (ecological) 'nature'? John Stuart Mill and the Victorian perspective

John Parham

Abstract

In *The Green Studies Reader* (2000) Laurence Coupe suggests that 'Nature is perhaps the most complex word in the language' and argues that 'green studies [...] hinges on the recognition of the complexity of that word and of our relation to whatever it denotes'. The opening section of this essay reviews the difficulties this question has posed to contemporary ecocritical theory. It discusses in particular the tension, identified by Martin Ryle, between 'nature-endorsing' approaches – those that take certain texts at face value as 'true' records of landscapes, natural processes and environmental practice – and 'nature-sceptical' approaches – those that interrogate the uses to which 'nature' is put in texts e.g. the social paradigms being proposed.

Part two of the essay argues that nineteenth-century critics have already confronted this specific question – what is nature? Parham then seeks to establish his own approach to what nature 'denotes' with reference to what he sees as the most thorough nineteenth-century attempt to theorize the 'natural world' – John Stuart Mill's essay 'On Nature' (1874). The body of his argument studies Mill's essay and highlights the following key arguments: that Mill's scientifically based understanding that nature has a 'primary' or 'original' meaning independent of human 'constructions'; an examination of Mill's definition of 'intelligent action' whereby 'the activities of men' are subject to nature's laws while, nevertheless, 'Nature [is] a scheme to be amended, not imitated, by Man' (i.e. within 'the absolute limits of the laws of nature' the human race should be free to make adaptations, as indeed do other species); Mill's conclusion that both human social organisation and the natural environment result from the choice made as to how we live within the ecosystem: 'by every choice which we make either of ends or of means, we place ourselves to a greater or less extent under one set of laws of nature instead of another'. Finally, the paper looks at how Mill employed this notion of 'nature' as the basis for social organisation in the ongoing development of his 'Principles of Political Economy'. The paper concludes in support of an argument, made by Ryle, that 'ecocriticism, like green politics, must be centrally concerned with the historical development of "human nature"'.

Prompted by the popular perception of actual or impending
environmental crisis, ecocriticism, as it emerged in the early 1990s,
responded with a re-assertion of nature in the face of the havoc
wrought by the 'anti-nature' discourses of Enlightenment rationality
and its related (industrial) practices (Bate 1991: 4; Glotfelty 1996: xv-
xvi). Located, also, in a more specific discussion about the 'place' of
ecocriticism in an academic literary studies contaminated (so it was
perceived) by critical theory, this response took a variety of interrelated
forms: the re-assertion of natural spaces, notably American wilderness;
the re-assertion of nature writing as a (culpably) neglected form of
writing in both academic theory and the literary canon (Buell 1995: 9-
10); and the re-invocation, in the study of genres and periods, most
notably Romanticism and American transcendentalism, that are seen to
affirm the intrinsic value of nature (see Bate 1991; McKusick 2000). In
a subsequent, what might be called, 'secondary phase' of ecocriticism
which has (often ruthlessly) dissected and identified the weaknesses of
the 'first phase', this valorisation, or idealisation, of nature has been
called into question (Cohen 2004; Phillips 2003: 40). In doing so,
ecocriticism has arrived at what, with hindsight, was an always
inevitable encounter with the age-old question 'what is nature?' As
Laurence Coupe argues, "it might be no exaggeration to say that green
studies [...] hinges on the recognition of the complexity of that word
and of our relation to whatever it denotes" (Coupe 2000: 3).

One of the main critiques to have emerged from this secondary
phase ecocriticism is that, in idealising nature, ecocritics have been
guilty of perpetuating the dualistic and alienated distinction between
nature and culture generally attributed to the Enlightenment.
Accordingly, the more recent ecocritics have insisted upon the
complex inter-linkage between the two terms (see, for example,
Phillips 2003: 30-34). The central pillars of this argument have been a
view that culture and nature exist in dialectical relationship and that
human constructions of nature underlie social and political discourse.
In a survey of ecocriticism, for instance, Greg Garrard argues both
these things. He writes "'nature' is in some ways culturally
constructed" but, at the same time, "really exists". However, he
continues, the ultimate impossibility, notwithstanding the apparent but
illusory promise of ecological science, of answering the question
'what is nature?' means that it will always be incumbent on humans to

take responsibility for both our discourses of nature and the social practices that organise our relationship to and treatment of the natural world (2004: 10; 71-2).

A similar argument is contained within what, for British ecocritics at least, has been an increasingly influential book, Kate Soper's *What is Nature?* (1995). Soper, too, assumes a dialectical position on nature. On the one hand, she suggests, we can only understand nature through the prism of human constructions or paradigms. On this basis Soper offers a partial recuperation of anthropocentrism:

> It is inevitable that our attitudes to nature will be 'anthropocentric' in certain respects since there is no way of conceiving our relations to it other than through the mediation of ideas about ourselves. To suggest that it could be otherwise is to be insensitive to those ways in which the rest of nature is different, and should be respected as being so. (Soper 1995: 13)

On the other hand, Soper insists that there is an "extra-discursive reality of nature" and that we need to "acknowledge the nature which is *not* a cultural formation" (Soper 1995: 8). Soper's main concern, however, is with the politics of the idea of nature, "the social and cultural demarcations which have been drawn through the concept" (Soper 1995: 3). And she brings the two together in the notion of a "new humanism" whereby we retain a sense of the integrity of human culture that nevertheless remains sensitive to the dictates and constrictions imposed by the (rest of) the natural world (Soper 1995: 13) (the principle, of course, underpinning sustainable economic practice).

If ecocriticism cannot, then, simply be about the revalorisation of an idealised nature, the implication of this later criticism would appear to be that its task is to study those literary sources that will guide us in our attempts to answer the philosophical question 'what is nature?' and/or tackle the pragmatic question of how to imagine a sustainable political economy. The problem with this project, as identified by Soper, is the difficulty of reconciling what she calls "nature-endorsing" and "nature-sceptical" approaches (Soper 1995: 4). Working with Soper's formulation, but writing within a specifically ecocritical context, Martin Ryle describes these as, respectively, belief in art as "a means to deepen our apprehension of 'nature'" and the interrogation of the way in which 'nature', as discursive term or as material space or place, is always implicated in social relations" (Ryle 2002: 11). Ryle's analysis exposes the complexity of achieving such reconciliation. For, on the one hand, he points to the importance of nature-endorsing positions as a cultural prompt, or useful construct, for inculcating a sense of inter-dependency with non-human nature; as he reminds us, "no one [...] will regard themselves as an 'ecocritic' unless they feel some sense of the power of the best writing about nature to delight and instruct" (Ryle 2002: 12). On the other, he highlights the cultural divisions that underpin Wordsworthian Romanticism or nature-endorsing positions in general (for instance, advocacy for the exclusion of the working-classes from the Lake District). In that sense one might argue that the Romantic poets, usually regarded as having originated the nature-endorsing position, are of little help either in understanding what nature is, or in indicating an ecological social philosophy. For their reflections upon the question of 'nature' were resolutely non-materialist with a tendency to be diverted towards the "egotistical sublime" (Wordsworth), or transcendental philosophy (Coleridge). Correspondingly, political models, visions and projects were far-fetched and, in the context of a developing industrial society, idealistic (notably the Swiss mountain republics praised by Wordsworth, or Coleridge's "Pantisocracy" scheme for creating an egalitarian natural community on the banks of the Susquehanna River (see Bate 1991: 25; McKusick 2000: 40-41).

While this is an argument that, admittedly, needs more analysis than can be given here, in this chapter I will develop the argument, made elsewhere, that it is Victorian literary figures and cultural critics who developed the Romantic conception of nature and its social criticism into something more in accordance with contemporary ecological theory (see Parham 2002: 156-71). Nevertheless, this discussion of 'nature' will be conducted in a spirit of reconciliation whereby the impetus provided by Romantic, nature-endorsing writing, can be seen to vitalise the more nature-sceptical Victorian mind. My focus will be on the philosopher and economist John Stuart Mill. For while, as I will argue, Mill bequeathed to our own ecological discourse both a detailed analysis of the philosophical question of 'nature' and thoroughly worked out principles of political economy, the foundation of his work in a personal perspective profoundly altered by Romanticism offers precisely the reconciliation of nature scepticism and endorsement that has been posited as the proper basis for an ecologically inflected 'new humanism'.

Born in 1806, Mill's childhood was spent being educated by his father, the Utilitarian philosopher James Mill, through whom he came into contact with other prominent figures in the fields of economic and political theory such as Jeremy Bentham and David Ricardo (see Mill 1964: 27-42). In 1826, however, he suffered what he calls, in his *Autobiography*, "a crisis in my mental history". While there is some uncertainty as to the exact nature of this "crisis" (though it appears to have been a form of depression), critics do agree that it was, as much as anything, an intellectual crisis brought on by Mill's sudden perception of the inadequacies of the Enlightenment thinking that shaped his education. Having initially turned to music and poetry simply for consolation, the "crisis" would eventually alter Mill's entire mode of thinking. Mill attributes this transformation primarily to Wordsworth. Wordsworth's poems, describing what he called "the love of rural objects and natural scenery", reminded him of what had been the source of "much of the pleasure of my life" and, in doing so, helped counteract "one of my longest relapses into depression". The poems, he says, excited not only beauty but also "the very culture of the feelings, which I was in quest of" (Mill 1964: 115-6). Ultimately, however, the influence of Wordsworth and other Romantic writers and critics, notably Carlyle (Mill 1964: 131-3), was not to negate, but to reinforce Mill's analytical tendencies. Describing the "crisis", Mill remarks "that the habit of analysis has a tendency to wear away the feelings" when remaining "without its natural compliments and correctives" and comments that "I, for the first time, gave its proper place, among the prime necessities of human well-being, to the internal culture of the individual" (Mill 1964: 109; 113).

In this context Mill has been invoked to redeem Romanticism from the new historicist criticism of writers such as Jerome McGann, that accuses it of evading politics in the concentration on nature writing. Nicholas Roe, for example, cites the next quoted passage, from the *Autobiography*, to argue that romantic poetry both exhibits and can prompt a commitment to humanitarian concerns as well as being able to address "the social and environmental problems of our modern world" (Roe 2002: xi; 197-98). From Wordsworth's poems, writes Mill:

I seemed to draw from a source of inward joy, of sympathetic and imaginative
pleasure, which could be shared in by all human beings; which had no connexion
with struggle or imperfection, but would be made richer by every improvement in
the physical or social condition of mankind. (Mill 1964: 116)

These poems, it is clear, re-vitalised and informed Mill's
commitment to social analysis. "The delight which these poems gave
me proved that with culture of this sort there was nothing to dread
from the most confirmed habit of analysis", he wrote (Mill 1964:
116). As a consequence, Mill subsequently envisaged his project in
terms of reconciling the pragmatism of utilitarianism with the life-
enhancing and visionary nature of Romanticism. He articulated this in
complementary essays on Bentham and Coleridge, written in 1838 and
1840 respectively, and explained it further in a letter to Carlyle: "If I
have any *vocation*, I think it is exactly this, to translate the mysticism
of others into the language of Argument" (cited in Capaldi 2004: 94-
5). As I will now argue, this fusion of Romanticism to a more
pragmatic "language of Argument" underpins the interrelationship
between political economy and the economy of nature established by
Mill in two important works: *Principles of Political Economy* (first
published 1848) and the essay 'Nature' (published in 1874).

Mill began to articulate his economic thinking in an essay, 'On the
Definition of Political Economy', that was one of his *Essays on Some
Unsettled Questions of Political Economy* (first published in 1844).
He argued that political economy "has remained destitute of a
definition formed on strictly logical principles", a definition which, he
believed, should be centred around the "laws which regulate the
production, distribution, and consumption of wealth" (Mill 1974:
125). However, this, it becomes apparent, was merely a necessary
abstraction through which "a nearer approximation is obtained than
would otherwise be practicable". For Mill continued by arguing that
conclusions reached from the pure study of political economy would
"fail to be applicable to the explanation or prediction of real events,
until [...] modified by a correct allowance for the degree of influence
exercised by [any] other cause" (Mill 1974: 140).

The two chief examples of these "other cause[s]" that Mill gave
were physical laws and social consensus (Mill 1974: 139-40). In the
first case, he argued, political economy

presupposes all the physical sciences; it takes for granted all such of the truths of those sciences as are concerned in the production of the objects demanded by the wants of mankind; or at least it takes for granted that the physical part of the process takes place somehow. It then inquires what are the phenomena of *mind* which are concerned in the production and distribution of those same objects; it borrows from the pure science of mind the laws of those phenomena, and inquires what effects follow from these mental laws, acting in concurrence with those physical ones. (Mill 1974: 132-3)

While the reference to "the production of the objects demanded by the wants of mankind" appears to sanction human 'exploitation' of nature, what Mill is actually arguing here is that any such human activity must always be "in concurrence with [...] physical [laws]". From reading and corresponding with the French social thinker Alexis de Tocqueville, Mill had come to understand, secondly, that the abstract focus by which "Political Economy considers mankind as occupied solely in acquiring and consuming wealth" (Mill 1974: 138) was always, ultimately, subject to modification not only by physical laws, but by social forces, values and desires – the "phenomena of mind" to which he refers (see Capaldi 2004: 127). To this conclusion, that political economy is contingent upon both natural laws and social consensus, can be added a third 'modification' signalled by the phrase "the pursuit of any other object". For Mill argued, also, that "wealth production" has always to be qualified by these "other object[s]" meaning, essentially, the spiritual, creative, and qualitative dimensions to life. It is this, as we shall see, which turns out to be the most fundamentally Romantic innovation in Mill's political economy. Taking each of the three 'modifications' in turn I will indicate how these fit into an ecological reading of the *Principles of Political Economy*. Specifically, it will be argued, first, that Mill's political economy is rooted in the natural economy ("physical laws"); second, that the "principles of political economy" are contingent upon "social economy"; and, finally, that the specific social economy that Mill advocates is centred around a conception of 'quality of life' that transcends the merely economic and resonates with contemporary social ecology.

With regard to the physical laws that underlie political economy, the main way in which Mill pre-figures contemporary ecological thought is to instigate a discussion concerning the limits to natural resources. He argues that wealth originates from nature in two senses – nature supplies both the raw materials and the sources of power. Concerning the latter, Mill argues that while human labour moves things into position, sowing seeds into earth, for example, it is "the properties of matter, the laws of nature", which "do the rest" (I, i, § 2).[1] "The matter of the globe is not an inert recipient of forms and properties impressed by human hands; it has active energies by which it cooperates with, and may even be used as a substitute for, labour" (I, i, § 1).

This awareness, of the absolute degree to which human political economy is embedded within (the rest of) the natural economy, prompted Mill's perspicacity with regard to the potential limitations to natural resources. As Ian Cook argues, however, his thinking in this area actually demonstrates a tension between faith in economic progress, derived from the influence of Adam Smith, and a consciousness of limits shaped by Malthus' teaching on population (Cook 1998: 88). This much is evident when Mill posits "two antagonistic principles" to political economy whereby the reaching of natural limits can be deferred by "the progress of civilization" which he defines as "any extension of [human] knowledge, and [...] consequent command, of the properties and powers of natural agents" such as improvements in land use, agricultural skill or transport networks (I, xii, § 2-3). However, while he believed that the "advancement in what is called material prosperity" was, for the time being, "perpetual" and "unlimited" (I, xii, § 1-2) it was not, he insisted, indefinite, a fact generally overlooked in his own time because, Mill suggests, those limits were still some way off. Nevertheless, he argued that this overlooking of natural limits to production was "not only an error, but the most serious one to be found in the whole field of political economy" (I, xii, § 1-2) and he

---

[1] There are numerous editions of the *Principles of Political Economy*. Consequently, I have followed Mill's own example, and that adopted by other critics, of citing material with reference to the (relatively short) sections into which Mill divides the book rather than to the page numbers of the particular edition used by myself (this is though included in the bibliography). In this first example, therefore, I, i, § 2, refers to Book I, Chapter I, Section 2. The exception to this is where I have taken material from Mill's 'Preliminary Remarks'.

went on to raise specific questions about the sustainability of natural resources. Suggesting that "it will be seen hereafter how much of the economy of society depends on the limited quantity in which some of the most important natural agents exist", Mill speculated about potential limitations in land, water, air, coal, and metallic ores, and even envisaged a possible depletion of fish stocks (I, i, § 4).

While Mill serves here as an important historical precedent for reminding us of the embeddedness of the political in natural economy, arguably his greater interest (for contemporary ecological discourse) lies in the way in which he extends these principles to consider, as stated in the book's sub-title, "some of their applications to social philosophy". This discussion, it would appear, begins with an analysis of peasant proprietorship that itself begins with Mill quoting, at length, Wordsworth's praise for the peasant proprietors of the Lake District (II, vi, § 1). The conclusions for political economy that Mill draws, while owing a little to the "perfect republic" depicted by Wordsworth, are, however, rooted far more in the structures, and political movements and philosophies, of the industrial Victorian society that he is actually addressing in the book.

In Book 1 of *Principles of Political Economy* Mill addresses the relative merits of large and small scale production and makes a distinction between industry, where he regarded large-scale operations as, by and large, beneficial (I, ix, § 3), and agriculture where the conclusions are more ambivalent. A detailed analysis of small-scale farming is then undertaken in the context of a discussion about the virtues of peasant proprietorship. Mill balances its negative aspects (absence of science, "deficiency of the spirit of improvement", the lack of means for enabling "systematic improvements which operate on a large tract of country at once" – for instance, drainage or irrigation schemes) with its positives (traditional knowledge, the benefit of "daily and close observation" and "an ardour of industry [...] unexampled in any other condition of agriculture" (I, ix, § 4)). Analysing examples of peasant cultivators in Switzerland, Norway, Germany and Belgium, he concludes that peasant proprietorship is "still, as a whole, probably the best agriculture in the world" making it apparent, furthermore, that the benefits are not limited to productivity alone:

> I conceive it to be established, that there is no necessary connexion between this
> form of landed property and an imperfect state of the arts of production; that it is
> favourable in quite as many respects as it is unfavourable, to the most effective
> use of the powers of the soil; that no other existing state of agricultural economy
> has so beneficial effect on the industry, the intelligence, the frugality, and
> prudence of the population, nor tends on the whole so much to discourage an
> improvident increase of their numbers; and that no existing state, therefore, is on
> the whole so favourable both to their moral and their physical welfare. (II, vii, § 5)

Notwithstanding the citation of Wordsworth, Mill's interest in peasant proprietorship was not so much the product of a nature-endorsing point of view but rather, as Stafford has argued, of a concern about the "improvident increase" in population (Stafford 1998: 74). Furthermore, believing that healthy political economy rests upon the establishment of a complementary social philosophy, Mill went on to make the connection between peasant proprietorship and a radical, if gradual, progression towards socialism that became apparent in successive editions of *Principles of Political Economy*. Though this shift had been influenced, in a theoretical sense, by European social thinkers such as Auguste Comte and the Saint-Simonian school (Mill 1964: 125-8) and, in a personal sense, by "my wife's [Harriet's] promptings" (Mill 1964: 177-8), it also derived, fundamentally, from the above views on land use. As early as the mid-1840s, in response to the Great Famine in Ireland, Mill had argued for the "formation of peasant properties on the waste lands of Ireland" (Mill 1964: 170). By the 1870s, however, as a member of the Land Tenure Reform Association, he was recommending the state purchase of land for the creation of small scale or large co-operative farms and was also hinting at the idea of nationalisation (Stafford 1998: 126).

As Nicholas Capaldi points out, Mill's conception of socialism was not so much the familiar twentieth-century model of state socialism, but rather that of a more localised, communal, co-operative socialism. This is clear from an amendment to the third (1852) edition of *Principles of Political Economy* in which he suggests that improvement would best be achieved by "the association of the labourers themselves on terms of equality, collectively owning the capital under which they carry on their operations, and working under managers elected and removable by themselves" (Capaldi 2004: 213). What this does mean, however, is that Mill's socialism broadly corresponds to the emphasis on sustainable, decentralised governance in contemporary ecological social philosophy. In that respect alone his analysis of the connections between political and social economy has much to offer. Of course, ecological philosophy and criticism has also addressed itself to the more nebulous task of re-articulating accepted notions of 'quality of life' towards, with regard to levels of material prosperity, more sustainable expectations, a point argued by Ryle:

> In my view, some sense of the possible pleasures of a materially simpler life (in terms of consumption), [and] of how we might live in ways more directly connected with (and respectful of) aspects of the natural world, should be part of the 'alternative hedonism' which green cultural critique has to envisage. (Ryle 2002: 19)

In a historical study of political economy, Phyllis Deane has suggested that Mill's contribution is noteworthy for its appreciation of the moral and cultural ramifications of the subject (Deane 1989: 100). And in that regard, perhaps the most interesting aspect of his philosophy is not so much the question concerning patterns of ownership, but the extent to which Mill envisaged, and therefore helps us to envisage, this "materially simpler life". This, as indicated above, is the element of his thought most directly derived from the Romanticism discovered in the midst of the personal "crisis". Specifically, it took the form, in this book, both of a revised concept of 'wealth' and the endorsement of nature as something other than mere resource.

Near the beginning of the book Mill criticises the common assumption "that wealth consisted solely of money" on the grounds both that money could be "extremely onerous to the real resources of the country" (a point made with specific reference to foreign trade) and that it ought only to be the means to an end, that of living a comfortable life (Mill 1920: 2, 6). Furthermore, he believed, so Cook points out, that while economic development initially stimulates intellectual development, it ultimately acts as an impediment (Cook 1998: 53). As Mill puts it, in a letter from 1847, "society at large should not be overworked, nor over-anxious about the means of subsistence" (Capaldi 2004: 220). Accordingly, he argued that, in Britain, the 'industrial spirit' needed to be 'moderated' and the character improved towards an appreciation of 'true' values, higher aspirations, and things that cannot be bought. Even in writing about the means to maintain productivity, he would suggest that "a certain quantum of enjoyment" is "consistent with the greatest efficiency of labour" (I, iii, § 6). While one might baulk here at the utilitarian connotations of a "quantum of enjoyment", Mill is arguing, more generally, that an appreciation of non-material things would minimise both human labour and the potential depletion of the earth's resources.

Mill articulates these ideas more fully in Book IV of *Principles of Political Economy* where he opposes a "progressive state" favoured by "the political economists of the last two generations" to a 'stationary state'. In an argument shaped both by Malthusian comprehension of natural limits and by a more romantic interrogation of progress, Mill argues that "one must always ask, the further question, to what goal? Towards what ultimate point is society tending by its industrial progress?" and, furthermore, "when the progress ceases, in what condition are we to expect that it will leave mankind?" (IV, vi, § 1). The ensuing advocacy of the stationary state amalgamates Mill's belief in socialism with the belief in (what we would now call) sustainable growth: "What is economically needed is a better distribution, of which one indispensable means is a stricter restraint on population". However, notwithstanding this question of limits, Mill also argues that, ultimately, industrial improvements ought, anyway, to "produce their legitimate effect, that of abridging labour" with the result that "a much larger body of persons than at present" would both be freed from the "coarser toils" and possessed of "sufficient leisure [...] to cultivate freely the graces of life" (IV, vi, § 2). It is this emphasis, on the enhanced quality of life obtainable in the stationary state, which is the distinct innovation that Mill offers to political economy:

> I am inclined to believe that it would be, on the whole, a very considerable improvement on our present condition. I confess I am not charmed with the ideal of life held out by those who think that the normal state of human beings is that of struggling to get on; that the trampling, crushing, elbowing, and treading on each other's heels, which form the existing type of social life, are the most desirable lot of human kind, or anything but the disagreeable symptoms of one of the phases of industrial progress. (IV, vi, § 2)

Stafford argues that Mill's concerns about the threat of over-population receded somewhat after the census of the late 1850s and that he subsequently adjusted his emphasis towards a consideration of the impact of a still significant human population on its surrounding environment (Stafford 1998: 74). This emphasis is also reflected in Mill's advocacy of the stationary state, for the underlying romanticism induces him to extend the argument towards an advocacy both of solitude and unspoilt nature. In this respect, as Jonathan Riley has remarked, Mill's conception of the stationary state differs markedly from the more spartan version that had been envisaged by Ricardo (Riley 1998: 318-19):

> A population may be too crowded, though all be amply supplied with food and raiment. It is not good for man to be kept perforce at all times in the presence of his species. A world from which solitude is extirpated, is a very poor ideal. Solitude, in the sense of being often alone, is essential to any depth of meditation or of character; and solitude in the presence of natural beauty and grandeur, is the cradle of thoughts and aspirations which are not only good for the individual, but which society could ill do without. Nor is there much satisfaction in contemplating the world with nothing left to the spontaneous activity of nature; with every rood of land brought into cultivation, which is capable of growing food for human beings; every flowery waste or natural pasture ploughed up, all quadrupeds or birds which are not domesticated for man's use exterminated as his rivals for food [...]. (IV, vi, § 2)

This fusion, of political economy and romanticism, in Mill's chapter on the "Stationary State" is generally regarded as his legacy to ecological theory. It is not, however, an entirely unproblematic one. For some environmentalists, at least, would be troubled by the fact that the value Mill attaches to unspoiled nature is still expressed largely in terms of its benefits to the human population. There is little sense, for instance, of any intrinsic value in non-human nature. Nevertheless, it is worth holding on to Mill's argument in *Principles of Political Economy* that political economy is shaped by humanity's conceptualisation of nature and its own place within it. Nevertheless, what the book does not do is to elaborate upon the more abstract question of how, precisely, we conceptualise 'nature' itself. That comes instead with the later essay, 'Nature', published in 1874 though probably written between 1850 and 1858 (Millar 1998: 176). Described by the ecological theorist Robert Goodin as an "unjustifiably neglected" piece of work (see Pepper, Webster and Revill Vol I: 200), the essay simultaneously augments Mill's work on political economy and pre-empts the contemporary ongoing ecocritical interrogation of the meaning of 'nature'.

Mill makes three key arguments in the essay that together constitute, I would suggest, a broadly ecological conception of nature. Though he begins by acknowledging the complexity of the word, the first of these, denoted by reference to nature's "true figure and position", and to its "primary" or "original" meaning, is simply that nature exists independently of any human linguistic construction. Consequently, Mill critiques various examples of such constructions arguing that 'nature' has "acquired many meanings different from the primary one" and that it has generated "copious sources of false taste, false philosophy, false morality, and even bad law" (Mill 1969: 373). As one of 'Three Essays on Religion' much of the essay is a treatise upon the implications of basing an ethical framework on the "vague notion that [...] we should on the whole be guided by the spirit and general conception of nature's own ways" (Mill 1969: 382). Mill dismisses such attempts on the grounds of their spurious and idealistic conceptions of a nature that, he points out, has traits of "recklessness" and violence that, if applied to human behaviour, would translate into a justification for tyranny or murder. Alan Millar has argued that whereas most people who advocate following the precepts of nature (including, presumably, the majority of environmentalists) view it as primarily benign, Mill takes an opposite position in placing his emphasis upon an innate (albeit partial) malevolence. Nevertheless, argues Millar, Mill does appear ultimately to accept "a naturalistic view of human beings" and to believe that we "are parts of nature like any other organisms and as such [...] as much subject to nature's laws as anything else" (Millar 1998: 188-9). Indeed, on this basis Mill disputes the convention "by which Nature is opposed to art":

> Art is but the employment of the powers of Nature for an end. Phenomena produced by human agency, no less than those which as far as we are concerned are spontaneous, depend upon the properties of the elementary forces, or of the elementary substances and their compounds. (Mill 1969: 375)

Mill's project can perhaps be defined, then, as one of contemplating not only what constitutes 'nature', but also what constitutes, more specifically, 'human nature'.

Accordingly, the second key argument of the essay is to define human nature through what Mill calls "intelligent action". In addition to the criticism of an ethics founded on the grounds of conformity to nature, Mill – divulging the limits of his romanticism – dismisses, also, "the vein of sentiment so common in the modern world [...] which exalts instinct at the expense of reason" (Mill 1969: 392). These two examples of "false taste" underlie the notion of "intelligent action". Mill believes that because of its innate malevolence, "Nature is a scheme to be amended, not imitated, by Man". However, this, in turn, is the province not of "instinct" or feeling, but of reason, or "intelligence". Nevertheless, while he regards humans as free to adapt and act upon the rest of nature these adaptations must be subject to, and informed by, an understanding of "the absolute limits of the laws of nature". All human activities are natural, Mill repeats: "the volition which designs, the intelligence which contrives, and the muscular force which executes these movements are themselves powers of Nature" (Mill 1969: 375); yet at the same time they are also transformative:

> We move objects, and by doing this, bring some things into contact which were separate, or separate others which were in contact: and by this simple change of place, natural forces previously dormant are called into action and produce the desired effect. (Mill 1969: 375)

While any environmentalist would, in all probability, pick up upon the connotations of "forces previously dormant" being "called into action", Mill's intention, befitting the ethical focus of the essay, is largely to stress the positive aspects to human action. In this regard, he speaks in a language similar to the environmentalist concept of 'stewardship', arguing, for instance, that humanity should be engaged in "perpetually striving to amend the course of nature - and bringing that part of it over which we can exercise control, more nearly into conformity with a high standard of justice and goodness" (Mill 1969: 402).

The third key argument contained within the essay, picking up the implications of "intelligent action" for political economy, is that human social organisation, the embodiment of the choices we make as to how to live within the ecosystem, must be based upon this "intelligent" conceptualisation of nature:

A rational rule of conduct *may* be constructed out of the relation which it ought to bear to the laws of nature [...] Every alteration of circumstance alters more or less the laws of nature under which we act; and by every choice which we make either of ends or of means, we place ourselves to a greater or less extent under one set of laws of nature instead of another. If, therefore, the useless precept to follow nature were changed into a precept to study nature; to know and take heed of the properties of the things we have to deal with, so far as these properties are capable of forwarding or obstructing any given purpose; we should have arrived at the first principle of all, intelligent action or rather at the definition of intelligent action itself. (Mill 1969: 379-80)

This essentially dialectical concept, embedded in Mill's essay, is, I would suggest, profoundly ecological: to speak only in terms of a 'sublime' or untouched nature is to posit it as 'other' and ultimately as separate from us. However, to see ourselves within an ecosystem is both to recognise the integrity of nature and to celebrate humanity's ability, where appropriate and sustainable, to modify that ecosystem precisely as other species do. At the same time, however, the assertion, that "by every choice which we make [...] we place ourselves to a greater or less extent under one set of laws of nature instead of another" reminds us of our ultimate dependence (or inter-dependence) upon the rest of the natural world and of the limits to which we, as a species, can modify this.

Mill, I have argued, lays the foundation for an ecological conception of nature that is compatible with the 'new humanist' perspective of recent ecocritical theory. Indeed, he pre-figures Garrard's argument that the impossibility of a definitive knowledge means that humanity must take responsibility for forming its own discourses of nature and for the social practices that result from this. For some time Mill has been acknowledged as one of the forebears of ecological theory with several citations, for example, in the recent, five-volume collection *Environmentalism: Critical Concepts*. This, however, has largely been restricted to a recognition of the influence exerted by his paradigm of the stationary state on 'green' political and/or economic theory (see Dobson 1990; Goodin 1992; Riley 1998; Wall 1994). The argument in this chapter is that Mill's rigorous philosophical attempt to conceptualise nature, and in turn human nature, offers something even more substantial to ecological theory – an ontological understanding of the human place in nature as an essential prerequisite to defining green political economy.

Bibliography

Bate, Jonathan. 1991. *Romantic Ecology: Wordsworth and the Environmental Tradition*. London: Routledge.

Buell, Lawrence. 1995. *The Environmental Imagination: Thoreau, Nature Writing,and the Formation of American Culture*. Cambridge: Harvard University Press.

Capaldi, Nicholas. 2004. *John Stuart Mill: A Biography*. Cambridge: Cambridge University Press.

Cohen, Michael P. 2004. 'Blues in the Green: Ecocriticism Under Critique' in *Environmental History* 9(1). On line at: http://www.historycooperative.org/journals/eh/9.1/cohen.html (consulted 10.06.2002).

Cook, Ian. 1998. *Reading Mill: Studies in Political Theory*. Basingstoke: Macmillan.

Coupe, Laurence (ed.). 2000. *The Green Studies Reader: From Romanticism to Ecocriticism*. London and New York: Routledge.

Deane, Phyllis. 1989. *The State and the Economic System: An Introduction to the History of Political Economy*. Oxford: Oxford University Press.

Garrard, Greg. 2004. *Ecocriticism*. London: Routledge.

Glotfelty, Cheryll, and Harold Fromm (eds). 1996. *The Ecocriticism Reader: Landmarks in Literary Ecology*. Athens: University of Georgia Press.

Goodin, Robert E. 1992. *Green Political Theory*. Cambridge: Polity.

McKusick, James C. 2000. *Green Writing: Romanticism and Ecology*. Basingstoke: Macmillan.

Mill, John Stuart. 1920 [1848]. *Principles of Political Economy with some of their applications to social philosophy* (ed. W. J. Ashley). London: Longmans, Green, and Co.

— 1964 [1873]. *Autobiography of John Stuart Mill* (Signet Classics). New York: The New American Library of World Literature.

— 1969 [1874]. 'Nature' in Robson, J. M. (ed.). *Collected Works of John Stuart Mill: Essays on Ethics, Religion and Society*. Toronto and London: University of Toronto Press/Routledge. 10: 373-402.

— 1974 [1874]. *Essays on Some Unsettled Questions of Political Economy*. Clifton, New Jersey: Augustus M. Kelly Publishers.

Millar, Alan. 1998. 'Mill on Religion' in Skorupski, John (ed.). *The Cambridge Companion to Mill*. Cambridge: Cambridge University Press. 176-202.

Parham, John. 2002. 'Was there a Victorian Ecology?' in Parham, John (ed.). *The Environmental Tradition in English Literature*. Aldershot: Ashgate. 156-71.

Pepper, David, with Frank Webster, and George Revill (eds). 2003. *Environmentalism: Critical Concepts* (5 vols.). London: Routledge.

Phillips, Dana. 2003. *The Truth of Ecology: Nature, Culture, and Literature in America*. New York: Oxford University Press.

Riley, Jonathan. 1998. 'Mill's Political Economy: Ricardian Science and Liberal Utilitarian Art' in Skorupski, John (ed.). *The Cambridge Companion to Mill*. Cambridge: Cambridge University Press. 293-337.

Roe, Nicholas. 2002. *The Politics of Nature: William Wordsworth and Some Contemporaries*. Basingstoke: Palgrave.

Ruskin, John. 1907. *Unto this Last* (The People's Library). Cassell: London.Ryle, Martin. 2002. 'After "Organic Community": Ecocriticism, Nature, and Human Nature' in John Parham (ed.). *The Environmental Tradition in English Literature*. Aldershot: Ashgate. 11-23.

Skorupski, John (ed.). 1998. *The Cambridge Companion to Mill*. Cambridge: Cambridge University Press.

Soper, Kate. 1995. *What Is Nature? Culture, Politics And The Non-Human*. Oxford: Blackwell.

Stafford, William. 1998. *John Stuart Mill*. Basingstoke: Macmillan.Wall, Derek. 1994. *Green History*. London: Routledge.

Fear and Flowers in Anya Gallaccio's *Forest Floor, Keep off the Grass, Glaschu* and *Repens*

Judith Rugg

Abstract

Nature's gendering as female and the perception of women as being closer to nature than men is exploited and resisted by Anya Gallaccio in her site-specific artworks such as *Forest Floor, Keep off the Grass* and *Repens*. Her use of plants as sculptural material questions their associations with femininity and the domestic, and can be historicized with the work of Land Artists such as Mierle Laderman Ukeles, Harriet Feuggenbaum and Dominique Mazeud. Utilising Kleinian theory and drawing on the ideas of Julia Kristeva, this essay argues that Gallaccio collapses artifice, representation and simulacra into the strange and sinister, upsetting assumptions about the cultural stereotypes of femininity and creating subtly anarchic feminist works. [1]

The association between women and nature has a long history in Western culture, from Aristotle to Rousseau to Nietzsche (Lloyd 1989: 1). The constructed link between nature and woman through woman's reproductive ability and capacity for mothering has given rise to the view that women have a greater affinity with nature than men. Historically, landscapes have been represented in terms of the female body and the garden was considered a feminine preserve because of its association with flowers, fertility and proximity to the kitchen garden and the preparation of food.[2] The idea that women have a special affinity with the earth, or that they are the caretakers of it, assumes an essentialism which prolongs dichotomies relating to the

---

[1] Illustrations reproduced by permission of Anya Gallaccio, with thanks from the author of this article and the editors of the volume.

[2] For an historical account of the associations between women and nature see Carolyn Merchant (1980).

culture/nature, male/female divide and maintains the *natural* associations of nature with ignorance, and culture with knowledge. These oppositional dichotomies have an ideological function, in that they maintain the social order and the hegemonic discourses of culture, science and medicine etc. (Jordanova 1990: 48). This binary paradigm reinforces the association of masculinity with the city, and so-called feminine 'innocence' with the countryside. Images of the landscape in the Victorian era show the countryside as tranquil and stable in opposition to those of the city, which is often depicted as polluted (Rose 1993: 96). These representations construct an association of passivity with the landscape (female) and activity with the urban (male). Further, nature (woman) is also synonymous with formlessness, unknown irrational forces, the unbounded and indeterminate – *woman* represents "the confused forces of life" (Lloyd 1989: 1). Disorder is inferior to the rational qualities of the mind and knowledge, associated with the male. In Hollywood film, the male conquering hero is associated with the unknown landscape to be conquered, since what is signified as masculine will be the dominant preoccupation of such films.

The garden as an intimate domestic space associated with the feminine is both resisted and exploited by the sculptor and land artist Anya Gallaccio in her use of plants and flowers. Her use of these as sculptural materials questions their associations with femininity which include the frivolous, delicate, meaningless, marginal, and the fragile, as against the 'real world' of commerce and culture. The garden is located within the domestic in Britain and is a place where nature itself can be domesticated. It is both an extension of the material home and a respite from the threat of the outside world. Plants and gardens also have associative meanings with the park, which Walter Benjamin (1979: 296) saw as a place of bourgeois domestic harmony. The use of floral designs such as in wallpaper and upholstery, and of flowers and flowering plants within the domestic space, reinforce the relationship between the enclosed garden and the domestic. The decay and destabilisation inherent in Gallaccio's site-specific works which use plants and flowers – *Forest Floor, Keep Off the Grass, Glaschu,* and *Repens*) – undermine the notion of the garden as a paradigm for order and containment, together with the associations of flowers with femininity and passivity. The anarchism inherent in these works confronts the notion of the garden as an extension of female domestic labour, ultimately creating disorder and overturning expectations of the feminine. *Forest Floor, Keep Off the Grass, Glaschu* and *Repens* all manipulated the assumption that the garden marks off the boundary between nature and culture, pleasure and chaos. To be in a garden is to be closed off from the world, yet the garden as an establisher of boundaries makes it a symbolic structure, a reminder of mortality. As a site of pleasure and loss (of nature and of paradise, respectively) the garden is a refuge. Gallaccio's strategy of allowing chaos to blur the boundaries undermines the paternalistic pleasure of control and domination elicited by gardens and their significance as cultural enclaves against fenceless anarchic nature. Gallaccio has called *Glaschu* and *Repens* a form of gardening (conversation between the author and Anya Gallaccio, 19 July 2000).

Glaschu (1999) was sited in Lanarkshire House, Glasgow, an old Court House built in 1840 on the site of a tobacco mansion. Glasgow was a major industrial city in the nineteenth century and is now a city with an industrial past and post-industrial present, a city in a state of flux. The nearby derelict buildings have acquired plants and trees growing from their cracks, suggesting the way in which life continues against the odds. 'Glaschu' means 'dear green place' and is the Gaelic name for Glasgow, signifying its closeness to the countryside. Gallaccio was born there. The idea of the pastoral garden developed contemporaneously with the industrial revolution (Pugh 1988: 28), and *Glaschu* is a displacement of this antithesis since it is set within an industrial building.

Glaschu consisted of a planted 'green line' of plants, flowers and grasses, set in concrete based on a floral carpet design by James Templeton and Co., owners of a carpet factory also founded in the 1840s. It occupied the entire floor of the site. The viewer encountered the work physically by standing at floor level and looking closely at its details of flowers and leaves within the design, but also through a photograph of the work (taken from a balcony above), where the swirling lines of flowers and leaves are perceived in their double artifice. The plants grew to produce a flourishing of greenery and small flowers over a period of eight weeks. The work was reminiscent of a knot garden, its entire design only visible from above, except that it was indoors in a hitherto neglected space.

1. Landscape and the domestic

In *Glaschu,* plants, flowers and grasses are invaders from the natural, external world into the manufactured, cultural, interior world. Its formal references to the 'secret garden' feminise the space, and the presence of organic matter inside signals dereliction and the anxiety that is caused by the displacement of the outside to inside. In its use of an 1840s carpet floral design, a manufactured design based on nature and associated with women and the domestic, *Glaschu* suggested a reference to the position of women in the process of nineteenth-century industrialisation. By pushing back the boundaries of nature industrialisation privileged the mechanistic over the organic, simultaneously controlling, dominating and violating nature as female "while excluding women from society and economically dominant ideology and practices" (Agrest 1996: 55).

Repens (2000) was commissioned by Locus + and sited at Compton Verney, a mansion in Warwickshire designed by the architect Robert Adam in 1763. Gallaccio cut the enlarged pattern of a ceiling rose (fifty-five metres across) into the grass in the grounds surrounding the house. The pattern was repeated five times. Designs for prayer rugs repeat their patterns to the edge, implying that there is no edge and therefore implying infinity. By repeating this pattern Gallaccio subverts the idea of the garden which, by definition, must have a boundary in order for it to be separated from the excess of space and the exclusivity of experience.

A number of women artists working in the 1970s and 1980s made statements about the wider environment and addressed the need for social reconstruction through the use of waste management. The work of feminist 'Land Artists' demonstrated a relationship between landscape and the domestic where the 'everyday' domestic activity of washing, cleaning, gardening and nurturing provided the raw material for art. For example, Harriet Feigenbaum's *Erosion and Sedimentation Plan for Red Ash and Coal Silt Area – Willow Rings* (1985) involved restoring a strip mined area and maintaining it as a wetland environment by planting a series of willow trees. Betty Beaumont's definition of environment is all encompassing: personal, political, social, spiritual, physical, cultural and economic. Beaumont sees relationships between conceptual, virtual and geographical landscapes and believes that art should explore that potential (Beaumont, www-greenmuseum.org/content/artistsindex, 5 September 2002). Dominique Mazeaud's *The Great Cleansing of the Rio Grande River* (1987) is an ongoing performance work involving the clearing of rubbish from the river and inviting participating viewers. Early feminist environmental artists drew on ideas from art, sociology and science in order to expand the terms of art practice, merging definitions of art, science and sociology. Their works critique capitalism's relationship to the environment in the form of global corporations' role in pollution. Mierle Laderman Ukeles has drawn attention to women's unseen labour by making art out of essentially domestic chores. A series of thirteen performances, from 1973 to 1976, involved sweeping the floors of the museum, dusting, washing and cooking, which Ukeles saw as part of a global context of maintaining the environment. Anya Gallaccio also has related the element of repetition in her work to "women's work – that we do everyday, we repeat actions the whole time, all those things that people don't notice like cooking and cleaning". She has compared her work in its performative aspects with domestic tasks and by implication, maintenance art: "It is like the hidden domestic activities of how many times you cook dinner and how many times you the clean the bath" (conversation between the author and Anya Gallaccio, 27 April 2000).

The garden is associated with repetition, life, death, re-birth and cyclical time and women's labour as an extension of domestic space. In 'Women's Time' Julia Kristeva identifies feminist and patriarchal identities as structured within different notions of time and identifies three concepts of time – linear, monumental and cyclical. Linear time refers to our place in history and civilisation, which Kristeva associates with masculinity. Monumental time cuts across linear time and refers to eternity, which Kristeva sees as incorporating universal traits such as maternity. Cyclical time involves the experience of female subjectivity and includes repetition and cycles such as menstruation and is linked to monumental time. Kristeva sees monumental and cyclical time as fundamental in many civilisations, particularly mystical ones. Gallaccio's works utilise Kristeva's concept of cyclical time through their use of repetition and the ongoing life and death of plants, and with monumental time by their continual growth. *Glaschu's* oblique similarity to the knot garden (a symbol of eternity), the siting of *Repens* within a landscape originally designed by 'Capability' Brown (1716-83) (an environment which has endured through linear time and was itself designed to recall an historical time of the rural idyll through its use of grazing animals in the landscape) can be considered within Kristeva's concept of 'women's time'.

Historically, there is a relationship between gender and the domestication of plants; their role in the establishing and shifting of boundaries can be linked to the mobility of women in early societies (Hastorf 1998: 776). Through the juxtaposition of the floral design and carpet, *Glaschu* echoes the relationship between women's involvement in early plant cultivation and their role in the creation of the domestication of territory. The carpet references in the works suggest associations with women's domestic labour and the house. Historically, grasses and flowers were strewn on the floors of houses to change the smell and to maintain a clean environment. Initially whole gardens were depicted in early Persian carpet designs which were originally intended to replace gardens. This relationship between the garden as a place of enclosure and safety, and as an extension of the domestic environment can also be seen as a place of entrapment for women. The carpet has become a cultural metaphor for suburbia, a phenomenon which also reinforces the idea of the isolation of women. Whilst the garden is essentially an artificial place, as part of the domestic it endorses the social structure, preserving the status quo of gendered divisions of labour. It is a place where, it has been suggested, female sexuality outside of domestic relationships is buried and suppressed (MacCannell 1990: 101). Within the suburb, gardens are an uncanny mirror of the interior of the house in their conventional arrangements of lawn and carpet, flowers and furniture etc. Historically, parterres were created close to the house and were visible from it as imaginary extensions of inside space into outside space.

Carpet-bedding was developed after 1840 where bedding plants were arranged in designs which echoed those found on carpets. Both *Forest Floor* and *Glaschu* use carpets in forms that suggest associations with housework and domesticity and of gender roles ascribed within a patriarchal society and Gallaccio has referred to

Glaschu as a "concrete carpet" (conversation between the author and Gallaccio, 19 July 2000). The original 1840s Templeton floral design which Gallaccio used for *Glaschu* was probably intended primarily for consumption by women within the domestic sphere and was likely to be situated in the parlour or bedroom which were considered 'feminine' spaces. Victorian England's ubiquitous use of floral designs within the home of lace, curtains, wallpaper, upholstery, together with the use of flowering plants as domestic decoration, reinforced ideas about femininity within the domestic sphere. By deploying a design used for the mass production of carpets, Gallaccio re-positions the domestic within the industrial, counterposing the interior (female) world with the exterior (male) world which is reinforced by the juxtaposition between the concrete and the plants and flowers.

In *Repens, Glaschu, Keep Off the Grass* and *Forest Floor*, Gallaccio's use of plants and their association with the garden is part of her assertion that the garden is both a deception and a commodification of nature. Like the plant design it appropriates, *Glaschu* emphasises that every garden is a simulation of nature. Although we may think of them as nature, gardens are intermediaries, the culturalisation of nature masquerading as the natural. Gallaccio questions assumptions about identity and the apparent fixity of things. None of the plants she used were indigenous to Britain but "all came from garden centres" (conversation between the author and Gallaccio, 19 July 2000). The contemporary ubiquity of the plants, which have scattered origins, she sees as a metaphor for the human relationship with Glasgow as a centre for trade in the seventeenth and eighteenth centuries – a place where people came and went, settled and scattered. The line is both a frontier and a series of routes and paths leading from one place to another. In *Glaschu*, Gallaccio used plants as a metaphor for the hybridity of culture within the wider context of Glasgow's colonial history and the origins of its wealth, built on slavery.

2. Invisibility

One of the issues that Gallaccio is interested in is the invisibility of her work (conversation between the author and Gallaccio, 25 April 2002). In *Repens* and *Glaschu,* the design was only visible in its entirety from above and this position was denied to the viewer. *Repens,* after a relatively short time, merged with the grass, becoming invisible and eventually disappearing: its cut edges gradually blurred and the work became increasingly hard to see. *Forest Floor* was deliberately placed inside the wood, away from the path, and involved concealment. It became further hidden by the growth of the forest and the deterioration of the carpet. There are other elements of invisibility in the works – the Robert Adam design for the ceiling rose was never installed and the Court House and tobacco mansion in *Glaschu* were covered over by redevelopment. Part of the intention of the works was to oppose the high visibility of other aspects of the sites – for example, the absent sculptural objects in *Keep Off the Grass* and the emphasis on views and vistas in the (apparently unending) 'Capability' Brown landscape in *Repens.* In *Keep Off the Grass* (1997), sited on the Serpentine Gallery's lawn (its sculpture garden), Gallaccio sowed root vegetables (carrots, turnips and beetroots) on the dead patches of grass which were the imprints of heavy sculptural works that had been removed and Gallaccio (unseen) observed people looking for (and sometimes not finding) the work. By planting root vegetables, she indicates her interest in how things underground are invisible and are, in any case, hidden from view as they do not resemble conventional object-based sculpture.

Keep off the Grass can be considered as a critique of the spaces of art and the nature of sculpture. It suggested (feminised) nature as both subdued and resistant, and by further implication, public sculpture as visible, heavy and masculine.[3] The work interrogated how things become culturally as well as formally visible as the plants became rampant within their assigned spaces, over-spilling their defined areas yet remaining largely invisible. The idea that nature, within the garden, is subordinate and passive is countered in the work by the disorderly and unchecked growth of the plants. *Keep Off the Grass,* whilst referring to the garden as a paradigmatic fragment of nature, extended the idea of what we understand by nature. Part of the problematic of the work becomes how to focus people's attention on

---

[3] This reading is apparent in Gallaccio's comment regarding the relative invisibility of *Keep off the Grass* "as compared to the sculpture that was there, all the other things would be much more obvious, like a sculpture on a plinth or a big truck with lights or whatever [...]" (conversation between the author and Gallaccio, 19 July 2000).

an apparently empty space.[4] In using an essentially transient material, Gallaccio drew attention to the transience of all things and suggested that even heavy sculptural objects, no matter how large and heavy you make them, have a limited time on earth. She implied that as a framework for the consumption of art, the environment (and the ideological conditions that create it) is itself a construct. The work appeared natural (as having been made by nature) which was an illusion perpetuated by the landscaped park surrounding it, but both it and Hyde Park were closed off from the wider everyday urban environment and the ordered world of streets and buildings.

Repens was set within a landscape constructed by 'Capability' Brown who set country houses amid a "sea of grass" and disposed of plants and flowers (Quest-Ritson 2000: 135), where Gallaccio hoped to show "that what we think of as natural, is in fact highly contrived" (conversation between the author and Gallaccio, 19 July 2000). 'Capability' Brown's landscapes were intended as vistas – viewed from various positions from within them – whereas *Repens* resembled a parterre which, in its proximity to the house, extended the domestic like an outside carpet.[5] Historically women have been associated with the kitchen garden and men with the distant landscape, the 'beyond' and the sublime.

Robert Adam used elements of the natural world in his interiors and Gallaccio, in her use of one of his designs, repositioned this back into the outside. In a play on the word 'rose' the culturalisation and appropriation of nature is also alluded to by her use of one of Adams's ceiling rose designs. She literally turned assumptions about nature upside down by her reversal of the rose design (normally on the ceiling) onto the ground, alluding to the attempted mirroring of nature by the landed class to reinforce the delusion that systems based on privilege are natural. The attempt of something to appear to be something else, either conceptually or formally, is the nature of art and

---

[4] Gallacio noted, when observing people encountering her work that "even with the plants growing, the work could still be invisible because there was no art, it was like an empty space" (conversation between the author and Gallacio: 19 July 2000).

[5] The work mirrored some aspects of a parterre which often used embroidered shapes cut into turf and was outlined in box hedging. The English parterre was made of cut grass work ('gazon coupe') and included a border of flowers. It was to be viewed from the upper floors, or planted on rising ground (Quest-Ritson 2000: 70).

often a requirement of survival in nature. This is reflected in the site-specificity of *Repens*. Compton Verney was used during World War II by the Ministry of Home Security as a centre for research into camouflage and was itself camouflaged by the burning of its grounds to change their texture and colour.

3. The works as feminist artworks

Gallaccio's interest in materials like flowers stems from her interest in working with things that women artists "are frightened of working with" as working with them "is a really crazy thing to do if you want to be taken seriously" (Bickers 1996: 5). The association of flowers with beauty has been used and subverted by a number of women artists and Gallaccio's use of flowers as a sculptural material can be seen as a way of addressing the gender implications of the relationship between art and beauty. As she has said, "in the late 1980s, (male artists) could maybe deal with beauty, but women certainly couldn't" (conversation between the author and Gallaccio, 25 April 2002). She sees the flower works as essentially feminist works, a way of addressing the formal and sensual elements of art, and a diversion from the more dominant academic, text-based feminist works of the late 1970s and early 1980s.[6]

The association of flowers with the feminine includes the convention of wearing flowers in the hair, on the body and on clothing. Flower-like associations have been integrated into the female identity through the use of girl's names such as Rose, Jasmine and Violet which ascribed to women and girls certain (feminine) characteristics such as perfection, sensitivity and modesty (Stott 1992: 71). Flowers have been used culturally to embody patriarchal myths about femininity including sexual purity, love, beauty, innocence and fertility. The historical link between women, art and flowers ranges from seventeenth-century still-life painters to Victorian china painting as women and flowers as subjects developed as a genre from Renaissance to the late nineteenth century. The associations with

---

[6] To 'deflower' is to rape – hence violence against women is paradoxically disguised by flowers (Jacobus 1997: 316). Gallaccio's use of them can be considered as extending this association.

fragility, passivity and the decorative have been conveyed historically through the juxtaposition of women and flowers and were cultivated by the white middle-class Victorians. The creation of a flower/woman genre in art coincided in the late nineteenth and early twentieth centuries with what Victorians called 'the woman question' in social and political life (the suffragette movement), functioning as a way to realign aspects of femininity with fragility (Stott 1992: 77). The rise of the use of women in floral art in this period was an attempt culturally to diffuse the growing economic independence of women. Representations of women with flowers were part of a wider attempt to relocate women back into the home and to re-ascribe gender roles. In her use of flowers, Gallaccio investigates how to subvert the frivolous, *feminine* associations in order to make something that is "powerful, frightening and messy and dripping down the wall" (conversation between the author and Gallaccio, 25 April 2002).

Gallaccio's flower works are in contrast to Judy Chicago's *The Dinner Party* (1979) which has been described as "essentialist" in its assertion of the universality of womanhood (Molesworth 2000:79). In their forbidden subjects and materials, Gallaccio's works question representation and femininity through their exploitation of the inherent obsolescence and decay of their materials which associated them with death and loss, not celebration. Although accused of simple essentialism, Judy Chicago's *The Dinner Party* posited an idea of biological femininity whilst confronting the interface between public and private. In its representation of a dinner table set with ceramic variants of female genitalia, shown in the museum space, *The Dinner Party* asserted the discursive space of the private (and previously historically and metaphorically hidden) within a public, culturally historical space. The representation of female genitalia by feminist artists has also been seen as a way of making visible what modernism had erased (Pollock 1992: 9-14). By assuming a universality of the female through the use of the female body, Chicago's intention was to challenge the exclusion of women from Western culture. In its use of china painting, the work collapsed two referents: a technique traditionally associated with women's handicraft and its association with flowers; and the flower as metaphor for the signifying aspect of a woman's body. Through *The Dinner Party,* the flower/vagina was placed in opposition to the centrality of the phallus in the history of

Western art. The notion that women artists have certain forbidden materials and imagery available to them is culturalised by fixed notions of masculinity and femininity, which *The Dinner Party* partly endorses.

The manufactured images of leaves and flowers signify the acculturalisation of nature, the replacing of nature with its other and the substitution of the real with the artificial. The garden could be seen as a way to deal with the imaginary threat of nature which must be subdued and assimilated into culture, but in place of artifice striving against wilderness, as in a conventional garden, Gallaccio set up the conditions of anarchic growth against cultural constraints. The association of *Glaschu* and *Repens* with parterres are references to the symbolised control over nature. Landscape gardening is about power relations in a given time and the picturesque hides capitalist and gender relations. Gallaccio's works parody the slippage between the garden as made and complete, and nature-as-making (natural-looking) environment. Whilst formal gardens aestheticise the power of the landowning (male) class and subsequently the state, as artworks, the performativity of Gallaccio's works lie in their 'overgrowing' in an antithesis of control. 'Capability' Brown's landscapes overturned the parterres and knot gardens of the English landed class to create the impression of uninterrupted natural landscapes. *Repens* signifies that the power that formal gardens symbolised in the seventeenth and eighteenth centuries is still in place, yet hidden.

4. Death and loss and disorder

Culturally, the garden is associated with loss – the Garden of Eden is a metaphor for the supposed site of lost innocence and all gardens are a metaphor for Eden, a place associated with loss. The 'vanitas' symbolism of flowers in still-life painting was replaced by skulls in the fifteenth and sixteenth centuries as a more literal representation of death (Elkins 1993: 90). It has also been argued that, culturally, images of 'mother nature' function to "assuage the loss of the pre-Oedipal mother" (Rose 1993: 56). *Glaschu* evokes meanings of loss and absence in the suggestion of the luxurious interior, which once would have been the interior of Lanarkshire House as a mansion built on wealth gained from the tobacco trade. Tobacco is also a plant, but one that destroys both its own environment (sites used for the growing of tobacco can be used for little else) and people. The reference to things growing in the cracks of buildings also signifies absence and abandonment, of time moving on, and the scene is suggestive of unruly nature reclaiming the environment – one that Gallaccio also uses in *Forest Floor* to very different effect. If the work has meanings of regeneration and growth, it is also at the expense of the opposite. *Glaschu* embodies the notion that all things must pass away in its suggestion of past opulence. Death is chaos and the appearance of nature inside suggests uncontrolled decay and the degeneration back into nature which, if left alone, is the fate of all things.

In *Repens,* the pattern cut into the grass initially appeared formal, like a parterre, but became chaotic as it grew, eventually becoming hard to distinguish from the rest of the grass. Like parterres, the work eventually became grassed over, merging back into the "sea of grass" of the (contrived) 'Capability' Brown landscape.[7] What is initially order – a repeating pattern – veers towards the end of its life as an artwork into chaos, making the work eventually invisible. Disorder – the despoiler of pattern – symbolises both danger and power (Douglas 1966: 94).

Normally, the appearance in mowed grass of a plant (like a weed) would indicate that "sloth has taken up residence in paradise" (Fulford 1990: 27) and Gallaccio, utilising only grass and cutting, messes up the billiard table surface of the mown grass (normally suggesting order and control), planting her plan for degeneration. Although mowing the lawn is seen as man's work and a sign of bourgeois dominance over nature, tending flower beds is associated with female activity as, historically, domestic gardens were women's work since the provision of food and medicine was largely their responsibility (Quest-Ritson 2001: 51). *Repens* brings to mind Gallaccio's previous works which use flowers, *Preserve Beauty* (1991) and *Preserve Sunflower* (1991), for example. They refer to the Victorian practice of pressing flowers which can be seen as the symbolic repression of female sexuality (flowers are the (bi)sexual organs of plants yet associated with the feminine). It is the dangerous and immoral woman who, by letting nature overtake the garden, represents a threat to

---

[7] The work was allowed to exist for six weeks.

civilisation. Gallaccio's *modus operandi* of letting things pursue their own nature, by growing or deteriorating, goes against the grain of woman as nurturer.

Repens is derived from the Latin *repere* 'to creep' and means 'to creep up, grow along, or be just below the surface of the ground', suggesting a return of the repressed and a threat to controlled order. What seems to be re-creating the order of the formal garden in *Glaschu, Keep off the Grass* and *Repens,* reverts back to chaos. The popularity of landscapes designed by 'Capability' Brown – he worked on over one hundred and seventy gardens (Edwards 2002: 134) – coincided with the publication of Burke's *Philosophical Enquiry into the Origin of our Ideas of the Sublime and Beautiful* (1756) and the genre of landscape painting that emerged with the rise of the bourgeoisie in land and property ownership (Quest-Ritson 2001: 148). The landscapes of 'Capability' Brown were a pastoral version of the sublime in that they attempted to create an illusion of infinite space. The notion of the sublime is gendered (Immanuel Kant saw beauty as female and the sublime as male), and scenes of the sublime were only accessible to men (explorers, engineers, architects etc). Elements of the sublime were only feminised when they were controlled. The instability of Gallaccio's works disturbs both the sublimity of the landscapes in which they are set and the gendered implications of the sublime by turning gardening into a form of chaos and disturbing the viewing space. In *Forest Floor,* the ground is omnipresent and threatens to *pull down* and overwhelm the carpet; for the viewer in real time there is an endless suspension of terror.[8]

Forest Floor, Keep Off the Grass and *Repens* blur the boundaries of culture and nature. The artworks and their environments merge in an understated 'loss of control' that is actually highly controlled.[9] *Glaschu* drew in the viewer who stepped over the linear cracks of the work, re-negotiating its space with her or his body. The work signified renewal and regeneration in a reference to the transformation of the

---

[8] Burke believed that the sublime was evoked by mingling pleasure and terror, but terror must be held back and suspended. 'What is terrifying is that it happens that it does not happen', an 'agitation in the mind [...] which reflects on what is or what was in order to determine what is not yet.' (Lyotard 1989: 204).

[9] Like the forest itself which appears wild but was in fact a 'factory of trees' (conversation with Gallaccio, 25 April 2002).

site itself (it was being converted into a bar and restaurant), and to nature as the primary source of constant regeneration. The plants, flowers and grasses of *Glaschu* seem to signify the impossibility of art (the source of the design) imitating life – manifested through a work of art. Like *Forest Floor*, the 'carpet' design in *Glaschu* disintegrates, but through a reverse process of constant becoming and abundance as the plants and flowers infinitely regenerate. In Foucault's (1986) third principle of heterotopias, the carpet is the two-dimensional condensed space of the garden where the four parts of the world are superimposed, at the centre of which is the garden itself. Gallaccio disrupts the order and places the feminine within the centrality of this heterotopic space which, by its nature, according to Foucault, exposes the ideological organisation of space.

Anya Gallaccio *Forest Floor*

Anya Gallaccio *Keep off the Grass*

Anya Gallaccio *Glaschu*

Anya Gallaccio *Repens*

Bibliography

Agrest, Diane. 1996. 'The Return of the Repressed: Nature' in D. Agrest, P. Conoway and L. Kanes Weismann (eds). *The Sex of Architecture*. New York: Abrams.

Benjamin, Walter. 1998 [1979]. *One Way Street and Other Writings*. London: Verso.

Bickers, Patricia. 1996. 'Meltdown', *Art Monthly*, 195: 3-8.

Douglas, Mary. 1996 [1966]. *Purity and Danger: An Analysis of Concepts of Pollution and Taboo*. London: Routledge.

Edwardes, Jane. 2002. 'Who Guards the Gardens?', *Time Out* (3-10 April 2002): 134.

Foucault, Michèle. 1996 [1986]. 'On Other Spaces: Utopias and Heterotopias', in Neil Leach, (ed.) *Rethinking Architecture*. London: Routledge. 348-367.

Fulford, Robert. 1998. 'The Lawn: America's Magnificent Obsession' in *Azure* (July/August 1998): 34-41.

Hastorf, Christine. 1998. 'The Cultural Life of Early Domestic Plant Use' *Antiquity*, 72 (27): 773-782.

Jacobus, Mary. 1987. 'Freud's Mnemonic: Women, Screen Memories and Feminist Nostalgia' in M. Loorie, D. Stanton and M. Vicinus (eds). *Women and Memory* Special Issue, *Michigan Quarterly Review*. Michigan: University of Michigan Press. 117-139.

Jordanova, L.J. 1990. 'Natural facts: a historic perspective on science and sexuality' in Carol MacCormack and Marilyn Stratheska (eds). *Nature, Culture and Gender*. Cambridge: Cambridge University Press. 42–69.

Kristeva, Julia. 1981. 'Women's Time' (trans. A. Jardine and H. Blake). *Signs*, 7: 13-15.

Lloyd, Genevieve. 1984. *The Man of Reason: "Male" and "Female" in Western Philosophy*. London: Methuen.

MacCannell, Dean. 1991. 'Landscaping the Unconscious' in Mark Francis and Randolf Hestor (eds). *The Meaning of Gardens*. Cambridge, Mass: MIT Press. 94-101.

Molesworth, Helen. 2000. 'Housework and Art work' in *October* 92: 71-97

Pollock, Griselda. 1992 in E. Wright, E(ed.) *Feminism and Psychoanalysis: A Critical Dictionary*. Oxford: Blackwell. 4-9.

Pugh, Simon. 1988. *Garden – Nature – Language*. Manchester: Manchester University Press.

Quest-Ritson, Charles. 2001. *The English Garden: A Social History*. London: Viking.Rose, Gillian. 1993. *Feminism and Geography: The Limits of Geographical Knowledge*. Cambridge: Polity Press.

Stott, Annette. 1992. 'Floral Femininity: A Pictorial Definition' in *American Art*, 6 (2): 60-77.

Like a Ship to be Tossed: Emersonian Environmentalism and Marilynne Robinson's *Housekeeping*

Hannes Bergthaller

Abstract

For Emerson and those nature writers who followed his lead, it is the belief in nature's permanence and consistency which allows them to pursue the project of deriving 'spiritual facts' from 'natural facts,' making nature the normative ground on which to raise their critiques of modern society.

In her novel *Housekeeping*, Marilynne Robinson unmoors this 'House of Emerson,' the intellectual heritage of American transcendentalism. In her representations of the natural world, the protagonist Ruth employs a typological language that reverberates strongly with that of Emerson and Thoreau. However, rather than using this language to gesture towards an originary moment of unmediated experience in which the individual mind is aligned with nature's transcendent design, her version of typology becomes a means of coping with the loss of her dead mother. This essay examines Robinson's paradoxical method of conjuring presence from absence – her metaphors become as transient as the lifestyle that she embraces at the end of the novel. It is a therapeutic effort to 'make the world comprehensible and whole' undertaken in full knowledge of its ultimate futility, 'a blossom of need', in Robinson's diction.

Housekeeping can be read as appropriating and rewriting a tradition which, while professing to leave behind the merely human for a higher order of being, has frequently ended up using nature to empower the subject, to validate its sense of ownership and to naturalise conventional assumptions about gender and nation. It takes seriously the notion of nature's radical otherness and develops a highly self-reflexive language dramatising the cognitive and ethical quandaries that it entails. Robinson sketches out a version of the sublime that does not subsume its moment of negativity in the sweep towards an affirmation of humankind's special place in the scheme of things. She reminds her readers that leaving behind anthropocentrism – if it is possible – also means abandoning the *oikos*, the idea of nature as *our home*.

Emerson, in his seminal essay *Nature*, affirmed a metaphysical faith
that is still fundamental, not only to the natural sciences, but to
environmentalism and nature writing as well:

> God never jests with us, and will not compromise the end of nature by permitting
> any inconsequence in its procession. Any distrust of the permanence of laws
> would paralyze the faculties of man [...] We are not built like a ship to be tossed,
> but like a house to stand. (Ralph Waldo Emerson, *Nature* (1957a: 42)

Perry Miller has called this essay, which was first published in 1836, a
central document of the "cult of nature" that flourished in the United
States during the nineteenth century (Miller 1967: 152). It is
undoubtedly one of the most eloquent expressions of a cultural
metaphysics whose hold on the national imagination remains
unbroken even today, although it has undergone significant
modifications since the advent of the environmental crisis in the
second half of the twentieth century.[1] In this discussion, I will begin
by pointing out some of the ways in which an Emersonian
metaphysics continues to inform both the literature of U.S.
environmentalism and the work of many literary critics affiliated with
it. In the second part, I read Marilynne Robinson's novel
Housekeeping as an attempt to reassess the continuing viability of this
tradition, and, by way of a conclusion, try to spell out the bearing that
her work may have for ecocriticism and the literature of nature.

1. Emersonian Environmentalism

At the core of the metaphysical faith which Emerson's essay
articulated is the following belief that Americans enjoy a special
relationship with nature. Wilderness, as the purest form of nature, is
the wellspring of democratic virtues and thus of American national
character – the place where immigrants come to strip away the
cultural baggage of their countries of origin and become 'naturalized'.
By confronting nature in solitude, the American beholds "God and

---

[1] The term 'cultural metaphysics' is borrowed from Sacvan Bercovitch. I take it to
denote a culture's fundamental beliefs about the way in which the world is organised,
about people's role in the world and about what constitutes proper behaviour – that is,
those notions which underpin what in a given culture passes as 'common sense'
(Bercovitch 1978: 12).

nature face to face" (Emerson 1957a: 21), rather than mediated through socially informed habits of perception, and aligns himself with the natural laws on which the American nation is founded. Emerson identifies the stars as the clearest manifestation of natural law:

> [If] a man would be alone, let him look at the stars [...] One might think the atmosphere was made transparent with this design, to give man, in the heavenly bodies, the perpetual presence of the sublime [...] If the stars should appear one night in a thousand years, how would men believe and adore; and preserve for many generations the remembrance of the city of God which had been shown! (Emerson 1957a: 23)

While Emerson is echoing here the conclusion of the *Critique of Practical Reason*, where Kant famously pairs the "starry heavens above and the moral law within", the passage also marks his departure not only from the German idealist, but from other European theorists of the sublime, as well. For Kant, the star-studded sky is far from comforting – quite the contrary: the sheer multitude of the stars overwhelms man and threatens him with insignificance and "annihilates" his "importance as an animal creature" (Kant 1997: 133). The perception of the infinite in nature is only the first step of a dialectic in which the failure of the imagination to represent infinity to itself leads to a countervailing and empowering upsurge of reason. In Emerson's account, the first step of dispossession and terror is curtailed, leaving only the exulting feeling of a frictionless merger with nature, where the individual mind is aligned with nature's transcendent design – the various emotions which nature is said to elicit in her "lover" are so many variations of the "wild delight" described in the famous "transparent eyeball" section of *Nature* (Emerson 1957a: 24).

To distinguish this peculiarly American type of sublimity as it is formulated in Emerson's *Nature* from its European antecedents, Howard Horwitz has proposed to call it the "manifest or typological [...] or the domestic sublime" (Horwitz 1991: 37) – 'domestic' because, according to its schema, America's wilderness is the providential home of its chosen people. The continent's landscapes here become the visible sign of God's transcendental design for the American people, assuming the place which scripture had formerly occupied in the belief system of their Puritan forbears. Nature is perceived, as James Batchelder wrote in 1848, as a "foster mother" to the "governing race of man" (quoted in Miller 1965: 57). Emerson's incessant troping on the "food" (Emerson 1957a: 24) which nature provides to man, also bears out Horwitz' comment that "the continent's sublimity is synecdoche for divinely nurtured, manifest destiny" (Horwitz 1991: 37). Emerson even extrapolates this idea to a planetary scale: "The misery of man appears like childish petulance when we explore the steady and prodigal provision that has been made for his support and delight on this green ball which floats him through the heavens" (Emerson 1957a: 25).

The nationalist overtones of the 'cult of nature' have gradually come to take a backseat in the course of the transformations that it underwent in the twentieth century and were superseded by an ethos in which nature is seen as a site of individual spiritual fulfilment or 'healing'.[2] Indeed, most of its contemporary devotees will insist that life in the U.S. at the beginning of the twenty-first century poses formidable obstacles to the experience of 'oneness' with nature which they prize, and readily concede the superiority of 'primitive' cultures in this respect. However, even this widely acknowledged sense of alienation from the natural environment testifies to the fact that the metaphysical base of the 'cult of nature' has remained largely intact. The artificial environments with which postmodern U.S. Americans have surrounded themselves are denounced precisely because they obscure their original relation to nature – because they prevent, as Emerson would have it, the alignment of the "axis of vision" with the "axis of things" (Emerson 1957a: 55). The moral thrust of this argument is predicated on the same assumptions which form the base

---

[2] How easily the latter can slide back into the former is forcefully demonstrated by Robert Redford's comments on the ANWR debate in an e-mail message to the members of the Natural Resources Defense Council, on whose board he serves, in the aftermath of September 11th 2001: "The preservation of irreplaceable wildlands like the Arctic Refuge and Greater Yellowstone is a core American value. I have never been more appreciative of the wisdom of that value than during these past few weeks. When we are filled with grief and unanswerable questions it is often nature that we turn to for refuge and comfort. In the sanctuary of a forest or the vastness of the desert or the silence of a grassland, we can touch a timeless force larger than ourselves and our all-too-human problems. This is where the healing begins. Those who would sell out this natural heritage – this spiritual heritage – would destroy a wellspring of American strength." The full text of Redford's email is available on the internet at: http://greenyes.grrn.org/2001/11/msg00054.html.

of Emerson's argument in *Nature:* that nature presents humans with a transcendent order which assigns to them their proper place, and can therefore be properly characterized as their 'home'. Furthermore, this order can be directly translated into normative claims as to how humans should comport themselves with respect to their natural environment.

Intimately linked with these ideas is a certain view of the relation between language and the experiential world which allows for the conversion of natural facts into ethical precepts, a view which in *Nature* is explicitly typological and which was implicitly taken up by such important protagonists of the modern environmental movement as Rachel Carson and Aldo Leopold. Let me briefly outline this theory of language as it is formulated in Emerson's essay. He opens the chapter on language with three axioms:

1. Words are signs of natural facts.
2. Particular natural facts are symbols of particular spiritual facts.
3. Nature is the symbol of spirit. (Emerson 1957a: 31)

In his explanation of the first axiom, Emerson states that all concepts originate in a tropological abstraction from material facts: "*Right* means *straight*; *wrong* means *twisted; spirit* primarily means *wind*" (Emerson 1957a: 31). Words receive their meaning from their original referents. In the crucial next step, Emerson takes this idea further: "It is not words only that are emblematic; it is things which are emblematic. Every natural fact is a symbol of some spiritual fact" (Emerson 1957a: 32). The meaning of the term 'spirit' in Emerson's texts is notoriously difficult to explain, but in this particular case, the following passages make it quite clear that what he refers to as "spiritual facts" are moral truths – facts that not only 'are' but 'ought to be':

> The axioms of physics translate the laws of ethics. Thus the whole is greater than the part; reaction is equal to action; the smallest weight may be made to lift the greatest [...] and many the like propositions, which have an ethical as well as a physical sense (Emerson 1957a: 35).

This correspondence between moral and natural law has been called the 'core doctrine' of New England Transcendentalism (Spiller 1971:

xiv), and it was in consonance with the natural theology which dominated scientific inquiry well into the nineteenth century. As Laura Dassow Walls puts it, this doctrine could be upheld against the seeming contradictions it invariably produced only because it was backed up by "the deep embrace of a divinely designed universe which excluded the unknowable by fencing in certainty with the guarantee of coherence" (Walls 2003: 49). This trust in the commensurability of the worlds of mind and matter is expressed in the quote which I have chosen as the epigraph of this essay, and Emerson held on to it even after the optimistic mood of *Nature* had given way to the more sombre and sceptical voice that can be heard in his later essays. He never abandoned the conviction that, as he was to put it in *Experience*, "underneath the inharmonious and trivial particulars, is a musical perfection; the Ideal journeying always with us, the heaven without rent or seam" (Emerson 1957b: 266-267).

So, in the same way that the Old Testament was taken to foreshadow the New, and to typify the Puritan errand, nature, for Emerson, came to contain those divine laws which govern human history in general and the development of American society in particular. To the extent to which language is distanced from the originary moment of figuration when a natural fact is apprehended and spontaneously transposed into a mental image, it also loses its power to reveal spiritual truths and becomes a mere "paper currency" (Emerson 1957a: 33) which is parasitic on "the language created by the primary writers of the country, those, namely, who hold primarily to nature" (Emerson 1957a: 34). It is those poets who are "bred in the woods" (Emerson 1957a: 34) and have, therefore, been directly exposed to nature's transcendental design who are in the best position to give proper guidance to their nation. Their "good writing and brilliant discourse" are "perpetual allegories", a "blending" of "experience with the present action of the mind" (Emerson 1957a: 34). Thus, metaphor (under which term one may subsume what Emerson variously calls "emblem", "analogy", "metaphor" and "allegory"), which establishes the typological relation between material and spiritual facts, is not only the basis of language, but an instrument of transcendence by which man partakes of the divine mind:

Have mountains, and waves, and skies, no significance but what we consciously give them when we employ them as emblems of our thoughts? The world is emblematic. Parts of speech are metaphors, because the whole of nature is a metaphor of the human mind [...] This relation between the mind and matter is not fancied by some poet, but stands in the will of God, and so is free to be known by all men. (Emerson 1957a: 35)

Many ecocritics have interpreted this thoroughgoing spiritualization of nature as a symptom of Emerson's abiding anthropocentrism, part and parcel with his Baconian conviction that history must result in man's complete dominion over nature. They have contrasted it unfavourably with the more properly 'biocentric' vision of his disciple Henry David Thoreau, whom they cast as the single most important precursor of modern environmentalism in the U.S.[3]

I believe that such a critique underestimates the extent to which not only Thoreau and canonical exponents of modern environmentalist literature such as Leopold and Carson, but even ecocriticism itself have remained in the thrall of an Emersonian metaphysics. This is evident from the widely held belief that the individual may indeed enjoy an "original relation with the universe" (Emerson 1957a: 21), that this feat is most easily accomplished by confronting nature in solitude, and that it is possible to capture the meaning of this experience in language. Moreover, it is held that this experience can furnish the most powerful ground for effective political action. While some ecocritics no longer assign to humankind a position of absolute centrality in the natural order, they do believe with Emerson that there *is* such a natural order, and that there is a proper place for humans within this order which the science of ecology can help them to determine and occupy. They may have repudiated Emerson's imperial stance towards nature, but – much more importantly – they have held on to his optimistic vision about the mutual adequacy of mind and language on the one hand, and nature on the other. With Emerson, they are convinced that to those who are willing to hear, the natural world can speak for itself.

---

[3] Michael Branch, for example, writes that "Emerson's spiritualized nature [...] also blocked his capacity to value nature for its own sake" (Branch 1996: 303). On the reluctance of ecocritics to grant Emerson a more prominent place in their genealogy, cf. Lundblad 2003.

Thoreau's painstakingly detailed descriptions of natural processes in his diaries, celebrated by ecocritics as a record of his struggle to arrive at a biocentric vision, rest on the conviction that these facts will "one day flower in a truth" (Thoreau 1975: 56). Ultimately, Thoreau believes, all factual knowledge about the natural environment will be amenable to a typological exegesis of the kind imagined by Emerson when he writes that

a life in harmony with Nature, the love of truth and of virtue, will purge the eyes to understand her text" so that "the world shall be to us an open book, and every form significant of its hidden life and final cause (Emerson 1957a: 36).

In the same vein, Rachel Carson can assert that the natural landscape "is spread before us like the pages of an open book in which we can read why the land is what it is, and why we should preserve its integrity" (Carson 2000: 69-70). This is a sentence in which the parallel deployment of the "why" elegantly smoothes over the semantic disparity between the two subordinate clauses.

Similarly, Aldo Leopold characterizes the work he does on his farm as a form of "reading" (Leopold 1966: 86). Indeed, one might go so far as to claim that the entire first part of Leopold's *Sand County Almanac* is prefigured by a brief passage in Emerson's *Nature*:

What is a farm but a mute gospel? The chaff and the wheat, weeds and plants, blight, rain, insects, sun, – it is a sacred emblem from the first furrow of spring to the last stack which the snow of winter overtakes in the fields (Emerson 1957a: 39).

The underlying metaphysical premises which inform the vision of nature in the texts of all of these writers are the same as in Emerson's doctrine of correspondence: nature possesses an intrinsic meaning that humans can decipher, if only they find the right language, the proper tropes. The bridge by which to cross the gap between the propositional and the normative, the material and the spiritual, between 'is' and 'ought', is a *true* metaphor – such as Leopold's "land pyramid" (Leopold 1966: 251) and Carson's "web of life" (Carson 2000: 69), both of which are advanced as being scientific truth and ethical precept at the same time. Many ecocritics are on the same Emersonian track when they credit the prophets of ecology with achieving precisely that which Emerson demanded from the true poet: to "pierce the rotten diction" of decadent and hypercivilized writers, and to "fasten words again to visible things" (1957b: 34). The recuperation of literature's 'referential dimension' urged by Lawrence Buell and other ecocritics can gain the force of an ethical imperative only on the premise that what is thereby recovered will *as such* have ethical weight – an assumption that in turn can appear convincing only if the tropological work described explicitly by Emerson is tacitly taken for granted.

At the danger of overgeneralizing, one may therefore venture that the *oikos* of the ecological movement in the U.S. is, regarding its basic structure, the house of Emerson. That is to say, it is built on the conceptual heritage of New England Transcendentalism.

2. *Housekeeping*

Marilynne Robinson's novel *Housekeeping*, which was first published in 1981 and was quickly recognised as a classic, is one of the most astute efforts in contemporary literature to engage in a dialogue with this tradition – an effort which, as I intend to show, arrives at conclusions that are very different from the ones propounded by Emersonian environmentalists.

Given the book's suggestive title and the many hauntingly beautiful descriptions of the natural environment which it contains, and also considering the fact that Robinson's second book, *Mother Country* (1989), was a scathing attack on the ecological abuses perpetrated by the British nuclear industry, it is hardly surprising that numerous critics have tried to enlist *Housekeeping* for an environmentalist and, more specifically, an ecofeminist agenda. The book's narrative clearly lends itself to such an approach, as it is so obviously a feminist revision of one of the classical *topoi* of American literature: the flight of the individual from the oppressive constraints of culture. Whereas in the canonical versions of this story, the escapee is typically a man whose virility is under threat from the feminising influence of culture (Edward Abbey's *Desert Solitaire* is perhaps the best-known example of this in more recent nature writing), *Housekeeping* presents the reader with a cast of characters that is composed almost exclusively of women. This transposes the story into a very different mode. When at the end of the novel the narrator and protagonist, an adolescent girl named Ruth, and her aunt Sylvie, a

drifter, burn down the house built by Ruth's grandfather and escape
over the railroad bridge that crosses Lake Fingerbone to take up the
life of transients, they do so not only in order to escape the
responsibilities of domesticity. It is also an attempt to save the
peculiar kind of domesticity – the fragile 'household' which they have
established between each other – from being severed by the law,
which is represented by the sheriff of the little town who is a man
(Robinson 1982: 188; quoted hereafter as *HK*). Accordingly, Katrina
Bachinger interprets the novel's narrative trajectory as a passage from
a "hoministic hierarchical social order" to a "power-muted,
gynecocratic one" (Bachinger 1986: 17). Joan Kirkby claims that it
enacts a reversal of historical process "from patriarchal to matriarchal
rule, then to a state of nature", suggesting "a sense of connection with
natural life and rhythms, and an erotic rather than manipulative
attitude to nature" (Kirkby 1986: 98). The novel's title would thus
have to be read as an ironic transfiguration: whereas 'housekeeping'
traditionally refers to a sphere of domesticity clearly marked off from
the 'larger world' of masculine business, Robinson assimilates it into
its etymological equivalent – *ecology* – thus simultaneously extending
the domestic to the environment as a whole and abandoning the
traditional sphere of domesticity, erasing the exclusions which
constituted it in the first place. Many critics have also commented on
the novel's affinity with Thoreau's *Walden*, which is suggested by the
very arrangement of its setting, composed, as it is, of a lake, a railroad
track, a house, and a nearby village. Martha Ravits argues that
Housekeeping is taking up Thoreau's project of establishing spiritual
freedom through the renunciation of worldly encumbrances (Ravits
1989: 664).

   Against this background, one may attempt to characterize the novel
as an ecofeminist radicalisation of what Lawrence Buell has described
as the "epic of voluntary simplicity", and there is ample material in
the novel to back up such a reading. According to Buell, the
relinquishment of material goods as it is dramatized in texts of this
genre ideally culminates in the achievement of a sense of oneness and
familiarity with the environment, a relinquishment of "homocentrism"
and, ultimately, even of the self as a discrete entity (Buell 1995: 145).
Sylvie's 'housekeeping' offers itself for a reading along such lines, as
an opening up and breaking down of the built house, where the house

would have to be understood as a metaphor for the separation of humans from their 'true' natural home. When a spring flood inundates the house shortly after her arrival in Fingerbone, Sylvie is unbothered by this intrusion of nature into their domestic space and even waltzes with Ruth through the icy water (*HK*: 64). She soon moves into the room that was formerly occupied by her father, a room that has

> glass double doors opening into the grape arbor, which was built against the house like a lean-to, and into the orchard. It was not a bright room, but in summer it was full of the smell of grass and earth and blossoms or fruit, and the sound of bees (*HK*: 89).

Later in the novel, she leaves the sofa in the orchard after dusting it and forgets to close the doors and windows, so that old leaves and paper scraps begin to accumulate in the corners, shivering in the draught:

> Thus finely did our house become attuned to the orchard and the particularities of weather, even in the first days of Sylvie's housekeeping. Thus did she begin by littles and perhaps unawares to ready it for wasps and bats and barn swallows (*HK*: 85).

If the function of a house is to provide a space in which its inhabitants are separated and protected from their natural environment, it is precisely this function which Sylvie sets out to sabotage:

> Sylvie in a house was more like a mermaid in a ship's cabin. She preferred it sunk in the very element it was meant to exclude. We had crickets in the pantry, squirrels in the eaves, sparrows in the attic. (*HK*: 99).

She has Ruth and her sister Lucille take their dinners in the dark, in order that they may better perceive what is going on outside the house:

> We looked at the windows as we ate, and we listened to the crickets and nighthawks, which were always unnaturally loud then, perhaps because one sense is a shield for the others and we had lost our sight (*HK*: 86).

At dusk, Sylvie sits in the kitchen for hours, silent and motionless, listening to the insects. Ruth emulates her, knowing, as she says, that "in such a boundless and luminous evening, we would feel our proximity with our finer senses" (*HK*: 100). Thus, solitude and the suspension of the restrictive routines of domesticity permit a heightened state of awareness in which the environment is felt as a distinctly familiar presence. The dichotomy between a domestic interior and an alien and threatening exterior, where the women are assigned to the former while the latter is the domain of men, is obliterated. As Marcia Aldrich has it, "Sylvie's housekeeping privileges natural flux and as such reverses the oppositional hierarchy at work in the dominant ideology of housekeeping" (Aldrich 1989: 138). While the house is assimilated to its surroundings, the natural environment in turn seems to assume for Ruth a quality of homeliness, as in the description of the shore of Lake Fingerbone as a place of "a distinctly domestic disorder, warm and still and replete" (HK: 113)

There are a number of similar passages in which the natural and the domestic commingle, and where Ruth's evocative descriptions of her natural environment suggest the kind of "luminous interchange with the external world" (Buell 1995: 155) which Lawrence Buell hails as a hallmark of Thoreau's progress in his passage from anthropocentrism – an

> intensely pondered contemplation of characteristic images and events and gestures that take on a magical resonance now that the conditions of life have been simplified and the protagonist freed to appreciate how much more matters than what normally seems to matter. (Buell 1995: 153)

Tempting as such a reading may be, it ultimately remains less than persuasive, for it has to turn a blind eye to the deeply ambivalent character of Ruth's "unhousing" (*HK*: 159). In her reading of *Housekeeping*, Christine Caver situates the text within the literature of trauma and convincingly argues that it can be understood as a neo-realist account of "a family unable to get beyond the shock they cannot speak of", namely, the violent deaths of Ruth's grandfather and mother – the first an accident, the second a suicide (Carver 1996: 120). Similarly, Maria Moss reads the novel as a story about the failure to satisfy a basic human necessity, the need for sanctuary (Moss 2004: 6). Following their lead, one must point out that the passages of the novel where house and nature are blended frequently strike a note of uncanniness, of painful self-consciousness and even terror that complicates any attempt to read the novel merely as a celebration of the passage from anthropocentrism.

Not coincidentally, the first section of the novel, where the sisters spend a whole week at the shore of Lake Fingerbone, occurs after Sylvie is unable to write them a note that would provide a satisfactory excuse for their truancy. They experience their sojourn in nature as a form of banishment. While the "unnaturally lengthy and spacious" (*HK*: 79) quality of their days at the lake may seem to suggest a Thoreauvian 'deliberateness' of living, the concurrent heightening of awareness is neither deliberate nor simply delightful. Rather, it is a precarious and decidedly "heavy-hearted" pleasure wrung from suffering: "The combined effects of cold, tedium, guilt, loneliness, and dread sharpened our senses wonderfully" (*HK*: 79). Later, Ruth insists that she – unlike her sister Lucille – goes to the "woods for the woods' own sake" (*HK*: 99), but the enjoyment these visits afford her is of a distinctly morbid cast: "We would walk […] hearing the enthralled and incessant murmurings far above our heads, like children at a funeral" (HK: 98). Here, nature is pervaded by a sense of death and decay, inducing not comfort, but anxiety. The sensibility which emerges in these passages is quite unlike the exalted mood typical of much nature writing, and more in line with Edmund Burke's account of the sublime as "a sort of tranquillity tinged with terror" (Burke 1998: 165) – a sensation which may signify alienation from divine purpose just as readily as communion with it. In the Emersonian tradition, nature can figure as a site of rejuvenation and spiritual regeneration because her 'lover' intuits the presence of a transcendent order that is sympathetic to, sustains, and nourishes him. Likewise, in *Housekeeping* the natural world, particularly the lake, is pervaded by the presence of a different order of being:

The mountains, grayed and flattened by distance, looked like […] the broken lip of an iron pot, just at a simmer, endlessly distilling water into light. But the lake at our feet was plain, clear water, bottomed with smooth stones or simple mud […], as modest in its transformations of the ordinary as any puddle. Only the calm persistence with which the water touched, and touched, and touched, sifting all the little stones, jet, and white, and hazel, forced us to remember that the lake was vast, and in league with the moon (for no sublunar account could be made of its shimmering, cold life) . (*HK*: 112)

In this passage, the lake is described as the boundary between two different realms, where the element of the one is continually sublimated into that of the other; where water is 'distilled' into light and the lake's "cold life" testifies to the existence of an ideal sphere of immutable order, governed by different laws from those which prevail in the world of humans, such as the Greek and medieval cosmologists imagined the heavens to be. The notion of the two realms is one that Ruth obsessively reiterates, and her reflections may be termed 'sublime' in the etymological sense, for they always dwell on the threshold – *sub limen* – separating these two realms. Thus early in the book, after the death of her grandmother, she dreams of

> walking across the ice on the lake, [...] but in the dream the surface that I walked on proved to be knit up of hands and arms and upturned faces that shifted and quickened as I stepped, sinking only for a moment into lower relief under my weight. The dream and the obituary together created in my mind the conviction that my grandmother had entered into some other element upon which our lives floated as weightless, intangible, and inseparable as reflections in water. (*HK*: 41)

The waters of the lake, which have claimed both Ruth's grandfather and her mother (who is alluded to later in this passage with the mention of Helen of Troy's comb [41]), are imagined as the medium where the dead reside and literally support the living yet are absolutely separated from them. Indeed, Ruth seems to imply, the dead may belong to the world in a way that the living do not – their non-existence is more substantial than the life of the living, which is merely a reflection on the 'element' which they inhabit, and which may at any moment be swallowed up by their denser world. The threshold which separates the world of the living from that of the dead is most often represented as the surface of a body of water, although sometimes as a window, sometimes as a mirror, and always it is this *limen* on which the figures of consciousness appear. In the following passage, these three tropes are superimposed on each other, to dazzling effect:

> What is thought, after all, what is dreaming, but swim and flow, and the images they seem to animate? The images are the worst of it. It would be terrible to stand outside in the dark and watch a women in a lighted room studying her face in a window, and to throw a stone at her, shattering the glass, and then to watch the window knit itself up again and the bright bits of lip and throat and hair piece

themselves seamlessly again into that unknown, indifferent woman. It would be terrible to see a shattered mirror heal to show a dreaming woman tucking up her hair. And here we find our great affinity with water, for like reflections on water our thoughts will suffer no changing shock, no permanent displacement. They mock us with their seeming slightness. If they were more substantial – if they had weight and took up space – they would sink or be carried away in the general flux. But they persist, outside the brisk and ruinous energies of the world. (*HK*: 163)

At the outset, Ruth is outside of the house and watches her mother, Helen, as she remembers her from her early childhood, looking at her own reflection and combing her hair, as she did the evening before she took her daughters to Fingerbone and drowned herself in the lake (*HK*: 131). Ruth tries to break the window, presumably to join her mother and to make her aware of her own presence, but the window immediately seals over, like the ice on the lake. Then Ruth is inside, looking at a broken mirror, which seals over to reflect to her an image like that of Helen, as though she had taken her mother's place. The boundary which separates them from each other is identified here with "thought" and "dreaming": consciousness itself frustrates the desire to finally cross over from one realm to the other, as it keeps the dead ever present and yet absolutely separate. Their presence in memory is a constant, harrowing, reminder of a loss that cannot be repaired or compensated for, even by literally joining the dead – that is, by drowning oneself in the lake, as Ruth's mother has done. This suicide Ruth now understands precisely as an attempt to put an end to the painful reproduction of memory she herself is so familiar with, and the consequences of whose failure she has to bear. Like her father before her, Helen Foster has not achieved complete disappearance. Instead, her absence returns to haunt Ruth.

Ruth's wish to be "unhoused", to let herself be drawn across the conventional boundaries of the domestic and even abandon it for good, must thus be read against the background of the single most formative event in her life: the sudden loss of her mother, which in turn is a repetition of the loss of the father which Ruth's mother had experienced. While it may be interpreted as a way of attaining a deeper relationship to the natural environment, or of achieving spiritual self-reliance, it must also be understood as an expression of deep psychological anguish. When Lucille and Ruth have to stay overnight at the shore of Lake Fingerbone, about midway through the novel, they awaken in the middle of the night. It is pitch dark and unidentifiable animals scurry around their improvised shelter. Lucille throws stones at them and sings, denying "that all our human boundaries were overrun" (*HK*: 115). Ruth, on the other hand, keeps perfectly still and lets "the darkness in the sky become coextensive with the darkness in my skull and bowels and bones" (*HK*: 116). This episode has frequently been discussed as a moment when Ruth's new consciousness begins to come into its own, "liberating the mind from old patterns and making way for new perceptions and modes of being" (Kirkby 1986: 104; see also King 1996: 573). What it more immediately signifies, however, is a desire for consciousness to cease altogether, relieving her of the excruciating burden of remembrance:

> Darkness is the only solvent. While it was dark, [...] it seemed to me that there need not be relic, remnant, margin, residue, memento, bequest, memory, thought, track, or trace, if only the darkness could be perfect and permanent (*HK*: 116)

Ruth's excessive attentiveness to "relics", "remnants", and "residues", and her readiness to attach meaning to even the most mundane details of life, is thus another aspect of her inability to come to terms with her mother's death. What Ruth says of her grandmother Sylvia – that "she seemed absent-minded" but actually was "aware of too many things, having no principle for selecting the more from the less important" (*HK*: 25) – also applies to herself, her mother Helen, and to her aunt Sylvie. All of them are so fully absorbed by their awareness of the transience of things that they lose touch with their social environment – in the case of Sylvie and Ruth, to the point where they fall into a death-like state of trance. Even Ruth's grandfather Edmund is imagined by Ruth after this pattern. Assuming the perspective of her grandmother Sylvia, Ruth reports that he

> would pick up eggshells, a bird's wing, a jawbone, the ashy fragment of a wasp's nest. He would peer at each of them with the most absolute attention, and then put them in his pockets [...]. This is death in my hand, this is ruin in my breast pocket, where I keep my reading glasses. (*HK*: 17)

The juxtaposition of "death" and "ruin" with "reading glasses" in this passage suggests that the attention to the transience of the phenomenal world functions as a distinct mode of seeing the world, more particularly of *reading* it, of scanning it for hidden meanings.

This description of the grandfather also goes to indicate that, rather than representing the patriarchal 'law of the father' happily exorcised in the course of the narrative, as many feminist readings of the novel have proposed, he provides the first model for a way of relating to the world that will come to fruition with Ruth's narrative – a point that I will return to shortly. The experience of loss thus provides the basic premise for Ruth's outlook on the world, for what might well be called an 'epistemology of loss': "[J]ust when I had got used to the limits and dimensions of one moment, I was expelled into the next and made to wonder again if any shapes hid in its shadows" (*HK*: 166)

This is precisely the ghost of pyrrhonism, the kind of radical scepticism which Emerson was at such pains to expel from his idealist philosophy, lest we be left to wander "in the splendid labyrinth of the senses" (Emerson 1957a: 49). It is empiricism in its most extreme form: that the sun rose yesterday does not guarantee that it will also rise tomorrow. There are no substances in Ruth's world, only fleeting phenomena. Where Emerson, with a nod to Descartes' *Meditations*, insists on the benevolence of a God who, he writes, "would never jest with us" (Emerson 1957a: 42), Ruth speaks of the phenomenal world as a "sheet dropped over the world's true workings" in order to "trick" her (*HK*: 116).

So, while the numerous speculative or meditative passages of the novel clearly echo the typological rhetoric of Emerson and his heirs, as well some of their favourite themes (see Schaub 1995: 311; also Hedrick 1999: 138), something important is missing, namely the faith in the mutual adequacy of the worlds of mind and matter which is the linchpin of transcendentalist metaphysics – what Emerson called the "sacred faith" in the permanency of nature's laws (Emerson 1957a: 42). It is this faith which, for Emerson, anchors language to the experiential world and guarantees that his typological flights of fancy can converge on spiritual truths.

In this context, typological rhetoric becomes for Ruth a paradoxical method for conjuring presence from absence, for achieving an imaginary restoration of her mother which she knows perfectly well can never be other than imaginary. So the many passages where she describes the resurrection of the ordinary read almost like a gentle parody of Emerson's rhapsodic prose style, at once whimsical and tragic. At one point she imagines how one of her aunts, floating above

Lake Fingerbone in "some small boat", would gather the souls of all
the drowned with a fishing net, restoring them to normality:

> It was perhaps only from watching gulls fly like sparks up the face of clouds that
> dragged rain the length of the lake that I imagined such an enterprise might
> succeed. Or it was from watching gnats sail out of the grass, or from watching
> some discarded leaf gleaming at the top of the wind. Ascension seemed at such
> times a natural law. If one added to it a law of completion – that everything must
> finally be made comprehensible – then some general rescue of the sort I imagined
> my aunt to have undertaken would be inevitable [...] What are all these fragments
> for, if not to be knit up finally? (*HK*: 91-92)

If the natural world here provides the types by which Ruth can
imagine redemption, both her persistent use of the subjunctive mood,
and the almost comical exhaustiveness of her aunt's rescue mission,
make it quite obvious that this is not a rigorous translation of material
facts into spiritual facts. Rather, it is wishful thinking, an anguished
effort to impose an order on the world which is at once necessary to
make life bearable and patently fictional – that is to say, something to
be achieved only in art. Art's function in the world of *Housekeeping* is
thus to achieve the precarious restoration of a loss that it cannot repair.
It is a way of coming to terms with what Ruth calls the "force behind
the movement of time": "a mourning that will not be comforted. That
is why the first event is known to have been an expulsion, and the last
is hoped to be a reconciliation and return" (*HK*: 192). In the long
meditation on Biblical stories of origin in which this statement occurs,
Ruth imagines that a "second creation" occurred when Cain killed his
brother Abel and sorrow entered the world (*HK*: 193). God's attempt
to "purge this wicked sadness away with a flood" only multiplied the
sorrow, and "Every sorrow suggests a thousand songs, and every song
recalls a thousand sorrows, and so they are infinite in number, and all
the same" (*HK*: 193-194). One may read this as a narrative about the
birth of art out of the experience of loss, where the songs and stories
that commemorate the dead are a way to keep them present to the
living. Art, like the taste of water in the longer passage from which
this comes, contains their memory. Sylvie is a story-teller in this sense
– in the rare moments when she becomes talkative, she repeats the
stories which the people she has met in her life as a transient have told
her, or which she has read in old newspapers, and they are always
stories of abandonment and loss (*HK*: 66, 87, 103) – but Ruth's own

narrative, which constitutes the novel, is, of course, the principal instance of it.

However, the first artist we encounter in the novel is Ruth's grandfather Edmund, who is introduced not only as a successful railroad inspector, but also as a self-educated painter. Never having seen mountains, he devours stories of mountains, and takes to painting mountains in a manner suggestive of the Edenic landscapes of Henri Rousseau (HK: 4).[4] It is his desire to see real mountains that leads him to leave the Middle West and take his family to Fingerbone. If it was a mere accident that this move ultimately resulted in his drowning in the lake, Ruth nevertheless imagines it as a fulfilment of the desires expressed in his paintings. Contemplating the brilliant colours of the morning sky as she rows across Lake Fingerbone with Sylvie, Ruth says that "they reminded me of my grandfather's paintings, which I have always taken to be his vision of heaven" (HK: 149). However, Ruth imagines that the lake is pulling them down into its waters, as her grandfather watches them from his "Pullman berth, regarding the morning through a small blue window" of the submerged train (HK: 150), just as Sylvie used to sit at the "luminous" window of the kitchen, "the battered table and the clutter that lay on it [...] one ultramarine chill, the clutter of ordinary life on the deck of a drowned ship" (HK: 102). In these passages, it becomes clear that the waters of the lake, and the realm of the dead which they represent, are also the place where the desire for wholeness and immutability which is expressed by art, but can never be stilled by it, would at last find its fulfilment. The watchfulness engendered by loss is connate with the desire for the 'real' engendered by art. This is borne out by the singular effect that one of Edmund's works has on his wife Sylvia. He has fitted the image of two seahorses into the case of a defunct pocket watch he has found by the side of the lake:

> It was the seahorses themselves that she wanted to see as soon as she took her eyes away, and that she wanted to see even when she was looking at them. The wanting never subsided until something – a quarrel, a visit – took her attention

---

[4] Rousseau worked for the Paris municipal customs office, collecting fees from local farmers who brought their produce to the markets. The parallel to Edmund Foster, who earns his living "supervising the loading and unloading of livestock and freight" (HK: 5), is striking.

away. In the same way her daughters would touch her and watch her and follow her, for a while. (*HK*: 13)

That the images which prompt grandmother Sylvia's reverie here are of submarine creatures reinforces the link between the ideal domain of art, the waters of the lake, and the realm of the dead.

Against this background, it becomes clear that Ruth and Sylvie's flight across the railroad bridge at the end of the novel figures not only as a kind of 'death' – social or physical – but above all as a withdrawal into language itself. The event is rendered with skilful ambiguity so as to leave the decision to the reader whether to accept Ruth's contention that they "caught the next westbound" (*HK*: 216), which she offers with an earnestness that seems designed to arouse suspicion ("I will try to tell you the plain truth" [*HK*: 216]), or to conclude that they have indeed drowned in the lake, as the newspapers report (*HK*: 213). At the end of the novel, Ruth speculates how their absence may affect Lucille, whom she imagines sitting in a house and looking at a black window. When she is there, Ruth and Sylvie would sweep through, "leaving behind us a strong smell of lake water" (*HK*: 218). Lucille's imagined comment at this sign of their absence/presence would confirm that they now exist in that element of immutability that is the medium of art: "They never change" (*HK*: 218). The whole last paragraph of the novel is a studied demonstration of language's capacity to evoke that which is not there, playing on the contrast between the fiction's degree of detail and its unreality – an unreality which in the very last sentence comes to engulf Lucille, as well:

> No one watching this woman smear her initials in the steam on her water glass with her first finger, or slip cellophane packets of oyster crackers into her hand bag for the sea gulls, could know how her thoughts are thronged by our absence, or know how she does not watch, does not listen, does not wait, does not hope, and always for me and Sylvie. (*HK*: 218-219)

2.1 Leaving the House and Keeping It Too

It will have become apparent that in order to read *Housekeeping* as a straightforward exposition of the virtues of a biocentric sensibility, one would have to suppress a great deal of the novel's complexity. If we insist on interpreting the relation of Sylvie and Ruth to their environment in these terms, it is much more plausible to understand it as a caveat not to take at their word the exhortations of those deep ecologists who tell us to break down the boundaries of the human. For a biological organism, to refuse exclusion and to become "coextensive" (*HK:* 116) with its environment is synonymous with dying; by the same token, Ruth's wish to be "unhoused" must be understood as a wish to die. Thus the experience of true 'oneness' with nature, not to mention the sense of a world "comprehensible and whole" (*HK:* 92) which this experience is sometimes said to afford, can be had only in death – and in art, albeit figuratively. If we come to seek comfort and sustenance at Mother Nature's bosom, we may find her beautiful, but unexpectedly barren. According to the cultural metaphysics which Emerson's *Nature* helped to inaugurate, the solitary engagement with the natural world allows the individual to catch a glimpse of God's design; nature is a repository of transcendent, immutable meaning. Most contemporary environmentalists have disavowed theism, and they are well aware of natural dynamism. Yet even if they do no longer capitalize the term 'nature', they still use it in the singular, and not merely in deference to linguistic convention. They like to believe that nature can be understood as a harmonious, purposive 'whole' that would provide the normative ground on which a comprehensive critique of modern society may be raised.

It is this tradition of thought, the *oikos* of Emersonian environmentalism, which in *Housekeeping* is unmoored from its metaphysical foundations. In the world of Robinson's novel, the experience of wholeness and stability is available only in the domain of art, whereas the phenomenal world is a quicksand of deception, disappointment, decay, and inevitable loss. The metaphors which Ruth employs to impose a measure of coherence on the world are as transient as the lifestyle she embraces at the novel's end. They can no longer be *anchored* in experience, because experience itself is fluid and fleeting.

One need not share Ruth's pyrrhonism to appreciate her insights. The natural sciences do offer a vision of nature as a more or less continuous field of forces, and they would hardly corroborate Ruth's fears that the world may suddenly come to an end. However, Emerson's optimism that the increase in scientific knowledge would also help to circumscribe humankind's proper place in the cosmic order has turned out to be unfounded. Our growing understanding of the material world has not assured us about our role in the great scheme of things – on the contrary: the erosion of nature's normativity has proceeded at exactly the same pace at which our understanding of its workings has grown. The more we know about nature, the less sure we seem to be about what to do with that knowledge. The *oikos* of the science of ecology has turned out to be not a 'household', after all, but merely a convenient shorthand for something that is more appropriately expressed in the form of mathematical formulae. Yet this does not excuse us from the task of keeping house – of defining and sustaining a meaningful relation to our natural environment. As *Housekeeping* reminds us, the most important tool that we have for this purpose is language, and it is appropriate to the task precisely because its meanings are of a different order than the material world of the natural sciences.

Bibliography

Aldrich, Marcia. 1989. 'The Poetics of Transience: Marilyn Robinson's *Housekeeping*' in *Essays in Literature* 16(1): 127-140.

Bachinger, Katrina. 1986. 'The Tao of *Housekeeping*: Reconnoitering the Utopian Ecological Frontier in Marilynne Robinson's "Feminist" Novel' in Truchlar, Leo (ed.) *Für eine offene Literaturwissenschaft:Erkundungen und Erprobungen am Beispiel US-amerikanischer Texte*. Salzburg: Neugebauer. 14-32.

Bercovitch, Sacvan. 1978. *The American Jeremiad*. Madison: University of Wisconsin Press.Branch, Michael P. 1996. 'Ralph Waldo Emerson' in Elder, John (ed.) *American Nature Writers Vol. I*. New York: Scribner's. 287-307.

Buell, Lawrence. 1995. *The Environmental Imagination: Thoreau, Nature Writing, and the Formation of American Culture*. Cambridge: Harvard University Press.

Burke, Edmund. 1998. *A Philosophical Inquiry Into the Sublime and the Beautiful and Other Pre-Revolutionary Writings*. David Womersley (ed.) London: Penguin.

Carson, Rachel. 2000. *Silent Spring*. London: Penguin Classics.

Caver, Christine. 1996. 'Nothing Left to Lose: *Housekeeping's* Strange Freedoms' in *American Literature* 68(1): 111-137.

Emerson, Ralph Waldo. 1957a. 'Nature' in Whicher, Stephen E. (ed.) *Selections from Ralph Waldo Emerson*. Boston: Houghton Mifflin. 21-56.

— 1957b. 'Experience' in Whicher, Stephen E. (ed.) *Selections from Ralph Waldo Emerson*. Boston: Houghton Mifflin. 254-273.

Hedrick, Tace. 1999. 'The Perimeters of Our Wandering Are Nowhere' in *Critique* 40(2): 137-151.

'Henri   Rousseau: Biography'.   On   line   at:
http://www.guggenheimcollection.org/site/artist_bio_139.html   (consulted
30.04.2005).

Horwitz, Howard. 1991. *By the Law of Nature: Form and Value in Nineteenth-Century America.* New York: Oxford University Press.

Kant, Immanuel. 1997. *The Critique of Practical Reason.* Mary Gregor, (ed. & tr.). Cambridge: Cambridge University Press.

King, Kristin. 1996. 'Resurfacing of *The Deeps:* Semiotic Balance in Marilynne Robinson's *Housekeeping*' in *Studies in the Novel* 28(4): 565-580.

Kirkby, Joan. 1986. 'Is There Life After Art? The Metaphysics of Marilynne Robinson's *Housekeeping*' in *Tulsa Studies in Women's Literature* 5(1): 91-109.

Leopold, Aldo. 1966. *A Sand County Almanac. With Essay on Conservation   from Round River.* New York: Ballantine Books.

'Letter from Robert Redford on ANWR'. On line at:
http://greenyes.grrn.org/2001/11/msg00054.html (consulted 30.04.2005).

Lundblat, Michael. 2003. 'Emersonian Science Studies and the Fate of Ecocriticism' in *ISLE: Interdisciplinary Studies in Literature and Environment* 10(2): 111-134.

Miller, Perry. 1965. *The Life of the Mind in America: From the Revolution to the Civil War.* New York: Harcourt.

— 1967. *Nature's Nation.* Cambridge: Belknap Press.

Moss, Maria. 2004. 'The Search for Sanctuary: Marilynne Robinson's *Housekeeping* and E. Annie Proulx's *The Shipping News*' in *Amerikastudien/American Studies* 49(1): 79-90.

Ravits, Martha. 1989. 'Extending the American Range: Marilynne Robinson's *Housekeeping*' in *American Literature* 61(4): 644- 666.

Robinson, Marilynne. 1982. *Housekeeping.* New York: Bantam Books.

— 1989. *Mother Country.* London: Faber and Faber.

Schaub, Thomas. 1995. 'Lingering Hopes, Faltering Dreams: Marilynne Robinson's *Housekeeping* and the Politics of Contemporary Fiction' in Friedman, Melvin J. (ed. & intro.) and Ben Siegel (ed. & pref.) *Traditions, Voices and Dreams: The American Novel since the 1960s.* Newark: University of Delaware Press.

Spiller, Robert. 1971. 'Introduction' in Spiller, Robert and Stephen E. Whicher (eds). *The Early Lectures of Ralph Waldo Emerson, 1833-1842. Vol.III.* Cambridge: Harvard University Press. i-xxiii.

Thoreau, Henry David. 1975. *The Portable Thoreau.* Carl Bode (ed.). Harmondsworth: Penguin.

Walls, Laura Dassow. 2003. *Emerson's Life in Science: the Culture of Truth.*   Ithaca: Cornell University Press.

In the Mirror of Middle Earth: Langland's use of the world as a book and what we can make of it

Gillian Rudd

Abstract

The natural world offers a series of examples by which, and through which, human-kind may learn to appreciate God: this is a familiar literary topos in Langland, often neatly summed up in the phrase, 'the world as a book'. Such a phrase, which carries implications of reading and interpretation, sets humans somehow apart from the volume we read. What is interesting is that although in one way the trope of world as book must rely on some degree of separation (how else is it possible to read?), it also fundamentally relies on inclusion and the question raised becomes precisely that of the relation of human to natural world; of reader to text. The analogy of reading is useful, because reading necessarily involves interpretation, understanding and, frequently, confusion, paradox, lack of resolution; all of which also arise in environmental or ecological discussion. In the middle ages, there was the added dimension of reading words being the province of the relatively few, whereas the book of nature was, in theory at least, open to all. How much is the apparently thoroughly literary topos of the Malvern Hills also informed by a personal reaction to a precise geography? And Langland has used the phrase "in a mirour that highte Middelerthe". Are we to conclude that what we see in the world around us is necessarily dictated by what we ourselves are? Is it the case that all that we can see is, in effect, ourselves? However hard we resist, are we inevitably anthropocentric and narcissistic? This discussion explores Langland's response to this problem, while recognising that he would not have articulated it in these terms.[1]

Langland:

> [...] and sithen cam Kynde
> And nempned me by my name, and bad me nymen hede,

---

[1] A complementary discussion of this topic in Langland may be found in Rudd, G. 2003. 'Thinking Through Earth in Langland's *Piers Plowman* and the Harley lyric "Erthe to of erthe"' in *Ecotheology* 8 (2): 137-149.

And thorugh the wonders of this world wit for to take.
And on a mountaigne that Myddelerthe highte, as me tho thoughte,
I was fet forth by ensaumples to knowe,
Thorugh ech a creature, Kynde my creatour to lovye.[2]

[...] and then came Kynde and called me by my name and told me to take heed
and gain understanding through the wonders of the world. And on a mountain that
was called Middle Earth, as I thought then, I was led forward to learn by
examples, to love Nature, my creator, through each individual creature.

(*Piers Plowman.* Passus XI. 319-325)

At some point, probably in the late 1370s, the poet we now know as
William Langland was revising his long, allegorical poem which we
refer to as *Piers Plowman*. Little is known for certain about the poet
and the text itself has been the subject of much scholarly research and
speculation over the centuries, but it seems to have been a life's work
(quite possibly the only thing the poet wrote) continually under
revision and never fully finished.[3] This unfinished aspect of the work
reflects the restless tone of the whole. It is made up of a series of
dream visions, including dreams-within-dreams, interspersed with
waking passages, throughout all of which the dream's protagonist, Wil
(who is part poetic-persona, part personification of the human faculty
of the will), constantly interrogates what he sees and the people and
personifications he meets in the hope of discovering what it means to
"do well". The poem is thus exemplified by ceaseless questioning,
always returning to this central query, which amounts almost to a plea.

Doing well emerges as an ethical and moral duty which takes on
the force of a spiritual imperative in what is, after all, a religious poem
deeply concerned with the question of individual salvation. Salvation
may be individual, but the individual is always linked to the whole
here, and that whole is not only the whole of humanity, but of the
created world as a whole. Doing well, and indeed doing better and

---

[2] Langland. 1987. All quotations of the original text are taken from this edition. The
translations are my own.

[3] A good, accessible introduction to the B-Text of *Piers Plowman* may be found in
Simpson, J. 1990. *'Piers Plowman': An Introduction to the B-Text*. London and New
York: Longman. The version most commonly used today is the one known as the B
text. Although this version was probably substantially revised the revision process
was never completed, leaving the B text as the most complete version of the poem
available to us and hence the text I have used here.

doing best, thus entails not only right relations within human society, but also a correct appreciation of the natural world of which we are a part. As the passage under consideration here reveals, that appreciation includes admiration as well as at least an attempt to understand. In the quotation which heads this chapter, Wil is summoned away from what has become an increasingly abstract and bookish disputation about the ways to salvation and the fate of the good Pagan, and whisked off to a mountain top in order literally to look around him. At this point he is not only in a dream, but in a dream within that, so this mountain is obviously figural, as its name of Middle Earth indicates. As such it must represent this mortal world, halfway between Heaven (above) and Hell (below). However, with typical dream geography, this mountain of Middle Earth offers panoramic views of what we surely recognise as being also our world, the natural world of animals, trees, fields and birds, that constitutes what we so readily term 'nature'. It is this non-human natural world and in particular the fauna ("ech a creature") that provide the examples through which Wil is being encouraged to learn. From the start, then, Wil is both above the world looking down into it, and part of it, as the mountain is both above and integral to the surrounding landscape.

The literary topos used here by Langland is a familiar one: the natural world and all that is in it is regarded as a series of examples by which, and through which, humankind may learn to appreciate God. This attitude is often neatly summed up in the phrase, 'the world as a book'; a phrase which carries implications of reading and interpreting, but above all of us, humans, being somehow apart from the volume we read. Initially, this seems an easy image to understand. We may well object to the implied separation of humans from the rest of creation, but that dispute springs from an ethical stance, not from confusion. What is interesting is that, although in one way the trope of world book must rely on some degree of separation (how else is it possible to read?), it also fundamentally relies on inclusion. Humans must be like the rest of creation if they are to learn through the examples the natural world offers. It is this dual stance that is so subtly reflected in Langland's use of the mountain vantage-point here. The exhilaration so many experience when standing on a height surveying the surrounding countryside springs in part from a sense of being apart from the world, literally above it, seeing it all spread before us. It is from such a high point that Wil's attention is drawn to the creatures that inhabit this panorama as he is instructed to take heed ("nymen hede") that he may thus acquire understanding ("wit for to take") and so his panoramic survey becomes a detailed scrutiny.

Langland has made use of the almost dual vision offered by viewing a landscape from a peak before. In the fifth line of the Prologue, right at the beginning of the poem, he specifically tells us that he, or Wil, his poetic persona, is walking the Malvern hills: he "wente wide in this world wonders to here./ [...] on a May morwenynge on Malverne hilles" (B.Prol.4-5) ('walked abroad in this world to hear wonders [...] on a May morning on the Malvern hills'). In this first case Wil falls asleep and although we are told he finds himself in a wilderness in his dream, we are not told explicitly that he is still on a height. Nevertheless, the lines that follow depict a landscape as seen from afar, with a tower on a hill, a dale with a second more forbidding tower (a dungeon) and a wide plane between, full of people. All of this is not only more easily imagined as seen from a height, but is, in fact, what one still sees if one stands on the Malvern Hills, looking over Great Malvern. The landscape is thus both credible and credibly linked to an actual geographical position. This is not the place to enter into discussion of how far Langland was a rural or a London poet,[4] and neither do I wish to suggest in any way that Langland is portraying a literal view. Rather, the point is that, by evoking a *specific* landscape, Langland is adding particular point to his more general argument. In the case of the Prologue, in which the action then zooms in to focus on the people and their social groups, this association creates a direct link between Wil's dream and Langland's (and his first audience's), social and historical contexts. In Passus XI, however, the link is between a figurative motif – that of the natural world being like a book – and the literal experience of looking across a landscape as one might look over pages of a volume.

The figure of the Book of Nature as a companion volume to the Book of the Bible has a long history and was well-established as a

---

[4] The case for Langland to be regarded as a London poet is made by Barron, Caroline, 'William Langland: A London Poet' in Hanawalt (ed.) 1992, 91-109.

literary and religious device by the fourteenth century.[5] This tradition suggested, as John Whitman has put it:

> the possibility of turning the exegesis of Scripture into the allegory of nature. The belief that God authored not one book, but two – the Bible and the world – implied that the elucidation of the one complemented the understanding of the other" (Whitman 1987: 126).

Langland was thus able to draw on this tradition tacitly: he does not have to say in so many words that Kynde (whose name indicates Nature and God the Creator as well as species), is presenting a living world to Wil which is also a collection of images created in order to have their metaphorical meanings decoded. Both those suggestions are contained in the single word "ensaumples", which combines "an instance typical of a class" with "an illustration of a general truth", and "symbol, sign or token" with "a comparison drawn from nature". It is essentially the same word as "exemplar" – a fair text used by scribes to create other copies.[6] However, there is an opposite danger here, one of which ecocritics will be particularly aware: that to regard the natural world primarily as a book seems to relegate the whole of the non-human realm to a secondary role. Further risks are attendant upon that, such as, if the animals are there solely as examples, they have no value in their own right. Moreover, such a view suggests that all things must have a meaning in order to have a value, and that that meaning is determined purely in terms of bearing relevance to, and being interpretable within, humanity's relation to God. Such risks are real, but appear only if we overlook the essential point that Wil, and hence we humans, are ourselves part of this book of nature. We may be standing on a mountainside, but we are still within and a part of (rather than apart from) the landscape that surrounds and so contains us. This aspect of the tradition is reflected in Langland's use of alliteration in B.XI.325 to mark the close association of all creatures,

---

[5] The standard overview of the trope of the book of nature is to be found in Ch 16 'The Book as Symbol' in Curtius E. R., 1953. *European Literature and the Latin Middle Ages* (tr. W. R. Trask). John Whitman provides an interesting and detailed consideration of this figure in relation to the development of allegory in Ch 4 of his book (Whitman, John, 1987. *Allegory: the dynamics of an ancient and medieval technique*) esp.: 126-130.

[6] See *The Middle English Dictionary* under "ensaumple".

each, including Wil, created by God in his aspect of nature: "Thorugh eche a creature, Kynde my creatour to lovye". The fact that Kynde is "my creator" ensures that humans can also be counted among the creatures of the world, but it also suggests that humans must look to all the others in order to come to a proper relation with God.

Thus the question raised has become precisely that of the relation of human to natural world, and simultaneously of reader to text. The analogy of reading is useful, because reading necessarily involves interpretation, understanding and, frequently, confusion, paradox, lack of resolution; all of which also arise in environmental or ecological discussion. In the middle ages, there was the added dimension of reading words, particularly the words of the Bible, being the province of the relatively few, whereas the book of nature was, in theory at least, open to all. That, of course, was itself a problem: if the natural world was to be a book open to the illiterate, how were either they, or the literate, to know if they read it correctly? The point is perhaps exacerbated by the fact that it is possible to link this kind of literary open book to an actual panorama – in this case, that available to anyone willing to climb the Malvern Hills. On the one hand, this deft device brings together the literal and the figurative acts of reading as we read both Langland's text and, through it, see and simultaneously read, the landscape he describes. On the other, it runs the risk of a reader finding Langland's description jarring with their own experience of the view from those same hills. In that case, the whole enterprise is put in jeopardy, as once we have lost belief in the landscape we are no longer bound to be drawn in to the allegorical experience and metaphorical reading presented through Wil. The close bond between us as readers and the book, whether the literal one of words on a page or the figurative one of the natural world, is broken and we are no longer either disposed or really able to learn from the examples therein.

This then raises the associated question: how much is this apparently thoroughly literary topos also informed by a personal reaction to a precise geography? The whole matter is further complicated by the fact that at the beginning of this same passus Langland has used the phrase "in a mirour that highte Middelerthe" – in a mirror called Middle earth. Are we to conclude that what we see in the world around us is necessarily dictated by what we ourselves are? Is it the case that all that we can see is, in effect, ourselves? Such a conclusion would fit well with the point, or is it an objection, often raised in ecological debate, that the human species is incapable of thinking itself out of the central place in the world. However hard we try, we are inevitably anthropocentric and narcissistic.

Certainly such anthropocentrism is evident in Hugh of St Victor's use of the world as a book trope. Writing in the twelfth-century, Hugh, a monk, mystic and theologian, is addressing his fellow theologians and intellectuals, - a narrower audience than the one of fourteenth-century clerics and pious layman, and possibly Lollards, whom we assume first read Langland,[7] but his words have resonance, nevertheless:

> Universus enim mundus iste sensibilis quasi quidam liber est scriptus digito Dei, hoc est virtute divina creatus, et singulæ creaturæ quasi figuræ quædam sunt non humano placito inventæ, sed divino arbitrio institutæ ad manifestandam invisibilium Dei sapientiam. Quemadmodum autem si illiteratus quis apertum librum videat, figuras aspicit, litteras non cognoscit: ita stultus et *animalis homo*, qui *non percipit ea quæ Dei sunt (I Cor. II)*, in visibilibus istis creaturis foris videt speciem, sed intus non intelligit rationem. Qui autem spiritualis est et omnia dijudicare potest, in eo quidem quod foris considerat pluchritudinem operis, intus concipit quam miranda sit sapientia Creatoris. Et ideo nemo est cui opera Dei mirabilia non sint, [...] Bonum ergo est assidue contemplari et admirari opera divina, [...]

> For the entire visible world is like a book written by the finger of God, that is, created by divine goodness, and the individual creatures are, as it were, figures, not invented by human pleasure, but devised by divine judgement to reveal the wisdom of the God of invisible things. Moreover, just as when an illiterate man looks on an open book, he sees the shapes but does not understand the letters, in the same way he is an ignoramus and the "simple man" who "does not perceive those things which are of God" (I Cor.2); in the case of those visible creatures, outwardly he sees their appearance, but inwardly does not comprehend their rationale. On the other hand, one who is spiritual and able to distinguish all things, while outwardly considering the beauty of the work, inwardly recognises how wonderful the wisdom of the Creator is. And indeed there is no one for whom the works of God are not wonderful [...] Therefore it is good to contemplate them carefully and wonder at the divine works [...]

---

[7] For a consideration of Langland's likely audience see Burrow, John. 1957. 'The Audience of *Piers Plowman*' in *Anglia* 75: 373-84.

(*De Tribus Deibus* as given in Migne vol 176. 1880: 814)[8]

This extract reminds us of how some aspects of a literary device can be set aside by an author eager to emphasise other things. Hugh is not concerned with the most obvious implication of the notion that the world can be regarded as a book, viz. that everyone has access to it and so may read it with advantage. Instead, Hugh moves swiftly over the notion of the world being a book for all to gaze upon, educated and ignorant alike, into the greater understanding that he asserts is the province of the learned alone. It is indicative of his priorities that the reference to 1 Corinthians provides a Biblical source for the non-spiritual or natural man, rather than for the manifestation of God's wisdom in the created world. For that one has to turn to the somewhat rather convoluted verse of Romans 1.20: "For the invisible things of him from the creation of the world are clearly seen, being understood by the things that are made, even his eternal power and Godhead". Interestingly, and appropriately for this discussion of Langland, the context for this quotation from Romans is that of knowing the wrath of God. Here we are to learn from the created world not merely in order to wonder at God's artistry, but to see the potential power of His anger manifested in the relations between beasts and in the natural phenomena we term 'disasters'. The 1388 Wycliffe Bible, which is more or less contemporary with Langland's B text, provides a more vivid rendition of this verse (here in modernized spelling): "For the invisible things of Him that are understood, are beheld of the creature of the world by those things that are made, yea, and the everlasting virtue of Him and the Godhead, so that they may not be excused". What is particularly interesting about this rendition is that here humankind is clearly placed, as Langland places us, within the world. Here we are "the creature of the world" understanding the invisible aspects of God through the visible ones which are made – and because those visible things of the natural world are indubitably physical there is no excuse for not seeing them.

---

[8] As pointed out by C. H. Buttimer (in Buttimer, C. H. 1939. *Hugh of Saint-Victor's 'Didascalicon, de studio legendi'; a critical text.* vii) this treatise is erroneously printed as book seven of Hugh's *Didascalicon*, in Migne, J. P. (ed.) 1880. *Patrologicae cursus completus series Latina.* Vol. 176. The extract quoted here may be found on p. 814 of that volume.

Hugh is keen to emphasise that only someone lacking in spiritual awareness could fail to recognise the wisdom of God when contemplating the beauty of the world around us. Much of the appeal of the topos is its suggestion that some apprehension of the Divine goodness and power (*"virtute"*) is available to all. Even if we cannot move beyond apprehension to comprehension, acknowledging the wonder of the created world goes some way towards acknowledging the power behind it. It is significant that for Hugh it is not just seeing but marvelling that is the key here as the wonder of creation is emphasised (*"Miranda"*, *"mirabilia"*, *"admirari"*). This is the right and immediate reaction of the ignorant and educated alike to the world around us, but it is the element most often overlooked. It is this sense of wonder that Stephen R. L. Clark suggests we now need to recover when thinking of the earth (Clark 1993). Without it and the reverence that comes with it, he argues, there is little hope of regarding earth, be it as soil, planet or creation, in a way which will compel us to treat it with respect. Significantly, this wonder, available, and indeed necessary, to all, is *expressly* not allegorical (Clark 1993: 31). It is, however, religious and as such integral to Langland's vision, as he, like Hugh, presents wonder as a mode of direct appreciation of the earth as something which surpasses the human imagination, and which is, simply, more important than mankind. Towards this the right response, as they both acknowledge, is marvel.

Langland presents that sense of wonder through Wil's detailed description of the landscape across forty-one lines (326-367) in which wonder appears twice (as "wonderful" in line 328 and "wonder" in 346), the verb 'marvel' twice ("marveilled", 350 and 359) and the noun "selkouthe", meaning "wonder" or "marvel", also twice (363 and 366). So far it appears that Wil's reaction is exactly the one both expected and required; like Hugh's ideal reader, intellectual and illiterate alike, Wil here proves that the best readers retain not only the ability to wonder, but also the desire to understand spiritually rather than intellectually. Kynde's use of examples in order to teach in this extract from *Piers Plowman* is thus an exact instance of learning from the book of the world. The implication is that Wil is being drawn away from abstract discussion into direct understanding, governed both by his own human nature and by the force which we still often refer to broadly as 'Nature'.

By having Kynde himself show Wil the world, Langland may be presenting a picture of the artist showing his work, but Wil himself seems unaware of this and, indeed, seems to draw a shadowy distinction between "Kynde" and "Kynde my creatour". It may be that this shift in phrase reflects the difference between Nature as regent power of God and God the Creator himself, but there is also some sense in which "kynde" is acting here as the equivalent of 'species' with its concomitant link to 'characteristic'. In this way the connotations of "kynde" are very close to those of current English 'nature' as found in such phrases as "in the nature of the beast" as well as 'human nature' or 'good-natured'. "Kynde" is thus a complex term, which is doubtless why Langland chose to employ it, but it seems to me that the Kynde in line 323, who calls Wil, carries with it a sense of "kynde" as an innate quality. Here it is, perhaps, human nature as it is supposed to be, that is, attentive and receptive to the wonders of the world around it; capable of perceiving the creative power that lies behind it. The hint that this is an innate quality of each individual human is signalled by Langland's phrase "nempned me by my name" (B.XI.320), which carries with it overtones of intimate recognition and knowledge of the one being summoned. Wil is in effect being called to himself, out of overly intellectual debates into a more affective mode. It is only when he is in this mode that he is able to look out at the world and learn from it.

What Wil sees is a delicate mixture of straightforward observation and informed reflection. He begins with a sweep across "the sonne and the see and the sond after" ("the sun and the see and the sand afterwards", 326). That view moves us finally from the particular landscape of the Malverns into the general, ideal panorama which embraces coastline and woodland alike, as Wil goes on to mention snakes in woods and birds of wonderful colours among his general view of birds and beasts, each, significantly, with its mate. As his eye moves on he sees "Man and his make" and although "make" is clearly "mate" it is ironically apt that the next lines mention poverty and plenty, peace and war, happiness and sorrow all together and all, arguably, the product of human activity. Having tipped over briefly into social comment, Wil pulls himself up again to look in more detail at the world of beasts and birds before him. Watching them, he is struck by the reason that governs the animals' habits, particularly regarding generation, as the males and females retreat to single-sex company after the mating season. The birds' skill in nest building attracts Wil's particular admiration, as he wonders who taught them their various tricks and admits that they outstrip humans in their ingenuity. Significantly, he notes that the many different places birds choose to lay reflect their need to hide their eggs from predators, including humans. Finally, his attention is drawn to the many colours of flowers in woods and the variety of greens of the grass ("how among the grene gras growed so manye hewes" 365). This level of detail, together with the snippets of medieval natural lore scattered throughout this descriptive passage (such as the belief that some birds conceived by breathing into each other's bills) indicates that there is much to be gained from simply looking carefully at the world around us. It suggests, too, that the aesthetic pleasure and straightforward admiration evoked by such moments of still observation may be worthwhile in themselves.

It is worth noting that none of the birds, animals or plants mentioned in these lines of this predominantly allegorical poem is actually read allegorically, not even the peacock, which is a favourite for such treatment. Instead, they are presented simply as themselves and allowed to remain as such. Repeatedly, words indicating wonder and admiration are used, as Wil enacts the very reaction to the pictures in the world outlined by Hugh. He can see the figures and admires them, but he does not know quite what to make of them. The whole passage is a series of precise observations, which combines sincere love of the world with an increasing sense of unease which culminates in a sudden change of mood as Wil switches his focuses from the wonders before him to the rationale behind them. What he sees now depresses and, indeed, angers him to the point where he takes Reason himself to task:

> Ac that moost meved me and my mood chaunged –
> That Reson rewarded and ruled alle beestes
> Save man and his make: many tyme and ofte
> No Reson hem folwede, [neither riche ne povere].
> And thanne I rebukede Reson, and right til hymselven I seyde,
> 'I have wonder of thee, that witty art holde,
> Why thow ne sewest man and his make, that no mysfeet hem folwe.'
> (B.XI.368-74)

> But what moved me most and changed my mood [was] that Reason rewarded and
> governed all beasts except man and his mate: many times and often no Reason
> followed them, neither the rich nor the poor. And then I rebuked Reason and right
> to his face I said, 'I wonder at you, who are considered wise, why do you not
> follow man and his mate so that no misdeed accompanies them.'

His choice of words is significant here; previously reason was said to
follow ("sewen" 334) the animals rather than govern them, and even
here "reward" implies something consequent upon their behaviour,
presumably such as the survival and hatching of those eggs which are
most effectively hidden. All this reflects the way we deduce reasons
for things from observing the effects and then attempt to work out the
cause. The natural world is thus seen to be an essentially reactive
rather than proactive one, and initially that was all part of the wonder
of it. Now, however, Wil's tone has changed from one of wondering
admiration to one of argumentative debate. The trigger has been his
awareness that somehow mankind is not fully part of this world
picture. It seems that every animal and plant naturally does what is
best, or (it is implied) suffers the consequences, but mankind seems to
go along without having to obey any obvious rationale and thus,
importantly, is not better off, but rather abandoned to self-destructive
inclinations by the benign force that seems to govern the rest of the
world. Put briefly, Wil's complaint is: if we are part of nature why are
we not treated like the rest and looked after properly? It is a complaint
that reveals the source of the underlying unease: mankind, it seems, is
separated from the rest and, worse, we are separated by our relation to
reason. The very capacity that enables us to draw comparisons
between ourselves and the rest of the world, indeed the one that allows
us to marvel at the intricacies of nature, is here portrayed as letting us
down. Far from endowing us with greater insight and understanding,
ensuring that we act correctly and thus assuring us of superiority, Wil
accuses Reason of, in effect, leading us astray.

It is easy not to notice the substitution that has occurred here. The
apparently benign and all-seeing Kynde has been replaced by the
rather different character of Reson. It seems that Kynde has slipped
away, or Wil no longer sees him; certainly he does not speak again in
this dream, nor is he referred to. Perhaps Wil's outburst effects this
change, as it is addressed directly to Reson, who may be a force within
nature, but is also an intellectual capacity. The shift in companion may

also indicate the ironic consequence of Wil's anger: frustration at not being able to understand what he sees distracts Wil from fulfilling Kynde's purpose in taking him up to the mountain in the first place. Wil is no longer viewing the world with wonder, instead he is once again embarking on argument.

As Reson takes over Kynde's place as the governing force of the world, that world is revealed as a less kindly place. Wil's rebuke meets with a response which hints at the possibility of vengence: "Amende thow it if thow myght, for my tyme is to abide" ("Amend it yourself if you can, for my time is to come" 377). "Abide" here carries the force of not only a time to come but also a power biding its time, waiting to strike finally and once and for all. This more menacing aspect is compounded in the next line in which several of the available meanings for 'suffering' come into play: "Suffraunce is a soverayn virtue, and a swift vengeaunce" (B.XI.376). Reson is thus presented as the force that allows things to happen, suffers from what happens and brings suffering in due course as a consequence of what has happened. In an extension of the course of events that leads birds to build nests in inaccessible places, Wil realises that we will only truly know how damaging our actions are when we are forced to face the consequences. Doubtless Langland is thinking primarily in terms of individual and religious salvation here, but his poem as a whole reveals that the right treatment of the world in general is an essential element of his concept of doing well. This particular passage also raises a question about the consequences of attempting to maintain an affective relation to the world through cultivating a sense of wonder. Does such an endeavour retain a sense of being part of it, or does it simply bring home to us our innate anxieties? Langland offers here an exploration of what happens when we regard the world as a book, and traces one possible outcome. The effort to recognise that we are part of that book is thwarted by the apparent difference between our habits and those of the other inhabitants of its pages. More damaging, however, is the sudden loss of the wonder that had accompanied the initial looking at nature. A more atavistic reaction surfaces, as Wil's angry outburst to Reson is fuelled by dreadful anxiety that there is nothing to keep an eye on humans to prevent us from going horribly wrong. Indeed, *Piers Plowman* as a whole implies that humanity will indeed suffer the consequences, both individually and collectively, if our behaviour is not moderated. The problem for Wil may, in fact, be that, as far as the world is concerned, man is treated much the same as any other beast: those who do the right thing survive, those who don't, die. It is the lack of warning, not the lack of consequence, that he bemoans; a particularly pertinent point, given the wider context of Romans 1:20, which seems to imply that creation gives warning, just as much as it reveals wonder.

However, Wil's very anger shows that, in fact, there is warning to be found, if we are willing to look. It has been his contemplation of the world, of this book of nature, that has led him to realise that humankind is out of step with the rest of creation. Yet at the same time, it is clear that vilifying the species and its integral components, like reason, will not mend matters. An optimist might assert that the very fact that we can read the warning signs gives us the chance to correct behaviour that Wil seems to demand. A pessimist might wish to point out that perceiving the signs doesn't mean we take any notice of them.

Langland thus presents us with two closely linked reactions elicited by regarding the natural world as a kind of book, both of which seem as pertinent today as they were in the fourteenth century. Looking into its pages has led to wonder, but also to frustration and a hopeless railing against one of the very faculties that allows us to regard the world as a book to begin with. Yet throughout his poem the search for a right way to live is accompanied by passages of sheer observation and straightforward appreciation of the world, and these moments survive the tussles with social ills that follow. I have already touched on one such moment in this passage, but it is worth quoting the whole section for the full effect:

> And sithen I loked on the see and so forth on the sterres;
> Manye selkouthes I seigh, ben noght to seye nouthe.
> I seigh floures in the fryth and hir faire colours,
> And how among the grene gras growed so manye hewes,
> And some soure and some swete – selkough me thoughte.
> Of his kynde and hir colour to carpe it were to long. (B.XI.362-367)

And then I looked over the sea and so out on to the stars; many wonders I saw, which I can hardly speak of now. I saw flowers in the woods and their fair colours, and how so many shades grew among the green grass, and some were sour and some sweet – I thought it wonderful. It would be overlong to talk about their kinds/nature and their colour.

The lightness of touch which brings so closely together the depth of the sea and the distance of the stars (suggested in looking "forth"), and then adds the detail of the variety of hue in grass, evokes an affective response which is the basis for the kind of emotional link to the non-human natural realm currently being advocated as one of the ways forward for an ecological understanding of the world.[9] Here in Langland's poem such contemplation is likewise presented as a spiritual restorative and, although his protagonist proves incapable of maintaining a purely admiring response for long, the short period spent standing next to Kynde, and marvelling at the world that surrounds us, continues to offer a paradigm as well as a reason for why we should study the pages of the book of nature.

Bibliography

Barron, Caroline. 1992. 'William Langland: A London Poet' in Hanawalt, B. (ed.) *Chaucer's England: Literature in Historical Context*. Minneapolis: University of Minnesota Press. 91-109.

Burrow, John. 1957. 'The Audience of *Piers Plowman*' in *Anglia* 75: 373-84.

Buttimer, C. H. 1939. *Hugh of Saint-Victor's 'Didascalicon, de studio legendi'; a critical text*. Washington: Catholic University of America.

Curtius, E. R. 1953. *European Literature and the Latin Middle Ages* (tr. W. R. Trask). New York: Pantheon Books.

Hanawalt, B. (ed.) 1992. *Chaucer's England: Literature in Historical Context*. Minneapolis: University of Minnesota Press.

Hugh of St Victor. 1880. (ed. J.P. Migne) *De Tribus Deibus* [erroneously, *Didascalicon* book 7] in *Patrologicae cursus completus series Latin*. Paris: Maine. Vol 176.

Kaplan, R. and S. Kaplan. 1989. *The Experience of Nature: A Psychological Perspective*. New York: Cambridge University Press.

Kellert, S. R. and E. O. Wilson (eds). 1993. *The Biophilia Hypothesis*. Washington: Island Press.

---

[9] Kay Milton's *Loving Nature: Towards an Ecology of Emotion* provides an assessment of what such an emotionally-based relation to the world might be like. Much work in this area is linked to notions of human health. See, for example, Kellert, S. R. and E. O. Wilson (eds). 1993. *The Biophilia Hypothesis* and Kaplan R. and S. Kaplan. 1989. *The Experience of Nature: A Psychological Perspective*.

Langland, William. 1987. *The Vision of Piers Plowman. A Complete Edition of the B text* (ed. A.V.C. Schmidt, 2nd edition) (Everyman Library) London: J.M. Dent.

Milton, Kay. 2002. *Loving Nature: Towards an Ecology of Emotion.* London: Routledge.

Rudd, G. 2003. 'Thinking Through Earth in Langland's *Piers Plowman* and the Harley lyric "Erthe to of erthe"', in *Ecotheology* 8(2): 137-149.

Whitman, J. 1987. *Allegory: the dynamics of an ancient and medieval technique.* Oxford: Clarendon Press. Ch. 4; esp.: 126-130.

Wycliffe New Testament 1388. 2002 (ed. W.R. Cooper) (The Tyndale Society) London: British Library.

Poodles and Curs: Eugenic Comedy in Ibsen's
An Enemy of the People

Greg Garrard

Abstract

Garrard begins with a discussion of Joseph Meeker's book *The Comedy of Survival*, where Meeker argues that comedy is the ideal mode for ecological writing since it subordinates the hero's self-assertion to the comic demand of survival – muddling through, making do, and so on. He then looks at the odd place of *An Enemy of the People* in Ibsen's *oeuvre*, a comedy situated between two full tragedies, and seeks to relate it to nineteenth-century eugenic thought. The suggestion is that Ibsen's comedy suggests some rather pressing political problems for Meeker's argument, and for ecological monism.

1. The Comedy of Survival

One of the earliest works of literary ecocriticism is a little-known book by Joseph Meeker called *The Comedy of Survival: Studies in Literary Ecology*, published in 1972. This odd and intriguing book, published around the high point of the first wave of environmental concern, was effectively forgotten until its resurgence in the late 1980s, which eventually led to renewed interest in the relationship of human cultural productions to the ecological conditions of life on earth. This second wave critical work called itself 'ecocriticism', and whilst it set about elaborating original and contemporary analyses of culture, it also appropriated important works of the past like Leo Marx's *The Machine in the Garden* (1964), Annette Kolodny's *The Lay of the Land* (1975) and Raymond Williams' *The Country and the City* (1973) under its new rubric. Meeker's book was an obvious beneficiary of this renewal, and the first major anthology, *The Ecocriticism Reader* (1996), included an important chapter from it on

'The Comic Mode'. I will refer mainly to the latter, since it is the most widely accessible version of the original text, whilst also making occasional reference to the revised third edition, published in 1997.

What is curious about *The Comedy of Survival* is that it deploys a simple mimetic theory of literature and a decidedly humanistic conception of the place of art in society in the service of an anti- or even in-humanist project. In this respect it is distinct from the other works of first wave environmental literary criticism, which tend to adopt a skeptical approach to literary representation, inclining to the broadly Marxist view that reads literature as *ideology*, or a potent form of false consciousness. Williams, for example, suggests that 'pastoral' is at least as likely to mystify economic and ecological history in the interests of a ruling or aspiring class as to present any radical or even oppositional perspective. Meeker, on the other hand, is prepared to "assume in a simpleminded way that literature does imitate human actions" (Meeker 1996: 155), so that through it we might look back upon the attitudes and practices of the culture which produced it. He is also more explicit about his environmentalist commitments than other first wave critics, defining "literary ecology" as "the study of biological themes and relationships which appear in literary works" (Meeker 1997: 7), and stating his determination to elucidate the contribution of literature to – or its detraction from – our ecological survival. Meeker therefore conforms closely to the definition of an ecocritic advanced by Richard Kerridge:

> The ecocritic wants to track environmental ideas and representations wherever they appear, to see more clearly a debate which seems to be taking place, often part-concealed, in a great many cultural spaces. Most of all, ecocriticism seeks to evaluate texts and ideas in terms of their coherence and usefulness as responses to environmental crisis. (Kerridge 1998: 5)

Meeker's basic thesis, as suggested by the title of the book, is that Occidental attitudes to nature are conditioned by – among other things – two opposed literary-philosophical modes of thought, the tragic and the comic. Of the first, Meeker claims that:

> The tragic view assumes that man exists in a state of conflict with powers that are greater than he is. Such forces as nature, the gods, moral law, passionate love, the greatness of ideas and knowledge all seem enormously above mankind and in some way determine his welfare or his suffering. Tragic literature and philosophy,

then, undertake to demonstrate that man is equal or superior to his conflict. (Meeker 1996: 157)

The noble confrontation with such powers exalts man (sic) in a spiritual sense even as he is humbled, usually with horrific violence, in a physical or perhaps *earthly* sense. The tragic mode therefore relies upon and reinforces a pre-existing notion of man's unearthly vocation, his transcendence of nature. In ecological terms, then, tragedy must come to seem a form of grotesque *hubris*: "The tragic view of man, for all its flattering optimism, has led to cultural biological disasters, and it is time to look for alternatives which might encourage better the survival of our own and other species" (Meeker 1996: 158).

Comedy, on the other hand, understands nature's necessities, and enjoins man to accommodate himself to them as best he can. It "demonstrates that man is durable even though he may be weak, stupid and undignified" (ibid) because it is basically "concerned with muddling through, not with progress or perfection" (1996: 160). In these respects comedy is analogous to a 'climax' ecosystem, in which, he claims, co-operation and symbiosis are more important than 'survival of the fittest', the needs of the individual are subordinate to the necessities of the whole, and where a 'cosmopolitan' tolerance of diversity in the interests of stability prevails over the 'pioneer' attitudes of tragedy. Comedy is therefore 'adaptive' for the human animal, because it ridicules idealistic aspirations and accepts the constraints of nature, implicitly endorsing a *monistic* ontology of human belonging against a *dualistic* ontology of transcendence. By extension, tragedy may be seen as 'anthropocentric' in its concentration upon the nobility of individual man in his confrontations with 'the gods' in their various guises, whereas comedy would express a 'biocentric' insistence upon relativity, adaptation, community and survival.

In these respects, Meeker's work endorses an assumption of ecological thought that goes back to the Monist League and to Ernst Haeckel, the coiner of the term 'ecology': that ecological survival requires an ethical reorientation away from anthropocentric theism and humanism towards a biocentrism informed, variously, by scientific monism, 'paleolithic' animism or deontological 'intrinsic value'. This assumption permeates modern environmental ethics,

ensuring   underlying   agreement   between   ostensibly   opposed
arguments:

> Although a wide variety of positions is discussed in the literature, the consensus it
> seems, is that an adequate and workable environmental ethics must embrace non-
> anthropocentrism, holism, moral monism, and, perhaps, a commitment to some
> form of intrinsic value. (Light and Katz 1996: 2)

The seminal texts in ecological thought share the consensus – having
helped to found it – from the 'land ethic' of Aldo Leopold's *Sand
County Almanac* through David Ehrenfeld's attack on *The Arrogance
of Humanism*, and the critique of mainstream Western Christianity by
Lynn White Jnr. to the contemporary animism of Max Oelschlaeger,
Christopher Manes and Dave Foreman. Manes argues, for example,
that "a viable environmental ethics must challenge the humanistic
backdrop that makes 'Man' possible, restoring us to the humbler
status of *Homo sapiens*: one species among millions of other
beautiful, terrifying, fascinating – and signifying – forms" (Manes
1996: 26).

   Both Meeker's thesis and the more general ecophilosophical
consensus that he reproduces are vulnerable to direct challenge, not
least in terms of the highly reductive way they tend to schematize
historically complex and contested intellectual and ethical traditions.
Meeker appeals to a wholly undifferentiated notion of 'the comic'
(which he equates with play in general) and a simplified pseudo-
Aristotelian notion of 'the tragic', which raises the problem that
comedy, in his sense, is ubiquitous, ranging from *A Midsummer
Night's Dream*, *Catch-22* and Monty Python through everyday jokes,
puns and farce to frolicking lambs and mudsliding otters. As Meeker
himself admits, great tragedy is severely limited to ancient Greece and
Elizabethan England – and, I would add, nineteenth-century Norway –
whereas ecologically-damaging practices could hardly be said to be so
limited. Moreover, although Meeker is critical of the 'nature red in
tooth and claw' tradition in biology, he is unable to see how his own
view of climax ecosystems as essentially symbiotic and harmonious is
conditioned by the cultural politics of 1970s environmentalism: not
only does it fail to acknowledge the role of symbiosis as a survival
strategy in a *competitive* environment, but the 'climax ecosystem' is
itself a concept that is coming to be seen more as an instance of

metaphysical wish-fulfilment than as scientific fact (see Garrard 2004: 56-8).

Meeker's idea of a diverse, balanced and harmonious community – a veritable anarchist commune of forest species – is then sharply counterposed against the radically simplified and hierarchical ecosystem of civilisation that "has only one animal to deal with, man, plus minor adjustments to keep alive the few domesticated plants and animals enslaved to man" (Meeker 1996: 162). But why should our immensely complex long term co-evolution with our 'domesticated' species be characterised as slavery, especially when Meeker is elsewhere at pains to remind us that "man is a species of animal whose welfare depends upon successful integration with the plants, animals, and land that make up his environment"? (Meeker 1996: 163). As Michael Pollan observes, "domesticated species don't command our respect the way their wild cousins often do" (2001: xvi). Meeker's contempt reflects the decidedly *humanistic* view of "domestication as something we do to other species, but it makes just as much sense to think of it as something certain plants and animals have done to us, a clever evolutionary strategy for advancing their own interests" (ibid). Our extraordinary ability to modify existing habitats to suit ourselves and our symbionts is a symptom of disastrous ecological success, not tragic failure. Human populations are, after all, still growing.

Meeker's analogy between comic survival and evolutionary adaptation is appealingly simple and provocative, but it also forces him to propose an absurd parallel relationship between tragic heroism and extinction:

> Fossilized remains attest to the many extinct animals who insisted on the propriety of their traditions in the face of a changing world. Of the estimated one billion different species produced so far by evolution, ninety-nine percent have become extinct. (1996: 165)

Either Meeker is really suggesting that Antigone's tragic refusal to abandon funerary tradition is somehow comparable to the dinosaurs' stubborn allegiance to their reptilian inheritance, or this is a tongue-in-cheek allusion to Western culture's adherence to self-destructive anthropocentric beliefs. While Meeker's approach is often light-hearted and genial, I suspect the former in this instance.

Nevertheless, it is worth interrogating Meeker's thesis on the terrain of its own choosing, namely literature. The next section of this chapter examines the explicit environmental problematic in Ibsen's *An Enemy of the People* in terms of environmental history and psychology, a practice I call *eco*criticism because it takes a generous and sympathetic approach to its object in the interests of environmental advocacy. The section that follows, however, will adopt a suspicious approach that compares the misanthropy of Ibsen's tragicomic hero Dr Tomas Stockmann to environmentalist inhumanism through the notion of 'eugenic comedy'. This exercise in eco*criticism* will investigate the consequences of different kinds of monism, or to put it another way, different ways of seeing humans as animals. The literary or cultural construction of humans as animals, called 'theriomorphism', has historically been used for satirical or abusive purposes (see Garrard 2004: 136-159). However, since Darwin's decisive intervention in *The Descent of Man*, theriomorphism has acquired a scientific dimension that is reflected – in a variety of ways – in environmentalism, evolutionary biology, eugenics and ecocriticism.

2. Eco*criticism*

An Enemy of the People is, to my knowledge, the only work by a major dramatist to incorporate an explicitly environmental dimension. As Michael Meyer points out, it was performed in Tokyo in 1898 "as a protest against dangerous effusion from a chemical factory" (Meyer 2000: 113n). Yet Ibsen's critics have generally chosen either to ignore the play – the dominant response – or to downplay its contemporary relevance. Perhaps because the field of Ibsen criticism in English seems dominated by neo-Leavisites, any such topicality in fact renders the play suspect, at least until the critic has carried the play away into a timeless realm of existential decisions or 'vigilant openmindedness'. Meyer, for example, overstates the case in an instructive fashion:

> *A Doll's House* is no more about women's rights than Shakespeare's *Richard II* is about the divine right of kings, or *Ghosts* about syphilis or *An Enemy of the People* about public hygiene. Its theme is the need of every individual to find out the kind of person he or she really is, and to strive to become that person. (Meyer 1971: 478)

To put it in this way seems perverse and ultimately self-defeating, because although undoubtedly being a woman, a king, or a victim of syphilis, ought hardly to exhaust one's sense of "the kind of person [one] really is", these factors cannot simply be dismissed to the realm of the arbitrary or historically-transitory. Indeed, what sense can we make of the halting efforts at self-realisation of Nora or Oswald without them? There is an especial propensity for critics to dismiss an interest in nature or environmental issues as merely allegorical or symbolic, which has led ecocritics such as Jonathan Bate and Lawrence Buell to a distinctive emphasis on *literality*. Buell, for example, argues for a "dual accountability" in criticism:

> This ambidextrous response avoids opposite reductionisms: reductionism at the level of formal representation, such as to compel us to believe either that the text replicates the object-world or that it creates an entirely distinct linguistic world; and reductionism at the ideational level, such as to require us to believe that the environment ought to be considered either the major subject of concern or merely a mystification of some other interest. (Buell 1995: 13)

Such a response, by the way, might help to mediate the fraught question of Ibsen's 'naturalism' and his 'symbolism', especially in the later plays.

An Enemy of the People is, then, literally an environmentalist comedy, centred as it is on Tomas Stockmann's discovery of the contamination of the town baths with industrial waste:

> These Baths are a whited sepulchre – and a poisoned one at that. Dangerous to health in the highest degree! All that filth up at Moelledal – you know, that stinking refuse from the tanneries – has infected the water in the pipes that feed the Pump Room. And that's not all. This damnable muck has even seeped out onto the beach. (Meyer 2000: 137)

Clive Ponting's *Green History of the World* identifies tanning as one of the earliest forms of industrial pollution:

> Although the reliance on human, animal, water and wind power for early industry meant that the energy inputs were largely non-polluting, the waste products of the earliest industries produced numerous pollutants, particularly in water courses. The tanning of ox, cow and calf hides and the tawing of deer, sheep and horse hides produced large quantities of acid, lime, alum and oil which, together with the remains of the hides, were usually dumped into the local river or stream. (Ponting 1992: 360)

Ibsen's toxicology is surprisingly detailed and accurate, identifying the specific type and nature of the biological pollution as well as its origins in the decaying organic remains:

> DR STOCKMANN [showing the letter]: Here it is ! This is proof that there's putrefying organic matter present in the water – millions of infusoria. This water, used either internally or externally, is a positive menace to health. (Watts 1979: 122)

This discovery of toxic decay at the smug, self-satisfied heart of the provincial spa town ought not to be taken *only* literally, of course. The play had probably been on Ibsen's mind for about two years before he sat down and wrote it, very rapidly indeed, in 1882, but the final version must be inflected by the savage critical and public response to *Ghosts*, which came out in 1881. There is an obvious analogy between the initial acclaim given Stockmann by the liberal press and Ibsen's popularity after the publication of *The Pillars of Society* in 1877. The craven kowtowing before Establishment values and priorities of the supposedly liberal journalist Hovstad once his vital interests are threatened must then be seen as a critique of the attitudes of contemporary journalists to the playwright's 'discovery' of an inner – though also literally biological – pollution in *Ghosts*.

The nature of the pollution is, in fact, insistently material during the first three acts of *An Enemy of the People*. The letter from "the University" containing their analysis of his samples is Stockmann's guarantee of rectitude in his own eyes, and helps him to sway the various third parties such as Aslaksen, Chairman of the Householders' Association. Its simple, incontrovertible objectivity is under threat very quickly, though, most particularly from Stockmann's father-in-law (and owner of the tanneries), Morten Kiil: the *ad hominem* argument that Stockmann is really trying to get his own back on his brother Peter, the Mayor, is articulated clearly here and repeated throughout the rest of the play. Moreover, Kiil finds the supposedly objective existence of these invisible "creatures" extremely dubious:

> KIIL: What was it now? Didn't you say that some animals had got into the water pipes?
> TOM: Yes, bacteria.
> KIIL: Quite a number of them, so Petra told me. Regular army!

TOM: Millions, probably.
KIIL: But no one can see them. Isn't that right?
TOM: Of course one can't *see* them.
KIIL: (chuckles silently) Devil take me if this isn't the best I've heard from you yet! (Meyer 2000: 142-3)

Kiil is so sure at this stage that Stockmann is making it all up that he simply ignores the implied threat to his industrial activities. The more the Doctor is censored and criticised, however, the more Kiil comes to recognise the real ramifications of the analysis:

KIIL: You were saying yesterday that the worst of the filth came from my tannery. If that's true, then my grandfather and my father before me and I myself must have been poisoning this town for years, like three destroying angels. D'you think I'm going to sit down under a reproach like that ? (Watts 1979: 209)

Kiil blackmails Stockmann, deliberately creating a conflict of interest by buying shares in the Baths with money that would otherwise have been left to his daughter. This evasion of responsibility is one of the typical responses to the identification of environmental problems listed by Ponting:

Fatalistic acceptance of pollution as an inevitable consequence of human activities; authorities balking at prevention or control measures; lack of foresight and technical understanding; the problem of allocating responsibility; a preference for short-term local fixes rather than long-term solutions and a failure of individuals or companies to take responsibility for their actions. (Ponting 1992: 346)
11

Kiil understands very well the nature of his responsibility for the pollution, and is prepared, in effect, to disinherit his daughter and grandchildren to protect his reputation. And yet it is not exactly clear who is responsible for the contamination, as the authorities were warned by Dr Stockmann when the Baths were constructed that the conduits were wrongly placed: "The intake's too low – it'll have to be moved to a point much higher up" (Watts 1979: 123). Thus the Mayor Peter Stockmann is implicated in the crisis – specifically for his lack of foresight – and quickly moves to silence his brother. In particular, he points out that word of contamination would ruin the reputation of the Baths and ruin the local economy, even if substantial ameliorative measures were undertaken, measures which would in any case be prohibitively expensive: following Stockmann's recommendation that "we must build a sewer to carry off the alleged impurities from Molledal, and that all the water-pipes must be relaid" would cost "several hundred thousand kroner" according to the Mayor (Watts 1979: 138). As long as local people believe the cost will be borne by the owners of the Baths, they are enthusiastic about his plans, but it seems that "The proprietors find themselves in no position to incur any greater expense than they are already bearing" (Watts 1979: 164). The spectre of a substantial increase in local rates leads to the rapid desertion of Stockmann's supporters, especially as the Mayor proposes instead – without scientific support – a "discreet" programme of "certain improvements". It may seem odd that the possibility of cleaning up or closing down the tanneries does not occur to anyone – until we look at Ponting's list again. Evidently the "fatalistic acceptance" of industrial pollution is just as much a recurring feature of environmental history as the other responses listed, that have – without exception – been identified in *An Enemy of the People*.

So Ibsen's handling of the quite literal problem of environmental pollution is unerring. But is it relevant to our sense of the *artistic value* of the play? Perhaps committed environmentalists will feel that it is, but this may appear a rather sectarian argument. In fact, it bears quite directly on some of the key aesthetic questions about the play. In R.D. Gray's view, the plot is implausible, because the "opposition seems at least a little unlikely", especially such universal and vociferous opposition (Gray 1977: 86). Apparently any businessman would see that "it would be worth losing money for two years to avoid the worse consequence" of an outbreak of typhoid fever which would ruin the reputation of the Baths for a long time. He concludes that Ibsen is led by his passionate identification with his hero to exaggerate the stupidity and hypocrisy of the opposition to an absurd degree. Admittedly there is much truth in the second part of this claim, but the first displays less perceptiveness than Ibsen concerning economic 'rationality'. Gray's assumption, shared by many who see the environmental idiocies perpetrated under the auspices of capitalist self-interest, is that those involved are just not being self-interested *enough*, that they need to take a longer-term, more rational view. The problem with this assumption is that it fails to acknowledge the operation in economic affairs of a form of systematic irrationality known as 'the tragedy of the commons'.

The phenomenon, which is actually an instance of the logical puzzle known as the 'Prisoner's Dilemma', was identified by fisheries economist Scott Gordon in 1954 and later popularised by right-wing biologist Garrett Hardin (Ridley 1996: 231). It occurs wherever common property such as fish, wildlife, air and water are at stake in an economy ruled purely by self-interest. Individuals, acting 'rationally' in these limited terms, maximize their use of the commons to the extent that eventually they are exhausted, thus denying them to all. As Matt Ridley puts it, "the rational individual would – did – kill the last two mammoths on the planet because he knew that another individual would get them if he did not" (231). Since Hardin assumes that everyone acts out of self-interest, he argues that only authoritarian means can prevent such a tragedy. However, according to Ridley, observation of traditional commons in the real world shows that 'irrational' strategies of non-competitive co-operation are commonplace. Regulated by custom and local laws, these yield greater individual utility over the long run than supposedly rational self-interest. They also tend to be much more successful than regulatory systems imposed by distant central governments.

Given their competitive relationship with other spas, the behaviour of the people of Stockmann's town is entirely 'rational' in economic terms, whilst nevertheless giving rise to a classic 'tragedy of the commons'. Moreover the bind generates some strikingly dissonant behaviour amongst the townspeople: their livelihoods threatened, they attack Stockmann at a tumultuous public meeting as an "enemy of the people", and yet the morning after Kiil reports that shares in the Baths "weren't hard to come by today" (Watts 1979: 208). It is not that dumping shares reveals the 'real' feelings of the people, rather that *both* responses issue from the same underlying motivation. Ibsen's comprehension of this dynamic is crucial to the aesthetic proportion of the play, and the ecocritical perspective especially competent to help us see it.

Furthermore, it would be a mistake to adopt Meeker's crudely mimetic model and assume that Ibsen's play simply reflects contemporary concerns about environmental pollution. While Meyer is able to draw attention to two historical situations known to Ibsen similar to that in *An Enemy of the People* (Meyer 2000: 114-6), it is equally important to note that the shift in the play from an emphasis on the actual pollution of the Baths to the symbolic pollution of the townspeople by greed and cowardice presents in reverse the development of the concept of 'pollution' itself. As I have observed elsewhere, 'pollution' originally had only moral and religious meanings, attracting and incorporating material and scientific ones from the seventeenth century onwards (Garrard 2004: 1-14). The combination of industrialisation and the emergence of toxicology in the nineteenth century played a decisive role in turning pollution from a primarily moral term to a scientific one that still retained a moral aura of contamination and defilement. Ibsen's play should therefore be seen as a *participant* in the shift in meaning that ultimately makes my ecocritical reading of his play possible.

3. *Eco*criticism

My analysis of the play so far has concentrated mainly on the first three acts. This is because the overt environmental agenda is overwhelmed by what appears to be a moral and spiritual crisis that reaches a crescendo in Act Four. Already enraged by the refusal of the 'liberal press' to support him, Stockmann's attempt to broadcast his findings at a public meeting is frustrated by his brother's machinations. Prevented from speaking to the subject directly, Stockmann announces "a discovery of much more far-reaching importance than the trifling fact that our water supply is poisoned, and that our curative Baths are built on infected ground" (Watts 1979: 181). Obviously from Meyer's elevated existentialist perspective, Stockmann's new 'revelation' is indeed qualitatively superior to the 'trifling' environmental crisis, although I would suggest that Stockmann's heavy irony here ought to alert us to the possibility that the two 'discoveries' are, for the Doctor at least, profoundly linked. The new realisation is "that it's the very sources of our spiritual life that are poisoned – and that our whole community stands on ground that's infected with lies!" (181). For the Ibsen enthusiast, this news will hardly be news – Ibsen was always preoccupied with the notion of spiritual 'pollution', which obviously gives weight to Meyer's abstract claims. *An Enemy of the People* would then become merely a token of the playwright's typical obsession with the role of 'the lie' in family and social life, and the environmental question merely a convenient 'plot' used to illustrate a pre-existent 'theme'. I want to argue, however, that the pollution 'plot' crucially affects – or perhaps *infects*, certainly *inflects* – the so-called 'spiritual' theme.

Once Stockmann has started talking in terms of "the sources of spiritual life", we might suppose that the appropriation of environmental crisis as *metaphor* signals a departure from the biological "comedy of survival". His struggle might easily come to seem identical to that of the tragic hero, positing a distinct, transcendent "spiritual life" of "much more far-reaching importance" than mere typhoid or gastro-enteritis. But it is not so, and the Doctor soon gives us an indication: "For many years I lived in a terrible hole up north; when I came to meet some of the people who lived there, thinly scattered among the rocks, I sometimes thought that what those poor stunted creatures up there really needed wasn't a doctor like me, but a vet!" (Watts 1979: 183). The righteous citizens are predictably offended by his 'joke', but there is more and worse to come. The 'majority' – the 'liberal' majority, the 'solid' majority of Aslaksen and Hovstad – is, we learn, "precisely what is poisoning our spiritual life at the source", (Watts 1979: 186) and Stockmann sets out to prove 'scientifically' that 'the minority is always right':

> Well, isn't that true with all the rest of living creatures? […] look at dogs, they're [near] to us human beings in lots of ways. First think of an ordinary mongrel – one of those filthy, ragged, plebeian curs that does nothing but run round the streets fouling the doorposts. Then put that mongrel beside a poodle with a pedigree going back through generations of famous ancestors – who's been properly reared, and brought up among soft voices and music. D'you really think the poodle's brain won't have developed quite differently from the mongrel's ? (Watts 1979: 189)

Meyer is probably right to replace "poodles" with "greyhounds" in his translation, arguing that the former have "rather the wrong kind of associations" (Meyer 2000: 223). In Arthur Miller's adaptation, published in 1950, the speech is missing altogether, emphasising Stockmann's moral heroism in the face of a repressive majority.[1]

In this passage Stockmann reveals an interest in eugenics that he shared with a great many scientists in the latter part of the nineteenth century. Of course, the idea is there at least as far back as Plato's *Republic*, along with the analogy from animal husbandry, but this articulation of it seems to owe much to the influential theories set out by Francis Galton, the father of modern eugenics, in his *Hereditary Genius* of 1869. Galton, like Stockmann, was not especially interested in propagating a 'race' of Aryan *Übermenschen* (although he was undoubtedly a racialist) nor a new 'aristocracy' of any conventional kind, but rather sought to use the insights of Darwin and Wallace to investigate the biological conditions of 'natural ability'. To be precise, Galton wanted the state to promote the "spawning of numerous eugenically golden offspring" by society's true leaders, its "originators" (Kevles 1985: 4). Heredity, he claimed, affected not only gross physiological characteristics, but also intelligence, moral character and artistic talent, so that when Stockmann identifies a 'spiritual' pollution we can see that it need not be qualitatively distinct from the 'physical': the spirit is, from this essentially monistic perspective, as much governed by the 'laws of nature' as the stomach. Using the familiar husbandry analogy, Galton asserted that:

> There is nothing either in the history of domestic animals or in that of evolution to make us doubt that a race of sane men may be formed, who shall be as much superior mentally and morally to the modern European, as the modern European is to the lowest of the Negro races. (Galton 1892: x)

Moreover, Stockmann's appeal to the different influences on the poodle and the cur – what we would call 'nurture' – are not, as we might think, in conflict with his obsession with heredity – what we would call 'nature'. Darwin, in the acknowledged absence of a

---

[1] It is intriguing that Miller's adaptation of *An Enemy of the People* was done (like Ibsen's original) in between two much better-known tragedies (*Death of a Salesman* and *The Crucible*). In McCarthyite America, Miller claims for himself Ibsen's apparent moral authority on the question of "whether one's vision of truth ought to be a source of guilt at a time when the mass of men condemn it as a dangerous and devilish lie" (Miller 1950: 8). However, Miller also has to sanitise the play so that its exponent of truth is not seen even today as 'dangerous', even 'devilish'.

mechanism of heredity and variation, argued for a qualified version of the Lamarckian view that acquired characteristics could be inherited, undermining our conventional distinction. Galton, too, believed in the inheritance of acquired characteristics in 1869, although he repudiated the theory in later editions. At the end of *An Enemy of the People,* Doctor Stockmann, isolated and under attack from almost every quarter, resolves to look to the future. He decides to set up a school, with the help of his talented daughter Petra and her besotted suitor Captain Horster, to teach his own children but also to try to make "free men" of any "street urchins" or "guttersnipes" they can attract:

> STOCKMANN: [...] Get hold of a few for me. I'm going to experiment with mongrels for once. They have good heads on them sometimes. (Meyer 2000: 221)

Stockmann too hopes to improve the stock of the human animal.

But how might Stockmann prove his main point – that the majority is always *necessarily* wrong? Biologists such as Darwin and Galton believed that species could *regress*, meaning that they could revert to an earlier, more 'primitive' form. In terms of the monistic perspective, the theory ought to apply to humans, and indeed John Laydon Down described a syndrome in 1866 that he called "mongolian imbecility" because sufferers were believed to have 'reverted' to a primitive human type that lingered in some of the races of Central Asia. Galton eventually came to believe, on the basis of statistical analyses, that all species adhered to a constant mean distribution of characteristics unless forced to 'progress' by the pressure of natural selection. Humans, who seemed to have exempted themselves and a few selected companion species from this exigency, would then be in constant danger from regression, or 'atavism'. Adducing a number of arguments for a differential rate of reproduction between classes, races and types, Galton expressed a fear that was to become endemic in eugenic thought:

> It may seem monstrous that the weak should be crowded out by the strong, but it is still more monstrous that the races best fitted to play their part on the stage of life, should be crowded out by the incompetent, the ailing, and the desponding. (Galton 1892: 243)

So Galton did not just believe that the majority *happened* to be morally-eugenically 'wrong', but that they always would be if allowed to reproduce unconstrained by eugenic considerations. For Stockmann, surrounded by a cowardly and uncomprehending 'majority', regression is a live issue, and eugenic selection a response just as rational and necessary to survival as relaying the conduits to keep toxic waste out of the drinking water. When a citizen protests "We're not animals, Doctor!" he replies:

> But bless my soul, that's exactly what you are, my friend – we're the finest animals anyone could wish for […] though you won't find many pedigree animals even among us. Yes, there's an enormous difference between the human poodles and the human mongrels. (Meyer 2000: 189)

Arthur Miller left out the eugenic speeches because of the historical association of eugenic theriomorphism with fascism, insisting that "in light of genocide, the holocaust that has swept our world on the wings of the black ideology of racism, it is inconceivable that Ibsen would insist today that certain individuals are by breeding, or race, or 'innate' qualities superior to others or possessed of the right to dictate to others" (1950: 10). So not only does his adaptation transform Stockmann into an unambiguous moral and existential hero, but Ibsen himself is given a posthumous pardon and allowed to join the postwar liberal consensus. Despite the fact that many regimes and political parties around the world supported eugenic policies, the fascist association drove theriomorphism into the intellectual wilderness for at least two decades after the war. Intriguingly given Meeker's thesis, the period also saw the rebirth of tragedy in the work of Arthur Miller, as well as accelerating ecological destruction. There is no evidence at all of an historical connection between the status of tragedy and environmental crisis.

As for *An Enemy of the People*, on one level it supports Meeker's thesis: it is an eugenic comedy which ends with survival of the poodles amid the baying curs, with Stockmann and his remaining allies hoping to 'muddle through' and avoid confrontation. As Robin Young points out, "much of the energy of play derives from the confrontation between Dr Stockmann – really a larger-than-life comic character – and a social situation which is and remains to the end of the play unregenerately serious and potentially tragic in its implications" (Young 1994: 65). In this respect Stockmann is similar to Hamlet, who is really a comic character according to Meeker: not only is he very funny, but he perpetually avoids confrontation and seeks to redirect the natural aggression aroused by his father's murder. In this he is like a predatory animal that has to restrain intraspecific aggression as far as possible. Ultimately Hamlet, under the tragic injunction of blood revenge inflicted by his father, is destroyed by men such as Laertes and Claudius who share his father's ethic. Meeker concludes that "Hamlet demonstrates [...] how impossible it is to be at the same time both a good man according to the criteria of tragedy, and a good human animal according to the requirements of nature" (Meeker 1997: 49). It is a remarkably persuasive interpretation of the play.

But *An Enemy of the People* poses problems because although it shares Meeker's theriomorphic premise, it raises questions about the very notion of "requirements of nature". Meeker says of Ibsen's heroes that "they are not superior to nature, nor are they judged by the gods", thus illustrating the decline of tragic assumptions. Nevertheless, their own transcendent uniqueness is never in question, so "the remarkable character is crucial to realistic tragedy, for it is all that remains of the classical prerequisites for a tragic view of life" (Meeker 1997: 33). But for Stockmann, it is precisely *nature* that makes men remarkable, and it is scientific knowledge of nature that gives him his unbreakable conviction of his own position. Moreover, his eugenics is of a piece with his toxicological concerns; both derive from the assumption that we are indeed animals.

Meeker's theriomorphism is very different from Stockmann's, however, and it worth drawing attention to both of them in part to measure the distance between them. Crucially, Stockmann's theriomorphism is hierarchical, whereas Meeker shares the deep ecological reading of evolutionary biology: that "in nature there simply is no higher or lower, first or second, better or worse" (Manes 1996: 23). For him, deep ecological theriomorphism means trying to be a "good human animal according to the requirements of nature" by adopting a "play ethic" of biocentric equality, compromise and ecological survival. Yet according to some proponents of evolutionary theriomorphism, such injunctions are merely pious hopes based on romanticised views of animal behaviour. Meeker and other deep ecologists promote the sort of animal they hope we could be, not the sort of animal we are. As Matt Ridley argues in *The Origins of Virtue*, a fascinating theriomorphic account of the biological foundations and limits of altruism, "environmental ethics are [...] to be taught in spite of human nature, not in concert with it. They do not come naturally. We all knew that anyway, did we not?" (Ridley 1996: 225). John Gray's theriomorphic polemic *Straw Dogs* portrays the demand for an environmental ethic as "another version of humanism, not an alternative to it" (Gray 2002: 17). If we are serious about seeing humans as animals, he claims, we will accept that "the mass of mankind is ruled not by its intermittent moral sensations, still less by self-interest, but by the needs of the moment. It seems fated to wreck the balance of life on Earth – and thereby to be the agent of its own destruction" (ibid). Inevitably eugenics will return, but not in the crude form of selective breeding or euthanasia. Rather humans will use bio-engineering to "remodel themselves, the better to survive in the wasteland they have made" (Gray 2002: 186). It is a vision remote from Meeker's genial "play ethic", but a reminder that the strange, challenging collocation 'eugenic comedy' cannot be located only safely in the past as a model for possible survival, and that there are ways of being a "good human animal" that are far from comic.

Bibliography

Buell, Lawrence. 1995. *The Environmental Imagination: Thoreau, Nature Writing and the Formation of American Culture.* Cambridge: Harvard University Press.

Galton, Francis. 1892. *Hereditary Genius: An Inquiry Into Its Laws and Consequences.* London: Watts.

Garrard, G. 2004. *Ecocriticism.* London: Routledge.

Gray, John. 2002. *Straw Dogs.* London: Granta.

Gray, Ronald. 1977. *Ibsen: A Dissenting View.* Cambridge: Cambridge University Press.

Kerridge, Richard. 1998. 'Introduction' in Kerridge, Richard and Neil Sammells (eds). *Writing the Environment.* London: Zed Books. 1-9.

Kevles, Daniel. 1985. *In the Name of Eugenics: Genetics and the Uses of Human Heredity.* Berkeley: University of California Press.

Light, Andrew and Eric Katz. 1996. 'Introduction: Environmental Pragmatism and Environmental Ethics as Contested Terrain', in Light, Andrew and Eric Katz (eds). *Environmental Pragmatism.* London: Routledge.

Manes, Christopher. 1996. 'Nature and Silence' in Glotfelty, Cheryl and Harold

Fromm (eds). *The Ecocriticism Reader.* Athens: University of Georgia Press.

Meeker, Joseph. 1996. 'The Comic Mode' in Cheryl Glotfelty and Harold Fromm (eds). *The Ecocriticism Reader.* Athens: University of Georgia Press.

— 1997. *The Comedy of Survival: Literary Ecology and a Play Ethic* (revised 3rd edn.). Tucson: University of Arizona Press.

Meyer, Michael. 1971. *Ibsen.* Harmondsworth: Penguin.

— 2000. *Ibsen: Plays Two.* London: Methuen. ['An Enemy of the People' tr. R Hart-Davies 1963.]

Miller, Arthur. 1950. *An Enemy of the People: Adapted from Henrik Ibsen.* Repr. London: Nick Hern 1989.

Pollan, Michael. 2001. *The Botany of Desire: A Plant's Eye View of the World.* London: Bloomsbury.

Ponting, Clive. 1992. *A Green History of the World.* London: Penguin.

Ridley, Matt. 1996. *The Origins of Virtue.* London: Viking.

Watts, Peter (ed. and tr.). 1979. *Ghosts and Other Plays.* Harmondsworth: Penguin.

Young, Robin. 1994. 'Ibsen and Comedy' in Macfarlane, James (ed.) *The Cambridge Companion to Ibsen.* Cambridge: Cambridge University Press.

The Hunter as Nature-Lover: Idyll, aggression and ecology in the German animal stories of Otto Alscher

Axel Goodbody

Abstract

The last native wolves in Germany were shot in the middle of the nineteenth century. The untamed landscapes of the American Wild West are without equivalent in a densely populated country where nature has been shaped and reshaped by its human inhabitants over the centuries. Nevertheless, the wild, be it in the form of those mountains and forests which are still perceived as constituting a challenge or threat to civilisation, or of Gypsies eking out a nomadic existence on the fringe of society, has exercised a particular fascination in German culture. This essay focuses on Otto Alscher (1880-1944), the "hermit of Orsowa", friend of Romanian gypsies, and hunter of bears and wolves in the Carpathian mountains. His novels and stories are examined for their political implications and situated in the context of shifting modern attitudes towards wild animals.

1. Hunting as a moral and environmental problem

The passionate debate about fox hunting in which British society has engaged in recent years has shown how emotive the ethical issues surrounding hunting are, and how complex not only its animal welfare consequences and ecological impact, but also its political, social and cultural implications remain. With the passing of the Hunting Act 2004, animal welfare activists, who believe hunting with hounds is a cruel sport which should be banned, appear to have won a historic victory over the pro-hunting lobby, whose principal argument has been that fox hunting is an effective and humane method of vermin control. Hunting fox and deer with hounds has been banned in Germany since the 1930s, and few Germans would wish to reinstate it. (Hunting with hounds is, however, still to be found in France and

Italy, as well as countries formerly belonging to the British Empire such as the US, Canada and India.) The control of predators and the regulation of wildlife are managed by shooting, and the German word for 'hunting' (*die Jagd*) today effectively means 'shooting'.

There is a long history of shooting as a German sport, in which the ancient traditions of the huntsman live on, and it still enjoys considerable prestige. At its height in the early years of the twentieth century, Kaiser Wilhelm II was famous for his lavish shooting parties. The Kaiser is reported to have shot 75 000 animals personally, over a period of 30 years – 7 a day on average (Bode and Emmert 2000: 128). His hunting activities have been interpreted as a form of compensation for feelings of inferiority stemming from physical disability (his left arm was shorter than his right), and they reflect a vain, impulsive and domineering personality which exacerbated international political tensions in the run up to the First World War. Personal obsession coincided here with the practice of hunting as a form of representation of power demonstrated by German rulers going back to the court of the Emperor Maximilian I in the early seventeenth century. After 1871, shooting parties on the Kaisers' East Prussian estates in Schorfheide and Rominten met the greatly increased representational needs of the newly founded Empire.

The custom fell into abeyance in the Weimar Republic, but was revived in the Third Reich, and continued in the 1950s, 1960s and 1970s, when West (and East!) German heads of state, senior politicians and top civil servants were members of the shooting fraternity, alongside members of the nobility, bankers and the captains of industry. With the growth of affluence, leisure time and mobility since the Second World War, shooting has grown in popularity as a field sport. Roe deer, wild boar, red deer and fallow deer, followed by chamois and moufflon (Corsican mountain sheep), and, of course, the 'lesser game' duck, pigeon, hare, pheasant and rabbit, are the principal animals shot. Today, however, state hunts have been discontinued, shooting sportsmen no longer possess the political clout they once had, and there is, as in the UK, a vociferous German anti-hunting lobby.[1]

Some of the particular arguments concerning fox hunting, such as the distress caused by the chase, do not pertain in the same measure to game shooting. However, shooting is also a blood sport, and as such poses the fundamental question whether it is legitimate to harm and kill animals for our pleasure. For there are manifestly other ways of procuring food, and probably other ways of managing the ecology of the countryside, which are more compatible with what many regard as our duty to treat animals with consideration as subjects of moral concern. It is commonly believed that hunting and shooting are remnants of (typically male) aggressive behaviour rooted in evolutionary psychology, and hence reflect innate human qualities. However, this view has been challenged by experts (see Fromm 1977: Chapter 8, 'Anthropology'). There is also a less than innocent political dimension to hunting. Historically, there have been many links between the control and exploitation of animals and of fellow humans. Big game has traditionally been the preserve of royalty and the upper class, who hunted in forests and other areas legally reserved from agricultural use and often forcibly depopulated. Social elitism has gone hand in hand with a problematic understanding of nature as a sphere of purity and authenticity. In Germany, the big game hunter and self-appointed *Reichsjägermeister* Hermann Göring, who took over the imperial estates, notoriously exemplified the link between hunting and the exclusion and extermination of beings not considered organic or 'natural'.

However, this chapter is less concerned with issues relating to animal rights or political oppression – and not at all with the arguments of those defending fox hunting in the UK relating to civil liberties (i.e. the right to shoot animals) and the impact of banning hunting on employment, the cohesion of rural communities or cultural traditions – than with the curiously complex relationship with wild animals and nature exemplified by hunters.

---

[1] See Nimtz-Köster 2001 and the webpages of the Initiative zur Abschaffung der Jagd (Initiative for the Abolition of Hunting), which has organised protest marches in Berlin, at http://www.abschaffung-der-jagd.de (consulted 17.07.2005).

Christian tradition, which underlies most Western attitudes, embraces two conflicting strands of thought about how animals should be treated. Both of these are founded on Bible passages. The first, 'dominionist' strand, which has tended to prevail since its 4th-century formulation by Saint Augustine, and remains influential today, emphasises humanity's separatedness from the rest of creation, and our legitimate right to make almost any use of animals for our own interests. In *Genesis* 1, 28 God blesses the newly created man and woman, and says to them: "Be fruitful, multiply, fill the earth and subdue it. Be masters of the fish of the sea, the birds of heaven and all the living creatures that move on earth" (*New Jerusalem Bible*). In *Genesis* 9, 1-4, Noah and his sons are even incited to be "*the terror and the dread* of all the animals on land and all the birds of heaven, of everything that moves on land and all the fish of the sea" (my emphasis). Every living thing is ours to eat.[2]

A second, subversive strand holds that human exploitation of nature (and predation in general!) entered history with the Fall, and will disappear when God comes again to reign on earth. It is visible in the teaching of Saint Francis and the writings of Albert Schweitzer. This counter-current in Western thought, which has come to the fore in recent decades, challenging humanity's exploitation of the animal world, is one which conceives of our relationship with animals as somewhere between brotherhood and stewardship. It is inspired by the ideal state of non-predation, in which all God's creatures coexist in peaceful vegetarianism, envisaged in the prophecy of Isaiah: "The wolf will live with the lamb, the panther lie down with the kid, calf, lion and fat-stock beast together, with a little boy to lead them" (*Isaiah* 22, 6-9). Many of the arguments around hunting today draw ultimately on one or other of these approaches.

The question whether hunting is 'natural' has long been a subject of philosophical debate. The justification for hunting in primitive societies is seemingly simple: wild animals were either a threat to human life or a source of food. Either way, killing animals was a

---

[2] There is, however, one exception: "You must not eat flesh with life, that is to say, blood, in it." In the immediately following lines, God also "demands account" of human *and animal* "life-blood", and goes on to establish a covenant with Noah, his descendants, and *every living creature on the ark*, that never again will He destroy all living creatures by a flood.

matter of survival.[3] The aim of the modern hunter is, in any case, to find and (usually) kill the animal, not for food or safety, but for recreation, self-realisation and the prestige associated with a fine set of antlers. Hunting today is, it is commonly claimed, 'natural' inasmuch as it is a disalienating activity. The hunter gains a knowledge of and develops a respect for his prey which is missing in ordinary life relations with animals as a result of the industrialisation of modern food production, and its invisibility to the consumer. By giving expression to the 'animal' or 'predator' within us, tracking, stalking and shooting are also an 'original' way of being human, in which normally suppressed instincts are reunited with reason. The Spanish philosopher José Ortega y Gasset's *Meditations on Hunting*, written in 1942, describe hunting as a "deep and permanent yearning in the human condition" (Ortega 1986: 29). The scarcity of game is an essential part of hunting, and it involves hardship, risk, physical effort and concentration. The rules of hunting are constructed such as to give the hunted animal a measure of equality with the hunter (though not necessarily a fair chance of survival!): as weapons become more effective, man has "imposed more and more limitations on himself as the animal's rival in order to leave it free to practise its wily defences, in order to avoid making the prey and the hunter excessively unequal" (Ortega 1986: 45).

Hunting is, then, a sport, but it cannot, for Ortega, be replaced by other competitive sports, or by photographing wild animals. For though the purpose of the hunt lies in the chase rather than in the kill (for the sportsman, that is; this does not apply to the utilitarian hunter), the death of the animal remains crucial. "Every good hunter is uneasy in the depths of his conscience when faced with the death he is about to inflict on the enchanting animal", and "the generally problematic, equivocal nature of man's relationship with animals shines through that uneasiness" (Ortega 1986: 88). However, without

> the harsh confrontation with the animal's fierceness, the struggle with its energetic defence, the *point of orgiastic intoxication aroused by the sight of*

---

[3] Anthropologists have, however, questioned whether hunting normally contributed significantly to the food of primitive *homo sapiens sapiens* hunter-gatherer societies. See Bode and Emmert 2000: 86-92.

blood, and even the hint of criminal suspicion which claws the hunter's conscience (my italics)

hunting in Ortega's view lacks authenticity: "the spirit of the hunt disappears" (Ortega 1986: 95). Ortega notes the 'extras' conveyed by hunting: "the immersion in the countryside, the healthfulness of the exercise, the distraction from [one's] job, and so on and so forth" (Ortega 1986: 97). However, hunting is far more than these. It is a spiritual act, a religious rite and an experience restoring us to authentic being. The 'equal' encounter with the wild is "a conscious and almost religious humbling of man which limits his superiority and lowers him toward the animal" (Ortega 1986: 97ff). Because hunting relies on intense observation of the animal, and a sort of imitation, or anticipation of its moves, Ortega writes of a "mystical union with the beast" (Ortega 1986: 124). In the "subtle rite" of hunting we divest ourselves of civilisation and return to nature (Ortega 1986: 123 and 116). Deprived by civilisation of our "ancestral proximity to animals, vegetables and minerals – in sum, to Nature", we take pleasure in the "artificial return to it" (Ortega 1986: 111). Hunting is a "vacation from the human condition through an authentic 'immersion in Nature'" (Ortega 1986: 121).

The argument that hunting gives temporary relief from the pain of individuation is returned to by Erich Fromm in *The Anatomy of Human Destructiveness*, but without Ortega's mysticism. Fromm distinguishes "elite hunting", which "satisfies the wish for power and control, including a certain amount of sadism, characteristic of power elites", from the actions of the primitive professional and the modern passionate hunter. The last of these is led by two principal motivations. The first is to return to the "natural state", become one with the animal, and be "freed from the burden of the existential split: to be part of nature *and* to transcend it by virtue of his consciousness". However, of *at least equal importance* is the hunter's enjoyment of his skill (Fromm 1977: 185). Neither the experience of "oneness with nature" nor the pleasure taken in the combination of skills and "wide knowledge beyond that of handling a weapon" (ibid.) required by hunting would seem to necessitate or justify killing wild animals today, though Fromm does not comment directly on this.

Val Plumwood's recent reflections on the "relational" or "respectful" hunt, one based on need and practised in a context which involves some elements of respect and sacredness, echo these arguments while accommodating recent sensitivities to animal rights and gender equality, the shift in thinking about nature from strong to weak anthropocentrism, and the return of the sacred. Plumwood limits her justification of hunting to forms which make use of the animal "responsibly and seriously to fulfil an important need in a way that recognises the 'more' that it is and respects both its individuality and its normal species life, in a reciprocal chain of mutual use which must ultimately include both hunter and hunted" (Plumwood 2000: 299ff). The principles of sacred eating are that in a good human life we must gain our food in such a way as to acknowledge our kinship with those whom we make our food, and may not forget the "more than food" that every one of us is (Plumwood 2000: 303). The "sensitive hunter" relies on his or her communicative skills, knowledge and, to a great degree, understanding of and rapport with the animals that are being hunted. The hunter will often be effective by adopting the intentional stance, conceiving the hunted animal as another mindful, communicative, and intentional being, and combining this rapport with the imperative of hunting food needed for the survival of self and loved ones.

Paradoxically, then, the hunter, whose killing of wild animals for mere recreation would seem to epitomise domination and anthropocentric utilitarianism, has, at least in theory, more intimate knowledge of these animals, and arguably practises greater steward- ship of them, than many contemporary city-dwellers concerned with animal welfare. Few cultures have understood animals better or had more respect for them as ends in themselves than hunting cultures, and hunting literature is full of compassion and respect for the quarry. Sporting pleasure also provides an incentive for the control of predator and pest populations, and for the retention and enhancement of habitats important for biodiversity.

Both Britain and Germany have witnessed a conservationist turn in hunting which began in the 1970s. The committed environmentalist Robin Page published a persuasive defence of hunting, *The Fox and the Orchid* in 1987 and today British professional associations stress the value of their efforts in preserving and creating habitat, managing populations of game animals and generally caring for wildlife.[4] In Germany, which possesses much larger areas of forest, hunting has long been regulated. The first significant provincial and national legislation to prevent the unnecessary suffering of hunted animals and preserve game was passed in the twenties and thirties, and further controls were introduced after the Second World War, since game stocks had been decimated by poachers and the occupying forces. Gun licences are only issued after the applicant has served a practical apprenticeship and passed an examination concerned as much with the needs of animals as with the code of practice in killing them. *Hege* ('care'/'protection') is a key term in German hunting vocabulary, and hunters feed deer and wild boar in winter and keep them free from parasites with antibiotics. As in Britain, German hunters see themselves as "applied conservationists", and hunting as an environmentally beneficial activity, contributing to the preservation of biodiversity.[5] For the German hunter, shooting has, then, two positive aspects which outweigh any doubts about the legitimacy of killing animals for sport. In addition to benefiting society by bringing people closer to nature and permitting them to escape at least temporarily from their alienation from their true human nature prevalent in modern society, it benefits the natural environment by preserving otherwise endangered species through the protection of their habitats.

Hunting deer continues to be a privilege of the relatively wealthy, and its residual upper class image is evident in the advertising and product design of consumer goods such as leisure clothing, cars and alcoholic drinks. But there has been a steady growth in the number of gun licences issued and the amount of game shot annually. The increasing commercialisation of hunting as a recreational activity has

---

[4] The British Association for Shooting and Conservation's website speaks of the association's mission "to promote and protect sporting and shooting and the *well-being of the countryside* (my emphasis)" and illustrates the importance it attaches to biodiversity and access with reference to a "Green Shoots" initiative launched in 2000. See http://basc.org (consulted 17.07.2005).

[5] See the aims of hunting as formulated on 'Jagd-online' http://www.jagd-online.de, the website of the Deutscher Jagdschutzverband (literally 'German Hunting Protection Association'). The page on *Waidgerechtigkeit*, the traditional ethos of hunting subscribed to by professionals and amateurs, lists regulations and practices concerning the care for and protection of animals (including the avoidance of unnecessary suffering), and environmental protection.

shifted it in practice further and further away from the interaction with the wild animal it traditionally involved, and stripped it of the schooling of the intellect and the disciplining of the instincts which had led Ortega to describe the code of ethics observed by hunters as comparable to those in monastic orders and the military (Ortega 1986: 31).

Tensions between the interests of hunters and conservationists have also come increasingly to the fore since the 1970s. A groundbreaking TV documentary on Red Deer by the pioneering environmental journalist Horst Stern broadcast on Christmas Eve 1971 showed how German forests were suffering widespread damage from over-stocking with deer. Stern repeated and developed his arguments in an open letter to the President, Walter Scheel, in 1975,[6] but the German Hunting Association has only grudgingly acknowledged their validity. Wilhelm Bode and Elisabeth Emmert have recently made the case for a "democratic legitimation" of hunting in Germany, by means of integrating hunting with conservation and forestry, in a transition "from nobleman's hobby to ecological handiwork". They call for three things: reduction of the stocks of game to a level which will prevent further irreparable damage to Germany's mixed forests,[7] a switch from trophy hunting to planned culling of the weaker animals, including does and fawns, and a reduction of winter feeding and medical intervention, which effectively turn deer and boar into domestic animals. As long as they continue to increase the number of deer by breeding and feeding programmes, hunters cannot claim to be standing in for extinct natural predators such as wolf, lynx and bear, or performing the ecologically valuable task of regulating game populations.

The reflection in literary texts of the public debate on hunting and of public attitudes towards animals over the past century has aroused

---

[6] Horst Stern, 'Jagd vorbei – Halali. Offener Brief an den Jäger Walter Scheel', *Zeitmagazin* 9 (21 February), 1975: 10-18. Reprinted in Bode and Emmert 2000: 12-25.

[7] Apart from general debarking, silver fir, maple, ash and beech have suffered disproportionately from deer grazing their young shoots, leaving behind a monoculture of planted spruce susceptible to storm damage and increasing erosion.

little academic interest in Germany so far.[8] Yet literature can, as a medium of non-trivial reflection on personal experience and received cultural values, offer insight into the complexity of our relationship with nature and animals. In what follows, I examine the hunting and wild animal stories of Otto Alscher (1880-1944) in the context of the ideological construction of nature in the early twentieth century and shifting understandings of hunting. Alscher, a hunter who also showed profound respect for wild animals and expressed concern at the erosion of their habitat, exemplifies the paradox in our attitudes towards animals. His writing illustrates the problematic political implications of the quest for authentic human experience, but also points towards the necessity for a 'partnership' with wild animals and a reconciliation of nature and culture, civilisation and the wild.

2. Otto Alscher as Hunter-Writer

Though forests, mountains and wild animals have exercised a powerful fascination over the German cultural imagination,[9] there is little more wilderness left in modern Germany than in Britain. The relatively densely populated central European landscape has been comprehensively shaped by its inhabitants since the middle ages, and the last native German wolves were shot in the mid nineteenth century. It is not therefore surprising that Otto Alscher, journalist, writer, smallholder and hunter, lived on the Eastern periphery of the German-speaking world, where the Danube traverses the Carpathian mountains.

Stories dealing with hunting and wild animals occupy a marginal status in twentieth-century German literature, and Alscher's reputation today is no more than that of a minor provincial writer. Yet he published four novels and six volumes of stories during his lifetime. In the years leading up to the First World War Alscher enjoyed

---

[8] See above all Thomas Dupke's study of the hunter and writer Hermann Löns (Dupke 1993), to which I refer above. Generally useful background information is also provided by Hermand (1991) and Meyer (2000).
[9] Simon Schama's *Landscape and Memory* (London: HarperCollins 1995) and Robert Pogue Harrison's *Forests: The Shadow of Civilisation* (Chicago: University of Chicago Press 1992), for instance, discuss these motifs in German myths and fairy tales.

considerable success with literary and journalistic works which presented his part of the world to a mainstream German readership as one remote from the European capitals, an exotic landscape of small towns, farms and forests inhabited by Gypsy woodcutters, Romanian farmers and Hungarian landlords. The novel *Gogan und das Tier* (Gogan and the Animal, 1912) and the two volumes of short prose *Die Kluft: Rufe von Menschen und Tieren* (The Gulf: Calls from Men and Animals, 1917) and *Tier und Mensch* (Animal and Man, 1928) were published respectively by a leading German publisher based in Berlin, and (in the case of the stories) by a reputable Munich firm. However, his later work failed to attract the attention of the public. The novel *Zwei Mörder in der Wildnis* (Two Murderers in the Wilderness, 1934) only appeared in abridged form, serialised in a popular journal, and his last collection of stories, *Die Bärin* (The She-Bear, 1943), which contains some of his best writing, was brought out locally in a small print-run by a friend of the author's.

Alscher began his writing career after a brief period studying photography and graphic design in Vienna in 1900. He moved to Budapest to work as a journalist in 1911, and at the end of the First World War he supported the short-lived Hungarian Socialist Republic. When this was crushed, he returned to the Banat (a region which had been German-speaking since the eighteenth century, but now be-longed to the Kingdom of Romania). For a time Alscher sought to work again as a journalist, and play a part in the cultural life of the German minority. However, political disillusionment, professional disappointments and the break-up of his first marriage led him to withdraw to the house in the woods he had built and lived in sporadically in the pre-war years. His efforts to live the simple life here, hunting, working a smallholding and writing, earned him the nickname of the "hermit" and "Mahatma Ghandi" of Orşowa. Grinding poverty and failure to find a publisher for his novels and stories left him open to the lure of fascism, whose glorification of the instincts he shared. As Germany lost control of Romania in the final months of the war, he was interned and died in a camp.[10]

---

[10] For a fuller account of Alscher's life and a general introduction to his writing see Goodbody 2003.

Alscher was a keen hunter in his youth, who seems gradually to have lost the desire to kill, and become more interested in observing and describing the bears, wolves, lynxes, polecats, martens, eagles and smaller creatures of the Carpathian forests. In his early stories, he celebrates hunting as an outlet for deep-rooted human instincts. However, his writing reflects a fundamental ambivalence regarding the shooting of wild animals. In the 1920s, the focus shifts away from the excitement of tracking animals down, towards respectful observation, appreciation of their grace and vitality, wonder at their autonomy and acknowledgement of their right to life. First signs of this may be found in the stories 'Der Marder' (The Marten) and 'Der Fremde' (The Stranger), written during the First World War. In the former, the author sets out with his dogs and his best rifle on a winter hunting expedition. It is the first good day after a depressing spell of bad weather, and the landscape is magically transformed by snowfall. He writes of the will to power and describes the exertion of hunting in terms reminiscent of Nietzsche, as a stripping away of the layers of effete civilisation, and, like Ortega, as a regaining of our lost animality:

> Is there anything more wonderful than the will to power? The will to violence, to overpowering, to cruelty, where necessary, when we only practise it because we are also prepared to suffer it, and it serves as a test of our strength against others [...]
>   The body steams and demands nakedness. The muscles, for which everything is irksome constriction when they are rejoicing, singing their melody, their powerful, monotonous, unwavering, flowing song. Life is the song of the body. Hard, will-pursuing, simple life, whose shame lies in the cloaked and concealed and not in the naked. (Alscher 1917: 20-22)[11]

Coming on the tracks of a pair of wolves, he muses:

> I would like to see a wolf again, his great, silent, strong grey form slipping through the woods, fearlessly approaching the hunter, who awaits him with beating heart. And see how all the wildness of the world suddenly lights up in his eyes, before abruptly fading, as his life force ebbs away, to reunite with some distant source of all being. (Alscher 1917: 24)

---

[11] All translations are my own.

Alscher laments the dilution of the life force in the process of civilisation, our recourse to increasingly sophisticated weapons, and the gradual displacement of strength by cunning, of the body by intellect. And yet this is no untroubled celebration of the Dionysian, for he also writes of modern man's unease at taking animal life. He experiences feelings of horror and shock at his own actions when faced with the death throes of a hare. There is a disturbing contradiction in man's dual nature, as both a creature of instincts and a reasoning subject guided by moral principles, capable of empathising with animals (Alscher 1917: 22). Brushing this aside, he shoots a wildcat which his dogs have flushed out of a badger's den. Reinvigorated, he strides out in search of further adventure and observes at the sight of the blood dripping from the animal strung from his rucksack:

> Perhaps the path of men is so strong and proud because it is marked in blood. Because every human step is one of destruction, destruction of time, space and impossibility. Is it not the most sublime aspect of our being that our acts of spoliation again and again lead to new life? It is the strong who prevail. Were not the development of man and animal based on this law, where would we be today? The right of the strongest will always hold sway; it will determine the future of humankind. Woe betide us should this no longer be so one day. Power must always precede the exercising of leniency, and the only true nobility is that of strength. (Alscher 1917: 28)

These commonplaces of Social Darwinism, in which Darwin's principle of the survival of the fittest (i.e. most able to adapt to environmental change) is replaced by a doctrine of the right of the strongest to dominate other species, and dubiously transferred to the human sphere, lead to reflection on the unlimited power of modern man over animals, and fantasies of his own prowess as a hunter:

> I am determined to exercise my superiority today. I want to see if there is anything that is a match for my will to conquer, whether the game of life and death in my hands can be disrupted by anything. (Alscher 1917: 28ff)

However, this moment of supreme hubris is a turning point. A marten, seemingly trapped in an isolated thicket, manages to escape his dogs and bullets to safety. He starts the homeward journey disappointed and perplexed that his shots could have missed their target. Gradually, these feelings pass, and his lasting memory is the sight of the marten's "wonderfully easy dashing", its "supple, agile gliding" across the snow, and the wonderment that prevented him from pressing the trigger until it was too late (Alscher 1917: 31ff):

> It does not jump, it does not run, it seems hardly to touch the snow, only to glide over its soft surface, without leaving a trace. I see the whole animal clearly, but I can discern no movement. Slim and slender, it flies off as if cast in bronze. (Alscher 1917: 31)

We humans will never be able to emulate such suppleness and lightness, that powerful yet invisible play of muscles whose action is of unfathomable origin. The secret of animals' strength lies in such seeming effortlessness, which contrasts with the struggle and sweat attaching to all our achievements. Indeed, it is shame over that sweat which drives us to seek artificial aid in weapons, to feign feverishly a strength which we do not possess, but with which the animal is born. Humans have sought to outstrip animals, he reflects, out of sheer *jealousy*. Our admiration for them is the purest thing of which we are capable (Alscher 1917: 33).

'The Stranger' recounts a comparable learning process in a Romanian shepherd's boy who is visiting his father in their summer grazing in the mountains for the first time. "What use are wolves?" he asks. "They're no good for anything, there's not even room for them in the forest any more – they should be exterminated!" (Alscher 1917: 44). He is puzzled by his father's equanimity when one of their dogs is killed by the leader of the wolf pack. The man accepts the presence of the wolves in the forest and argues for coexistence with them:

> "What's to be done? The wolf won't just accept us behaving as if we were masters in his forest. In the old days there were never any shepherds up here, the wolves did too much damage, the eagles took lambs too. But now we've come all the same, and if they defend themselves, we've simply got to put up with it! Forest is forest, and wolves belong to the forest." (Alscher 1917: 48)

Towards the end of the story, the boy finds the leader of the wolf pack trapped in the shepherds' hut. Having entered to steal a new-born lamb the shepherds are looking after, the animal has been caught by the wind blowing the door shut. Alone and without a weapon, the boy can do no more than shout abuse at the animal through the window. It turns to look at him:

How big the wolf was. How powerful his skull, his stocky breast and longhaired back. His eyes glowed. They stabbed towards him. Yet it was as if this strange, wild gaze did not rest on him, but went through him and beyond. (Alscher 1917: 57)

Overcome with the feeling that it is impossible for anyone to capture or defeat such "immense, indomitable wildness" (Alscher 1917: 58), which would merely be inherited by some other creature in the forest if this wolf should suffer harm, and with the sensation that he himself will "collapse and fade away" if he does not remove the barrier which separates him from the great power of the animal, the boy eventually throws open the door and releases the wolf. As it passes him, it is as if his existence "shakes from the steps of a great, strange life" (Alscher 1917: 60).

The stories narrated from the perspective of the hunter which predominate in Alscher's early work are increasingly balanced by tales and passages in the novels told from the animal's perspective. At the very heart of his mature writing is the encounter with the wild, which is crystallised in the experience of being looked at by the animal. By returning our gaze, animals make us aware that they are subjects and not merely objects. They assert an autonomy which decentres our anthropocentric world view momentarily. In an autobiographical note entitled 'Von mir über mich' (By and about myself), written in 1934 to accompany the serialisation of his novel *Two Murderers in the Wilderness* in the magazine *Daheim*, Alscher describes a formative experience in his childhood:

My life passed like that of many children of German émigrés until I was thirteen years old [...] Then, however, a by no means particularly unusual event had a powerful influence on me. [...] One day in October I was coming home with other comrades from a trip in the mountains. I was in front. It was already getting dark. It had become cooler, and, announced only by the occasional startled blackbird, night was approaching. I climb a slope and in front of me a small clearing opens in the woods, surrounded by low brush. Suddenly a large grey animal pushes across the open space. It is scarcely thirty paces from me, and does not notice my presence, since I had stopped to look out for my comrades. It moves casually and inaudibly through the half-light, then suddenly halts and turns towards me. I see its powerful skull, the hairs standing out on its cheeks, its short, pointed ears and the sturdy build of its chest. I know immediately - it's a wolf! But I just stare at it in total astonishment. There is no fear in me, only joyful shock, and question upon question [...] It is as if I were witnessing the beginning of a great friendship, but one which never got beyond a promise. I was filled with doubts and admiration for the free, wild animal, and left with a multitude of questions for which the boy had no answer. (*Daheim* 70(15): 4)

The encounter, which is perhaps as much imagined as experienced, corresponds to several passages in Alscher's fiction. He describes himself as a child of "German émigrés": his parents were both from Silesia, and the family only moved to Orşova when he was 11 years old. Hence the young Otto was an outsider, who sought solace in nature (and companionship with other social outsiders). The encounter with the wolf is presented as a solitary one, and the animal holds out a "great friendship" as a tantalising possibility. Significantly, Alscher does not seek to go beyond this and claim such friendship existed in reality, for that would domesticate the animal and sentimentalise the experience. Its freedom and wildness at the same time serve as a model for his own non-integration in society. Further, with the absence of fear, the boy has entered manhood: the incident resembles an initiation into the great community of nature.

Coming eye to eye with a wild animal, or hearing its call nearby, is described repeatedly in Alscher's stories as a mystical moment giving meaning to life. "It is strange", he concludes the autobiographical sketch,

that the long years I subsequently lived in the city, my work with a newspaper before the War [...], the War itself, [...] then the rewarding years of *völkisch* political activity – that all of this now seems to me merely an interlude making those moments stand out all the more clearly when in the warm wind of early Spring I heard in the forest below me the hoarse, plaintive cry of the lynx [...] Short, indeed, are the moments of true feeling of life that we experience, yet they alone are the very essence of our existence. (*ibid.*)

Alscher takes understanding of, and respect for, the wild animal a step further than previous German writers such as Karl May, Ludwig Ganghofer and Hermann Löns. Löns (1866-1914), who is remembered as the 'poet of the Lüneburg Heath' and 'father of the German wild animal story', was one of the first German writers to empathise with animals and write from their perspective. His early stories, written from the mid-1890s on, present real animals rather than the allegorical figures of animal fables, but still tend to humanise them as quaint rustic figures. His mature writing is more factual and naturalistic, and combines precise personal observation with scientific knowledge. Alscher's depiction of animals is from the start less cosily anthropomorphic than that of Löns, who was a mere 14 years his senior, and is more sensitive towards the reality of animals' lives and perceptual worlds.

The similarities between Löns and Alscher are nevertheless considerable: outsiders by birth in the regions to which they gave literary voice, they can be said to have constructed their identities by idealising the local landscape as wilderness, and stylising themselves as hunter-writers. For both, nature serves a dual function (see Dupke 1993: 107ff): on the one hand, it is a harmonious, often idyllic refuge from society, a source of pleasure which compensates for the alienation, disorientation and fragmentation of city life and modern industrial society, and for problems in the authors' private lives. (See especially Chapters 4 and 8 of Dupke 1993.) On the other, it is presented as a site of Darwinian struggle. The rule of the strongest is a quasi-divine order, a stern but ultimately reassuring life principle. The influence of Nietzsche's critique of civilisation is evident in Löns's and Alscher's celebration of the law of nature as one contrasting with the 'artificial', 'degenerate' laws of modern society, and standing as a model for social regeneration and the future state. (It is likely that Alscher absorbed Nietzsche's ideas indirectly, like Löns and many other contemporaries, from the popular works of Julius Langbehn and Paul de Lagarde – see Dupke 1993: 167-172). It is no accident that, although they displayed left-wing sympathies in their youth, both authors turned to *völkisch* (i.e. racist-nationalist) conservatism, and ended up in compromising proximity with the Nazis.[12]

The dual function of nature is perhaps clearest in Alscher's first novel, *Ich bin ein Flüchtling* (I am a Refugee, 1909). The forest provides a haven for the two Gypsy protagonists, who have been

---

[12] In the case of Löns, this was, of course, posthumous. In Chapter 1 of his book Dupke discusses the role of the monument erected to Löns in the Lüneburg Heath in Nazi ceremonies, and how the author became a symbol of rearmament in the Third Reich, self-sacrifice for the fatherland, and Blood and Soil. It is worth noting the ideological parallels with internationally better known contemporaries writing on nature and animals such as Knut Hamsun (*Growth of the Soil*, 1917) and Henry Williamson (*Tarka the Otter*, 1927) – see Chapter 7 ('The Literary Ecologist') of Bramwell 1989.

wrongly accused of theft and attempted murder. Its majestic calm
impresses itself on them: "Here they were at home, here, where they
had so often spent the night, in the months they had worked felling
timber, always with peace around them and in them" (Alscher 1909:
13). Such passages on the comforting safety the virgin forest affords
by day alternate with others where the giant trees tower over the two
tiny figures by night, the darkness gathering in their branches
suggesting the insignificance and powerlessness of human beings
against nature. The forest, the mountains and the starry skies above
them are visible tokens of *das Gesetz*, the law of nature. Its constant
self-renewal of the species in the great cycle of birth and death is aloof
and indifferent to the fate of individuals (Alscher 1909: 17 and 52).
Like Löns, Alscher seeks to reconcile ultimately contradictory faces of
nature: its unfathomable, hostile power over life and death, and the
comforting security of its seeming peace and harmony. One of the
gypsies lies awake:

> His gaze was fixed on the night, as if he saw the incomprehensible circling in it,
> something which came at him with furious power and which he was unable to
> oppose. But after a few hours' sleep, when he woke by chance, and saw the fire
> calmly flickering, and felt the deep silence of the night in the depths of the forest,
> a comforting sense of security came over him, a joyful feeling of being at home,
> so deep and certain that he thought it would never leave him. (Alscher 1909: 19)

Idyll and aggression were complementary aspects of international
cultural criticism at the turn of the twentieth century. They are present,
for instance, in the wilderness writing of Rudyard Kipling and Jack
London, and were exemplified as opposite poles in the nature
literature of the Weimar Republic by Waldemar Bonsels's much-loved
children's story *Die Biene Maja* (Maya The Bee, 1912), with its
monist spirituality, and Löns's Blood-and-Soil historical novel *Der
Wehrwolf* (The Warwolf, 1910). Löns and Alscher blend them
together in their animal stories and novels. (For Löns see Dupke 1993:
123-5 and 110) They construct nature as an expression of longings
and hopes shared by their contemporaries, but also of their fears and
fantasies of violence. The 'myth' of nature which comprises their
response to the scientific world view of the age embraces both
harmony and a destructive tendency. Alscher shares with Löns a
problematic fascination with the survival instinct and ruthless self-

assertion of predators. In *Two Murderers in the Wilderness* the protagonist Hugo Frahm recognises in a lynx which appears to him at various points in the forest, and personifies the wild, a model for his own behaviour:

> What if the appearance of the lynx before him had some meaning? Perhaps it was that a secret link might come into being between himself and this mightiest representative of the wilderness, one which brought his life closer to that of this bold robber? An act of violence had led him into the ancient forest, here, where only naked strength won out. Then he too must become a person who gained recognition through strength alone. That must be what the lynx was telling him. (*Daheim* 70(17): 7)

As Helga Korodi has pointed out, the animal effectively becomes his totem (Korodi 2003: 138).

However, there are also significant differences between Alscher and the North German Löns. Coming from a multi-ethnic stopping point for river traffic on the Danube on the edge of the Austro/Hungarian empire, where a sprinkling of Austrians and Hungarians lived alongside 'Swabian' Germans (who had emigrated there in the eighteenth century), Romanians, Gypsies and Jews, Alscher is relatively free of Löns's racism. His interest in Gypsies fused his vision of a natural way of life reintegrating dimensions of our being suppressed in modern civilisation with concern for the under-privileged and socially disadvantaged in pre-First World War society (for instance tramps, casual workers and shepherds). His political views were unprincipled: in the early years of the First World War he penned chauvinistic propaganda, and during the Second World War he wrote politically compromising articles in return for a small regular income – yet his individualism, tolerance and interest in a multi-cultural society were less compatible with Nazi ideology.

Alscher shared with Löns a celebration of hunting as a variant of the vitalist philosophy so widespread around 1900. This had ambi-valent consequences: on the one hand, the hunt was an innocent opportunity to enjoy nature and regain naturalness by watching, listening and putting physical strength, endurance and skill to the test. On the other, it enabled them to live out latent violent tendencies. Observing animals is a source of pleasure in itself for Löns, but it always leads to the destructive act. Dupke shows through close

reading of selected passages how hunting is erotically charged in
Löns's work. Suppressed libido is transformed into aggression, and
the kill is described in terms of sexual possession (Dupke 1993: 78-85
and 117ff). In some of Alscher's early stories and in places in *Two
Murderers in the Wilderness* nature also seems to be eroticised.
However, this is relatively insignificant in Alscher's work as a whole.

Löns's espousal of the conservationist cause (he supported efforts
to found the first German national park in the Lüneburg Heath,
opposed building in intact landscapes, spoke out against the clearing
of trees and hedges by 'improving' estate owners, campaigned for the
protection of birds and pleaded for consideration of animal suffering)
led environmentalists in the 1970s and 1980s to describe him as a
pioneering ecologist and an early Green (Dupke 1993: 20). However,
Dupke has shown how he was motivated by aesthetic and political
concerns rather than ecological considerations (Dupke 1993: 277).
Alscher reflects more on issues raised by the erosion of habitat of
wolves and eagles by mineral extraction, industrial development and
population growth in the Carpathians, and on the long-term
consequences of the impact of war and population displacement. He
pleads for an understanding of the plight of the native fauna and
tolerance of their existence.

In Alscher's late work, animals also become models for humanity
in caring and loyalty. This is particularly true of his last volume of
stories, *The She-Bear*, whose sub-title, "Contemplative Animal Stories" signals the author's relinquishment of vitalist activism. In the title
story he writes of a boy who has stolen an infant bear cub from its
den, and is bringing it back to show proudly to his teacher. Events
lead to dawning recognition that the mother bear is anything but a
"dumb animal", and the cub's life and happiness are worthy of his
respect and care. In 'Mein Freund Walter, der Uhu' (My Friend
Walter, the Owl: Strange Bonds between Men and Animals) Alscher
writes of his relationship with an eagle-owl which he had been given
as an owlet and raised to maturity. It continues to visit him after its
release into the wild. Closer knowledge of animals leads us to
recognise them as friends, he argues. Even predators are not enemies,
but competitors, and potential partners of man:

> There are bonds between humans and animals which we are yet far from
> fathoming. What little do we know of the true feelings of animals, we can only

guess at the point at which conditioned responses and instinct shade over into reflection and possibly even coherent thought. But of one thing I am certain: that the strong, free animal, the predator, is not necessarily the enemy of man, but rather man's partner and competitor, if it senses the same strength and freedom in him. (Alscher 1943: 22)

The need to coexist with animals and respect the natural environment is also the prime message of the late novel *Der Löwentöter* (The Lion-Killer). Alscher's most thoughtful treatment of our relationship with animals and with our own animality is, however, to be found in the early novel *Gogan and the Animal*, which explores the possibility of a reconciliation of civilisation with the wild, of reason with instinct. His most successful longer work in terms of structural cohesion and symbolic richness, the book tells the story of the illegitimate offspring of a Hungarian countess and a travelling Gypsy. Through Gogan's search for his true parents and his quest for an identity involving integration of his - at times - violent impulsiveness (described as the "unredeemed wildness" and "simplest, most violent instincts" within him – Alscher 1970: 118), Alscher undermines ethnic and social barriers. Gogan is bent on tracking down his father, in order to avenge his mother's rape and rid himself of the "curse of animality" he has inherited (Alscher 1970: 112). However, the novel ends with him resolving to accept what he owes to his father, and "grasp and transfigure" the "animality" within him (Alscher 1970: 113). When two college friends ask him to join them in a business project to exploit the forests on the estate, he rejects a strictly rational usage of the natural resources, saying this would compromise his personal freedom:

If I take on this property, I do not do so in order to regard it as forestry and arable land, but as a piece of land which belongs only to my feet [...] I do not wish to see the earth as an animal which has to work for me, no more do I intend to be its lackey, to live and bleed for it. I do not wish to possess, nor do I wish to be possessed, but rather to add myself to the soil as a part of nature, as a part of the landscape. Even if this means its ploughed fields lying fallow, and its woods becoming wilderness, it will remain the landscape with which my breath is one. (Alscher 1970: 116)

It becomes his aim in life to "convert the animality in us into conscious life practice" (Alscher 1970: 118), and avoid the pathology of an age in which human libido is suppressed. Gogan's newfound purpose finds confirmation in the trusting obedience of a pointer he has just purchased, "a large, powerful dog [...] with the muzzle of a badger, but the eyes of a wolf" (Alscher 1970: 115). Its hunting urges are half the result of training and half inborn hunting instinct. As "the product of man, yet animal enough [...] to testify to its belonging to the great unity of life with every breath" (Alscher 1970: 119), it stands as a model for the reconciliation of the tensions within him between longing for the freedom to follow his impulses and recognition of the necessity for reason and its disciplined application.

3. Conclusion

Animal rights advocates accuse hunters of treating animals as if they were a renewable resource, whose value is measurable solely in terms of human recreation, culinary pleasure, and aesthetic and social interests. However, as we have seen, hunting can equally be understood as a participation in normal ecological processes that celebrates and respects the value of the natural world, including the quarry. Alscher emphasised the otherness and autonomy of the wild animal as a source of enrichment in our lives. Wildness, he suggests, is important to us as something we are in danger of losing ourselves. This can be a justification for hunting, as in Gogan's explanation of an unannounced absence from the estate:

> "It's the same for me as for my new dog there. He must be able to simply disappear for a few days every now and then. Perhaps to chase a fox, for once free of all his training, or to work off his surplus energy, and in return for his exhaustion make a greater gain [...] It's the same with me!" (Alscher 1970: 115)

The book ends with Gogan taking the dog out hunting.

Alscher was of his time as a hunter and nature lover: the same paradox is observable in contemporaries such as the novelist William Faulkner, whose tale *The Bear* (written, like Alscher's last collection of stories, in the 1940s), is a paean to the wild and a lament at its passing, and Aldo Leopold, whose *Sand County Almanac* has earned him the title of founding father of environmental ethics. Both were life-long hunters. Alscher's narratives of conversion depicting hunters coming to recognise they derive greater pleasure from *observing* than from *killing* the animal also anticipate recent, more critical works, such as Horst Stern's *Jagdnovelle* (Hunting Novella, 1989).

Alscher's best writing avoids the Social Darwinism which is present as a disturbing ideological subtext in so much of his work, and anticipates the efforts of later nature writers to lead readers to reflect on the loss of our naturalness in modern society, and ways of recuperating it. His novels, which are flawed by structural weaknesses, implausible plots, clichéd characters, and intrusive religious-philosophical commentary, are on the whole deservedly forgotten today. But he was a master of shorter prose, excelling in brief, atmospheric pieces which seek, like wildlife photographs, to record the momentary encounter with the wild and the experience of nature. His deftly and economically structured and often beautifully written animal stories, which combine authentic knowledge of the animals with vivid landscape descriptions, will continue to find readers. Unsurpassed in evoking the atmosphere of the forest, they remind us of the presence of the wild, and the need for wildness in our lives.

"In the last two centuries, animals have gradually disappeared. Today we live without them", writes John Berger in his 1980 essay 'Why Look at Animals?' (Berger 2003: 264). Most of us know only our pets, which have been transformed into human puppets, and wild animals in zoos, or on television. These are "always the observed". The fact that they can observe us has lost all significance: they are the "objects of our ever-extending knowledge" (Berger 2003: 267). This reduction of the animal to an object is "part of the same process as that by which men have been reduced to isolated productive and consuming units" (Berger 2003: 265). Historically, animals have been "subjected *and* worshipped, bred *and* sacrificed":

> Today the vestiges of this dualism remain among those who live intimately with, and depend upon, animals. A peasant becomes fond of his pig and is glad to salt away its pork. What is significant, and is so difficult for the urban stranger to understand, is that the two statements in that sentence are connected by an *and* and not by a *but*. (Berger 2003: 261)

Simultaneously like and unlike us, animals lead parallel lives. They offer humans "a companionship which is different from any offered by human exchange. Different because it is a companionship offered to the loneliness of man as a species" (Berger 2003: 261). "The eyes

of an animal when they consider a man are attentive and wary",
Berger comments. "Man becomes aware of himself returning the
look" (Berger 2003: 260). For Alscher, hunting is a unique possibility
of experiencing the animal's gaze.

Bibliography

Alscher, Otto. 1909. *Ich bin ein Flüchtling*. Berlin: Egon Fleischel.
— 1917. *Die Kluft. Rufe von Menschen und Tieren*. Munich: Albert Langen.
— 1928. *Tier und Mensch. Geschichten*. Munich: Albert Langen.
— 1934. 'Zwei Mörder in der Wildnis. Roman' in *Daheim* (Leipzig) 70: 15-25 (11
   January – 22 March).
— 1970. *Gogan und das Tier*. Bucharest: Kriterion. [1st edition Berlin: S. Fischer,
   1912]
— 2000. *Die Bärin. Natur- und Tiergeschichten aus Siebenbürgen*. Rangsdorf,
   Brandenburg: Natur und Text. [1st edition Temeşvar: Anwender]
Berger, John. 2003. *Selected Essays* (ed. Geoff Dyer). New York: Vintage
   International.
Bode, Wilhelm and Elisabeth Emmert (eds). 2000. *Jagdwende: Vom Edelhobby zum
   ökologischen Handwerk*. 3rd edition. Munich: Beck.
Bramwell, Anna. 1989. *Ecology in the 20th Century: A History*. New Haven and
   London: Yale University Press.
Dupke, Thomas. 1993. *Mythos Löns. Heimat, Volk und Natur im Werk von Hermann
   Löns*. Wiesbaden: Deutscher Universitäts-Verlag.
Fromm, Erich. 1977. *The Anatomy of Human Destructiveness*. Harmondsworth:
   Penguin.
Garrard, Greg. 2004. *Ecocriticism*. London and New York: Routledge.
Goodbody, Axel. 2003. 'A Life Among Gypsies and Wolves: Otto Alscher's Quest
   for an Alternative to Modern Civilisation' in Wallace, Ian (ed.) *Fractured
   Biographies* (4th Yearbook of the Research Centre for German and Austrian Exile
   Studies). Amsterdam and New York: Rodopi. 181-208.
Hermand, Jost. 1991. 'Gehätschelt und gefressen. Das Tier in den Händen der
   Menschen' in *Im Wettlauf mit der Zeit. Anstöße zu einer ökologiebewußten
   Ästhetik*. Berlin: Edition Sigma. 53-74.
Korodi, Helga. 2003. 'Die Täuschungen der Wildnis. Der Roman *Zwei Mörder in der
   Wildnis* von Otto Alscher' in *Südostdeutsche Vierteljahresblätter* 52 (2003: 2):
   135-140.
Meyer, Heinz. 2000. '19./20. Jahrhundert' in Dinzelbacher, Peter (ed.) *Mensch und
   Tier in der Geschichte Europas*. Stuttgart: Alfred Kröner Verlag. 404-568.
Nimtz-Köster, Renate. 2001. 'Da kommt das Blut ins Kochen' in *Spiegel* 29 October:
   210.
Ortega y Gasset, José. 1986. *Meditations on Hunting* (tr. Howard B. Wescott). New
   York: Charles Scribner's Sons.

Page, Robin. 1987. *The Fox and the Orchid: Country Sports and the Countryside.* London: Quiller Press.

Plumwood, Val. 2000. 'Integrating Ethical Frameworks for Animals, Humans and Nature: A Critical Feminist Eco-Socialist Analysis' in *Ethics and Environment* 5 (2): 285-322.

Postcolonialism, Ecocriticism and the Animal in Recent Canadian Fiction[1]

Graham Huggan

Abstract

Huggan's essay argues the case for a productive alliance between postcolonialism and ecocriticism and acknowledges that such a case is not immediately persuasive. Deep ecologists might argue that postcolonial criticism has been, and remains, resolutely human-centred (anthropocentric). Committed first and foremost to the struggle for social justice, postcolonial critics have been insufficiently attuned to life-centred (bio- or ecocentric) issues and concerns. A growing body of work exists, however, to suggest a convergence between the interests of postcolonial and ecologically minded critics. Huggan examines debates about the parallels between racism and *speciesism* before he looks at two recent Canadian novels in which the production of a nonhuman "ecological subject" by no means precludes human social and political concerns. The novels are Yann Martel's *Life of Pi* (2002) and Barbara Gowdy's *The White Bone* (1998). In the course of his analysis Huggan gauges the implications of the differences between the presentation of the human and animal worlds respectively, given the novels' 'postcolonial' status. He considers their respective engagement with the racism/speciesism nexus, and their treatment of the discourses of both human and animal liberation, particularly with regard to the captivity of animals and to the alleged violation, through captivity, of their basic moral rights.

A characteristic response by literary scholars to an embattled perception, inside the academy as well as outside it, of the social irrelevance of their discipline has been to advertise the 'worldliness' of literary criticism, its responsibility not just to its subject but to the wider world. This 'worldliness' is less a throwback to Arnoldian

---

[1] Huggan, Graham. Greening Postcolonialism: Ecocritical Perspectives. Modern Fiction Studies 50:3 (2003), 701-733. © Purdue Research Foundation. Reprinted with permission of The Johns Hopkins University Press.

notions of the high moral seriousness of literary criticism than it is the product of a fundamental shift in modern critical sensibility closely allied to the so-called 'ethical turn'. The 'ethical turn' is not, as is sometimes imagined, an alarmed reaction to the perceived excesses of postmodern/poststructuralist criticism, but rather a conscious bringing to the surface of postmodernism's/poststructuralism's underlying social and moral concerns. The typical concerns of the ethical turn – an analysis of the relationship between self and other; an attempt to find new models of community; an interrogation of human subjectivity and, in some extreme cases, a challenging of the category of the 'human' itself – can be found in two recently established but rapidly expanding fields of critical enquiry, both of which make implicit claims for the reshaping of university humanities study in the future. These fields are postcolonial criticism and ecocriticism, and there are signs that, despite their seemingly incompatible interests, the two are converging. What happens when these two highly disparate bodies of knowledge collide is the subject of this chapter; but the chapter also enquires into the implications for the humanities (and, more specifically, for English Studies) of that collision. First, however, a few general definitions are required before any more specific sense can be developed of what the two fields, despite their obvious methodological and ideological differences, share.

Sceptics – and there are plenty – might well say that what the two fields most have in common is their almost congenital inability to define themselves. Definitions of postcolonialism abound, but very few practitioners are agreed on them – to the extent that Terry Eagleton jokingly claims that the first thing any self-respecting postcolonial critic does is to disown his or her status as a postcolonial critic; as if postcolonial criticism had become the academic subdiscipline that dare not speak its name (Eagleton 1999). Serviceable definitions of postcolonialism exist, nonetheless: Ato Quayson, for instance, offers a succinct, if highly expansive, definition that pushes the field far beyond the boundaries of English literary criticism. Postcolonialism, he says, involves

> a studied engagement with the experience of colonialism and its past and present effects, both at the local level of ex-colonial societies as well as the level of more

general global developments thought to be the after-effects of empire (Quayson 2000: 2).

Quayson's definition clearly stakes a claim for the interdisciplinarity of postcolonial studies – a claim also made on behalf of contemporary ecocriticism by several of its most prominent practitioners, such as the distinguished American critic Glen A. Love. Love's most recent book, *Practical Ecocriticism: Literature, Biology, and the Environment* (2003), looks to move beyond conventional understandings of ecocriticism as a sustained critical investigation into the relationship between literature and the physical environment, an investigation which requires of its practitioners that they plant "one foot in literature, the other [foot] on land" (Glotfelty and Fromm 1996: xix). While definitions such as this one go some way toward accounting for the "multiplicity of subjects and approaches" (Love 2003: 5) that come under the rubric of ecocriticism, they still fall short of its remit to include those "nonhuman contexts and considerations" that might provide a basis for its "challenge to so much postmodern critical discourse as well as to the critical [and philosophical] systems of the past" (Love 2003: 1). Nor is it just, as Love suggests, that an "extension of morality to the nonhuman world" implicitly challenges literary studies' distinctly "limited human vision, [and its] narrowly humanistic perception of what is consequential in life" (Love 2003: 25). It also implies the need for a cross-disciplinary approach to environmental and bioethical issues which, in bridging the humanities and the sciences, mounts a powerful challenge to traditional disciplinary configurations and, potentially, to the very meaning of the humanities themselves.

These are grandiose claims, and as ecocritics (like their postcolonial counterparts) are well aware, they don't usually match up in practice. Postcolonialism and ecocriticism remain, by and large, marginal to the concerns of most university humanities departments in Europe, although they have arguably achieved greater recognition in other parts of the world. Off-the-record views of postcolonial critics as exotic firebrands and ecocritics as misty-eyed romantics have proved difficult to dismantle even if, officially speaking, the subjects they represent are watchfully acknowledged, usually in conservative

English departments where the impact they might have on the humanities at large is strictly limited, and the damage they might do – not least to themselves – is carefully controlled. Given the limited foothold the two (sub)disciplines have so far been able to gain within the European academy, it might seem premature to look for ways of bringing them together in the interests of transformative social/ cultural criticism. Yet that is precisely what the rest of this chapter does, motivated as it is by the felt conviction that postcolonialism and ecocriticism have a great deal to offer one another at a time of perceived turbulence within the discipline of English Studies; and at a time of acknowledged global environmental crisis.

1. Common ground?

The case for a productive alliance between postcolonialism and ecocriticism is not immediately persuasive. Deep ecologists might argue that postcolonial criticism has been, and remains, resolutely human-centred (anthropocentric); committed first and foremost to the struggle for social justice, postcolonial critics have been insufficiently attuned to life-centred (bio- or ecocentric) issues and concerns. A growing body of work exists, however, to suggest a convergence between the interests of postcolonial and ecologically minded critics (O'Brien 2001). From recent reports on the devastating impact of transnational corporate commerce on local/indigenous ecosystems (Young 1999), to more theoretically oriented reflections on the efficacy of postcolonial literatures and/or literary criticism as vehicles for Green ideas (Head 1998), postcolonial criticism has effectively renewed, rather than belatedly discovered, its commitment to the environment, reiterating its insistence on the inseparability of current crises of ecological mismanagement from historical legacies of imperialistic exploitation and abuse.

Conversely, recent evidence can be cited of a 'postcolonial turn' in environmental criticism and philosophy which combats the tendencies of some Green movements toward Western liberal universalism and "[white] middle-class nature-protection elitism" (Pepper 1993: 246), and which rejects the lunatic-fringe misanthropy that hovers at the edges, and threatens to discredit, some of the more radical schools of ecological thought' (Curtin 1999: 18-20). The American environmental philosopher Deane Curtin's *Chinnagounder's Challenge* (1999) is a paradigmatic example here, arguing that moral debates about land use, bioethics and the rights of (threatened) indigenous peoples are always culturally coded, and that cross-cultural understanding is needed as much as an ability to decide what is right or wrong in any given event. "What makes sense as a preservation strategy in the first world", argues Curtin, "often has disastrous consequences in the third world" (Curtin 1999: 5). Curtin's concern echoes frequent complaints from Third World scholars that First World environmentalism, in assuming that its protest rhetoric and palliative measures are universally applicable, runs the risk of turning itself into another, late-capitalist form of 'ecological imperialism' (Crosby 1986; see also Curtin 1999: 5-7, 18-20). No one would dispute that Western environmentalist groups have been effective in attracting negative publicity for, say, technocratic World Bank/IMF-sponsored development programmes, several of which (the Green Revolution, for instance) have ironically emerged as examples of cultural arrogance masquerading as global philanthropy. But in seeking to foist their ethical agenda onto non-Western peoples and cultures, some of these groups risk being seen as arrogant in their turn (Arnold and Guha 1995: 19; see also Curtin 1999: 100; Gadgil and Guha 1995; Guha 1989).

Curtin's legitimate concern is that cultural difference should be factored in to ecological decision-making so as to avoid, or at least contest, the top-down managerialism that so often characterises First World arbitrations on environmental and human rights. Curtin's case studies, however, concentrate almost exclusively on instances of *human* conflict management; little consideration is given in them to *animal* concerns. The question of the animal, very much at the centre of current debates in philosophy, ethics and cultural theory (see, for example, Agamben 2004; Wolfe 2003), is thus curiously bracketed in Curtin's otherwise broadly inclusive study. Curtin acknowledges, at least, that careful arbitration has been needed in a number of conservationist ventures where conflicts come into play between apologists for human and animal rights. Here is another instance where the traditional concerns of ecocriticism and postcolonialism might well seem to be at loggerheads; but as Helen Tiffin among others has argued, these concerns are better seen as being closely linked. Following Jacques Derrida, Tiffin suggests that the category of 'human' appears to require some kind of sacrifice of the 'animal', an institutionalised speciesism that has been used to justify the mistreatment or even slaughter not just of animals, but of other, putatively 'lower-order' humans as well (Tiffin 2002; see also Wolfe 1998). The link between racism and speciesism has several provocative implications for postcolonial literary/cultural criticism, not least the possibility of an analogy between the "enslavement of black people (and by implication other enslaved peoples) and the enslavement of animals past and present" (Walker, qtd in Spiegel 1988: 9). As Tiffin suggests, slavery and imperial/colonial genocide were both often "justified on the grounds of categorizing other peoples as 'animals', a categorization [formerly] colonized communities understandably reject, but [one] which [still] leaves the foundational species/race boundary itself in place" (Tiffin 2002: 215). At the same time, discourses of revolutionary transformation during the turbulent decolonisation movements of the 60s also often reinforced the species boundary: Fanon, for instance, famously referred to decolonisation as a dynamic evolutionary process through which the colonised, uplifted from the animal state of their oppression, would triumphantly emerge into the sunlight, confirming what he called "the veritable creation of new men" (Fanon 1986 [1961]: 36).

That many of these liberationist discourses were, like Fanon's, unreflectingly patriarchal has frequently been noted by postcolonial critics; that several of them were just as explicitly speciesist has not. This has to do, to some extent, with Marxism's embattled relationship with 'nature', a relationship recently rehabilitated by scholars like David Harvey, who are sympathetic to both ecological (animal, environmental) and postcolonial (human, societal) concerns. As Harvey says, sensibly enough, "all proposals concerning 'the environment' are necessarily and simultaneously proposals for social change" (Harvey 1996: 120). But this doesn't stop him, like most other Marxists, from prioritising the human, and from demonstrating a profound impatience with the type of ecocentric thinking that posits the intrinsic value of all life-forms and the fundamental interconnectedness of the phenomenal world. Scoffing at such soft-boiled romanticism, Harvey suggests at one point that "[i]t is almost as if a fetishistic conception of 'nature' as something to be valued and worshipped separate from human action blinds a whole political movement to the qualities of the actual living environment [the city] in which the majority of humanity will soon live" (Harvey 1996: 427). Harvey's urban (urbane?) sensibilities are presumably at fault for his own blindness to the fact that many of the world's most impoverished people are precisely not city-dwellers, and that their daily lives are played out against the background of a desperate struggle over the control and management of life-sustaining natural resources. Notwithstanding, I would agree with Harvey that there is a pressing need to narrow the gap between an environmentalist and a socialist politics that have "by and large remained antagonistic to each other" (Harvey 1996: 120); and I would argue, further, that there is a need for a more conciliatory, though still appropriately critical, dialogue between often vehemently opposed advocates of animal and human rights. That the former have their origins in philanthropy is a point worth making; that the two regularly come into conflict is a given. But neither of these caveats in itself constitutes grounds for not considering the interests and concerns of animals; indeed, as the philosopher Tom Regan asserts, "[t]he animal rights movement is part of, not opposed to, the human rights movement. Attempts to dismiss it as antihuman are mere rhetoric" (Regan 1983: xiii). In the next part of this chapter, I will seek to play the part of both postcolonial and ecocritic by looking at two recent Canadian novels in which the production of a nonhuman "ecological subject" (Dobson 1990) by no means precludes human social and political concerns. However, in the works in question, Yann Martel's *Life of Pi* (2002) and Barbara Gowdy's *The White Bone* (1998), the relationship between human and animal worlds is presented very differently. In what follows, I will gauge the implications of these differences for the novels' nominally 'postcolonial' status; for their respective engagement with the racism/speciesism nexus; and for their treatment of the discourses of both human and animal liberation, particularly with regard to the captivity of animals and to the alleged violation, through captivity, of their basic moral rights.

2. States of captivity. State no. 1: The Zoo

Yann Martel's Booker-prizewinning novel *Life of Pi* has been gushingly described by one newspaper reviewer as "an adventure tale so filled with love for the animal kingdom that it ought to roar" (*Denver Post*, qtd in Martel 2003: n.p.). The story, narrated by the eponymous Pi, aka Piscine Molitor Patel, now living comfortably with his new family in Toronto, tells of the shipwreck that took his parents' lives, along with those of the zoo animals they were planning to transport from southern India to North America, their proposed new home. Pi, the sole human survivor, is cast adrift on a lifeboat on the Pacific with only a hyena, a zebra, an orangutan and a Bengal tiger for company. These animals, however, with the exception of the tiger - bizarrely named Richard Parker - prove to be only temporary companions. Darwinism prevails, with the zebra eaten first, then the orangutan, then the hyena. Pi is left with the tiger, whom he has to 'train' if he has any chance to survive. 227 days later, both fetch up unharmed on the Pacific coast of Mexico, where Pi proceeds to tell a number of ever more outrageous versions of his story to two bewildered officials from the Japanese Ministry of Transport, who have been instructed to find out what 'really' happened to the sunken ship. *Life of Pi*, as this inadequate synopsis suggests, is a multilayered fable that draws on a number of disparate sources. To some extent, the moral the fable draws is that of respect for animal difference. Pi survives, not only because of his formidable practical skills but because he understands, as a zookeeper's son, the territorial instincts of a tiger and recognises the need to stake his own territorial claim. Respect for animals is due, in part, to an acknowledgement of the everpresent threat of violence - a violence, born of the simple need to eat, that Pi is moved to re-enact:

I broke [the bird's] neck by leveraging its head backwards, one hand pushing up the beak, the other holding the neck. The feathers were so well attached that when I started pulling them out, skin came off – I was not plucking the bird; I was tearing it apart [...] I took the knife and skinned it instead [...] In its stomach, besides the morsel of dorado I had just given it, I found three small fish. After rinsing them of digestive juices, I ate them. I ate the bird's heart, liver and lungs. I swallowed its eyes and tongue with a gulp of water. I crushed its head and picked out its small brain. I ate the webbings of its feet. The rest of the bird was skin, bone and feathers. I dropped it beyond the edge of the tarpaulin for Richard Parker, who hadn't seen the bird arrive. An orange paw reached out. (Martel 2003: 311-12)

A similar lack of sentiment is shown in the early sequences of the novel at the family zoo in Pondicherry, which give short shrift to the anthropomorphism that creates an "animal even more dangerous than us, and one that [is] extremely common too, found on every continent, in every habitat: the redoubtable species *Animalus anthropomorphicus*, the animal as seen through human eyes" (Martel 2003: 41). It is "the obsession with putting ourselves at the centre of everything" that creates the effect of "look[ing] at an animal and see[ing] a mirror" (Martel 2003: 41), an unconsidered anthropomorphism also exposed in the sentimental view of wild animals as noble victims, subject to the apparently limitless cruelties of their nemesis in the animal kingdom, Man:

The life of the wild animal is simple, noble and meaningful, [such deluded romantics] imagine. Then it is captured by wicked men and thrown into tiny jails. Its "happiness" is dashed. It yearns mightily for "freedom" and does all it can to escape. Being denied its "freedom" for too long, the animal becomes a shadow of itself, its spirit broken. So some people imagine.

This is not the way it is.

Animals in the wild lead lives of compulsion and necessity within an unforgiving social hierarchy in an environment where the supply of fear is high and the supply of food low and where territory must constantly be defended and parasites forever endured. What is the meaning of freedom in such a context? Animals in the wild are, in practice, free neither in space nor in time, nor in their personal relations. (Martel 2003: 20)

This pragmatic view is then used to support what some might argue is the equally sentimental principle of contentment in captivity, the idealistic concept of zoos as places of "carefully worked-out coincidence" under whose conditions of "diplomatic peace" animals are happy "and we can [all] relax and have a look at each other" (Martel 2003: 24). The impassioned defence of zoos in the early section of Martel's novel runs counter to the view, perhaps expressed most vividly by John Berger in his celebrated essay 'Why Look at Animals?' (1980), that zoos constitute a monument to the disappearance of animals from many people's everyday lives. Zoos, says Berger,

> with their theatrical decor for display [are…] demonstrations of how animals have been rendered absolutely marginal […] The zoo to which people go to meet animals, to observe them, to see them, is, in fact, a monument to the impossibility of such encounters. Modern zoos are an epitaph to a relationship which was once as old as man (Berger 1980: 24, 19).

It is worth reflecting on why Martel's novel rejects this increasingly standard argument against the indignities of captivity and the conversion of animals into commodities, empty receptacles of value as much to be consumed as they are to be observed. The novel seems torn here between the production of a version of what is sometimes called the animal-rights 'respect principle' (Regan 1983) and the rejection of a liberationist position that assumes a continuing history of "the tyranny of human over nonhuman animals" while recognising that "the exploited group cannot themselves make an organised protest against the treatment they receive" (Singer 1976: vii, xii). Apparently parting company both with the utilitarianism of Singer and the modified anthropocentrism of Regan, Martel seems to come closest to a position based on neither sentience (Singer) nor sympathy (Regan), but rather on a respect for the radical otherness of wild animals, whose world is governed by targeted hostility and predation as a fact of life (Westra 1989; see also Martel 2003: 41 – "an animal is an animal, essentially and practically removed from us").

A trickier proposition still is Martel's stance toward colonialism, as mediated through his Indian boy-hero Pi, a seafaring version of Kipling's Mowgli in the unashamedly colonialist (and, for that matter, speciesist) *Jungle Books* (1894/5). Certainly, the novel can be read to some extent as a multilayered colonial allegory, in which the establishment of the family zoo at Pondicherry – a former French colony – is made to coincide with the moment of Indian national independence. On the other hand, the novel tends to mock such crudely 'explanatory' allegorising gestures, as is made particularly clear in the final sequence, when the Japanese officers despairingly try to make sense of Pi's alternative story, in which he arbitrarily substitutes people for animals, and the fable of his improbable survival against 'nature' and the elements is once again turned on its head (Martel 2003: 417-18). *Life of Pi* appears torn here, as well, between its attraction to colonialist nostalgia and its postcolonial/ecological counter-impulses toward the transformation of the beast fable: that paradigmatically anthropocentric, and often explicitly imperialistic, genre (Fernandes 1996). A further interpretative strand is provided by the novel's Canadian perspective, which implicitly engages with the variegated orientalisms of Canadian, particularly French Canadian, literature, and which considers the ambivalent status of Quebec as a sentimentalised colony-within-a-colony and an equally mythic 'India' as object of North American, as well as European fantasy – a colony of the imagination.

2.1 State no. 2: The Wild

At the conclusion of his tale, Pi gives profuse thanks to Richard Parker, who, shortly after their safe landing, unceremoniously takes off into the jungle, never to be seen again:

> 'Thank you for saving my life', says Pi, '[a]nd now go where you must. You have known the confined freedom of a zoo most of your life; now you will know the free confinement of a jungle' (Martel 2003: 384).

This dialectical interplay between freedom and confinement can also be found in another recent Canadian novel, Barbara Gowdy's subtitled "novel about elephants", *The White Bone* (1998). *The White Bone* tells the story – from their own point of view – of an East African elephant herd's struggle for survival in a desiccated landscape racked by drought and periodically invaded by predatory humans who hunt the elephants for ivory (and, so it seems as well, for their own twisted sport). The fallen world the elephants inhabit, codified in their own lore as the Domain, has obvious mythic resonances, while also recalling the crisis decades of the 60s and, particularly, the 70s, when elephants were hunted in some parts of postcolonial East Africa to the brink of extinction. Here, while no longer officially endangered, elephants must still compete for territory with rapidly increasing human populations, producing a "conflict of space [which, gradually] compressing them into smaller and smaller areas", threatens to reduce their viable habitat to the relatively protected enclaves of the wildlife parks (Douglas-Hamilton 1975: 256).

It is ironic, in this context, that the legendary Safe Place the elephants are seeking is envisioned at one point in the novel in terms of the modern tourist industry, as a game reserve where peaceful "hindleggers [humans] … [g]ape at she-ones [elephants] … [a]ll day long", as if, by "star[ing] at us hard enough, they [might] inflate back to what they were. Grow their ears and so on" (Gowdy 1999: 74). In passages like this one, Gowdy moves between the tongue-in-cheek attempt at a zoomorphic perspective on humans, seen here as the degenerate descendants of elephants, and the ironic awareness of the thoroughgoing anthropomorphism of her own, ostensibly animal-centred text. The Safe Place turns out to be just another human construct, as of course is the entire elaborate cosmology Gowdy dreams up for the elephants, which is reminiscent less of Kipling – Gowdy's most obvious literary precursor – than of assorted ecofeminist variations on the dubious 'spiritual awakening' of New Age thought (see Merchant 1992, Chs. 5 and 8). Although rendered biologically and culturally plausible, Gowdy's elephants can thus be seen as semi-mythic subjects for a form of zoological primitivism, inhabiting a fully fashioned tribal world of ancient superstitions and ancestral beliefs. In the modern version of this world, defined as much by human as by animal savagery, the fragile ecological alliances on which the elephants previously depended for their safety has been thrown violently, perhaps irrecoverably, out of place:

The emergence of humans did not, as is widely assumed, initiate a time of darkness. On the contrary, in the first generations following the Descent [the advent of human beings], the Domain [Earth] was a glorious place, and this is partly because humans back then were nothing like today's breed. They ate flesh, yes, and they were unrepentant and wrathful, but they killed only to eat [and there] weren't any massacres or mutilations. There was plenitude and ease, and between she-ones [elephants] and other creatures was a rare communion, for ... all she-ones were mind talkers, and the minds of all creatures were intelligible. (Gowdy 1999: 42-3)

In her insistence on the fully developed consciousness of elephants, among other animals, Gowdy implicitly supports Regan's view that animals are "psychophysical individuals who have an individual welfare", and that, by extension, they have "certain basic moral rights, including in particular the fundamental right to be treated with the respect that, as possessors of inherent value, they are due as a matter of strict justice" (Regan 1983: 121, 329). However, in the Manichaean world of *The White Bone*, the respect accorded to animals arguably comes at the price of contempt for humans, more particularly Gowdy's unnamed 'Africans', who, much like Conrad's, are allowed no language of their own and are chiefly characterised in the novel by their alarming predilection for performing unspeakable rites. This begs the question of the tacit racism of Gowdy's novel. Certainly, *The White Bone* can be assimilated easily enough to the long, ideologically objectionable tradition in which a mythicised 'Africa' has functioned as negative projection screen for a variety of hallucinatory white European fears, fantasies and desires (Hammond and Jablow 1977; Mudimbe 1988). It is tempting, in this context, to see the novel as a kind of neo-primitivist morality play in which the elephant features as a noble victim in a traditional society thrown disastrously off kilter, and the continuing assault on African wildlife contains within it a history of European imperial greed. This sentimental view is endorsed by the English journalist Richard Gavron, whose tiresome travelogue *The Last Elephant* (1993) is listed at the end of Gowdy's novel as one of her primary sources. For Gavron, the elephant is nothing less than a "flesh-and-blood symbol of [...] the most important question of all for Africa: the struggle of ancient traditions and resources to survive and contribute in the modern African world" (Gavron 1993: 3). After independence, Gavron claims,

> the first instinct of Africans was to turn around and wipe out their elephant populations: not merely to use the ivory to buy material goods, but also, it seems to me, to destroy their world's wildness and danger, to eradicate what many Africans regard as a primitive and shaming past. (Gavron 1993: xii)

Gavron's view, besides being smugly Eurocentric, risks relegating animals once more either to commodities – exchangeable trophies of post-imperial conquest – or to romantic embodiments of an atavistic 'wildness' in which the ambivalent inscriptions of Western modernity on the African continent are strategically erased. Gowdy's novel, to its credit, endorses neither of these untenable positions. It is ironically distanced, both from the genre of the apocalyptic "declensionist narrative" (Vance 1995: 172) and from the type of mock-historical fable in which animals are enlisted for the nostalgic production of a lost precolonial past. Ironic self-consciousness, however, is not enough to rescue the novel from a highly anthropocentric sentimentalism embodied in the all-too-familiar trope of the mourning elephant (see Masson and McCarthy 1996). This suggests, in the end, that for all the author's remarkable powers of sympathetic imagination, *The White Bone* is paradoxically marked by the detachment that accompanies attempts to solicit sympathy for animals by making 'them' seem more like 'us', and by making their plight our own.

2.2 State no. 3: The Beast Fable

The White Bone is characterised by entrapment, both literally in the shape of its persecuted elephants and metaphorically by the cloying sentimentality with which these creatures are often treated in the text. It is also worth considering whether there is a third source of entrapment here, namely the genre – the beast fable – around which the narrative is structured and upon which the novel, like its Canadian counterpart, *Life of Pi*, at once implicitly comments and explicitly draws.

In a sense, *The White Bone* and *Life of Pi* can both be seen as attempts to decolonise the beast fable, either by interrogating its imperial/ colonial origins (Fernandes 1996), or by turning its symbolic animal figures into fully fashioned ecological subjects, not lifeless relays for abstractions but living creatures of flesh and blood. Needless to say, however, the idea of bringing animals to life in literature remains just that, an idea; while the intrinsic anthropocentism of the beast fable proves in either text to be impossible to overcome. Indeed, traditionally humanistic genres such as the beast fable where animals speak with human voices are very much part of what the visual theorist Steve Baker calls the "instrumental characterisation" of animals in literature and the arts (Baker 2000: 175). This remains true whether such characterisation is "animal-endorsing" in its attempt to celebrate animals and advocate fairer treatment of them, or "animal-sceptical" in its recognition of the impossibility of speaking animals without also speaking for them, and its acknowledgement of the inevitable constructedness of "culture's means of [...] classifying the animal in order to make it meaningful to the human" (Baker 2000:175; see also Soper 1995).

The White Bone and *Life of Pi* are simultaneously "animal-endorsing" and "animal-sceptical" novels. They gesture, on the one hand, toward the transformation of a genre traditionally deployed to support moralistic, often highly conservative views of the human education process and, more recently, to prop up the social hierarchies and disciplinary regimes that legitimise imperial rule (Fernandes 1996; Vance 1995). But on the other, they acknowledge the impossibility of reaching out to the animal world without also to some extent humanising it. Martel's text does this by mocking anthropomorphism while also inevitably practising it; Gowdy's by registering a tension between the attempt to inhabit the mental and emotional spaces of animals' lives through a sustained act of the sympathetic imagination and an ironic awareness of animals as persistent objects of human desires and needs: objects of exploitation and abuse; objects of charity and affection. At the same time, both novels suggest that a leap of faith is needed to overcome the gulf of consciousness that separates humans from animals; otherwise, animals will continue to be captives in the world – and captives to the literary text.

3. Conclusion

What lessons might be learnt from the yoking of postcolonial and ecologically oriented criticism? A number of overlapping fields may be identified – most of which go far beyond the scope of this particular chapter – in which a critical dialogue between the two 'schools', still in its infancy, might usefully be pursued. The first of these fields, more explicitly activist, takes in historically situated critiques of capitalist ideologies of development; the second, more text-based, foregrounds the traditional discourses of environmental representation. Both fields combine a political concern for the abuses of authority with an ethical commitment to improving the conditions of the oppressed.

A third field concerns the cross-cultural implications of current ecocritical debates. Here, postcolonial criticism, despite what might still be seen as an unduly anthropocentric bias, offers a valuable corrective to a variety of explicitly or implicitly universalist ecological claims: the unexamined claim of equivalence among all "ecological beings" (Naess 1995), irrespective of material circumstances; the peremptory conviction, itself historically conditioned, that global ethical considerations should override local cultural concerns.

A fourth field addresses the problem of the rationalism/emotionalism dichotomy in postcolonial and ecocritical discourses. This field suggests the need for a more properly historicised, self-reflexive debate on the rhetorical function, as well as direct material effects, of Western-oriented discourses of intercultural reconciliation and anti-imperialist resistance; for a critical assessment of the ideological work performed in romanticising exploited indigenous peoples, endangered animals, and the encroachment of modernity on the 'wild'; and for a sustained challenge to the dominance of instrumental reason as a means of justifying authoritarian behaviour, both now and in the (colonial) past, both within and beyond the (human) species.

A fifth field, partly contained within the fourth, concerns the representation of the other. Here, the crucial questions of who speaks and for whom require constant critical attention, particularly in cases where 'othering' is the inadvertent result of an act of well-intentioned political advocacy, or where the attempt to reach out to one oppressed group runs the risk of further marginalising another.

Finally – and despite the problems mentioned above – it seems necessary to reaffirm the potential of the "environmental imagination" (Buell 1995) to envision alternative worlds, both within and beyond the realm of everyday human experience, that might reinvigorate the continuing global struggle for social and ecological justice. To be sure, the utopian aspirations of postcolonial criticism might well conflict, rather than coincide, with those of ecocriticism; while the early history of the twenty-first century, already darkened by a series of preventable human/ecological disasters, might well suggest that there is little room left for utopian thought. For all that, some form of active exchange between the critical projects of postcolonialism and ecocriticism now seems urgently necessary – not just as a collaborative means of addressing the social and environmental problems of the present, but also of imagining alternative futures in which our current ways of looking at ourselves and our relation to the world might be creatively transformed.

Let me close with two very brief comments on the implications of postcolonialism and ecocriticism for English Studies. The first is that both fields, internally conflicted though they are, appear united in their requirement for a cross-disciplinary approach to their wide range of chosen subjects. What this suggests is that neither postcolonialism nor ecocriticism can be practised alone within the confines of English literature departments (while postcolonial studies, in particular, would also benefit from a multilingual, as well as a multi- or interdisciplinary approach).

Whether university administrators have the means or inclination to make interdisciplinarity happen is, of course, another matter, while some scholars may well feel that the extended range of options offered by a contemporary, culturally oriented English Studies is interdisciplinary enough. But even if they are to be housed within predominantly literature-based English Studies programmes, postcolonialism and ecocriticism retain transformative potential, with the former offering a reminder that 'English Literature' is, after all, only one of many English literatures; and the latter a part-corrective to what Glen Love calls the "textbook anthropocentrism" of a traditional literary-studies approach (Love 2003: 23).

The second comment concerns the eternal debate over the future of the humanities. Here, postcolonialism and ecocriticism offer at least two possible alternatives. The first is a revitalised or, perhaps better, a re-extended form of humanism – a reaching out beyond the European boundaries of humanist philosophy, or a "pan-humanism" (the term is Gary Snyder's) that enthusiastically accommodates the nonhuman within humanistic thought. The latter is a continued critique, or a renewed rejection, of humanism. As Cary Wolfe suggests in the introduction to his collection, *Zoontologies: The Question of the Animal* (2003), academic researchers, both within and beyond the humanities, are increasingly confronting a "social, technological, and cultural context that is now in some inescapable sense posthuman, if not quite posthumanist" (Wolfe 2003: ix). According to Wolfe, much of the recent high-profile theoretical work on animals has had the effect, not just of probing the limits of the human, but of reconfirming the crisis of humanism in the academy at large (Wolfe 2003: x-xii). The humanities will probably survive this latest, perhaps exaggerated threat to their integrity. Whether they will adapt to it is another matter; the intriguing possibility of a 'posthumanist humanities' remains moot. Whatever the case, the tension between 'pan-humanist' and 'posthumanist' approaches to academic research – one already inscribed within emergent fields like postcolonialism and ecocriticism – should prove to be a feature of contemporary English Studies as it continues to struggle with its humanistic legacy for the foreseeable future.

Bibliography

Agamben, Giorgio. 2004. *The Open: Man and Animal* (tr. K. Attell). Stanford: Stanford University Press.

Arnold, David and Ramachandra Guha (eds). 1995. *Nature, Culture, Imperialism: Essays on the Environmental History of South Asia.* Delhi: Oxford University Press.

Baker, Steve. 2000. *The Postmodern Animal.* London: Reaktion Books.

Berger, John. 1980. 'Why Look at Animals?' in *About Looking.* New York: Pantheon. 1-26.

Buell, Lawrence. 1995. *The Environmental Imagination: Thoreau, Nature Writing, and the Formation of American Culture.* Cambridge: Harvard University Press.

Crosby, Alfred W. 1986. *Ecological Imperialism: The Biological Expansion of Europe, 900-1900.* Cambridge: Cambridge University Press.

Curtin, Deane. 1999. *Chinnagounder's Challenge: The Question of Ecological Citizenship.* Bloomington: Indiana University Press.

Dobson, Andrew. 1990. *Green Political Thought: An Introduction.* London: Unwin Hyman.

Douglas-Hamilton, Iain and Oria. 1975. *Among the Elephants.* London: Collins, Harvill Press.

Eagleton, Terry. 1999. 'Postcolonialism and "Postcolonialism"' in *Interventions* 1(1): 24-26.

Fanon, Frantz. 1986 [1961]. *The Wretched of the Earth* (tr. C. Farrington). New York: Grove Press.

Fernandes, Marie. 1996. *The Animal Fable in Modern Literature.* New Delhi: D.K. Publishers.

Gadgil, Madhav and Ramachandra Guha (eds). 1995. *Ecology and Equity: The Use and Abuse of Nature in Contemporary India.* London: Routledge.

Gavron, Jeremy. 1993. *The Last Elephant: An African Quest.* London: HarperCollins.

Glotfelty, Cheryll and Harold Fromm (eds). 1995. *The Ecocriticism Reader.* Athens: University of Georgia Press.

Gowdy, Barbara. 1999 [1998]. *The White Bone.* London: Flamingo.

Guha, Ramachandra. 2000 [1989]. *The Unquiet Woods: Ecological Change and Peasant Resistance in the Himalayas.* Berkeley: University of California Press.

Hammond, Dorothy and Alta Jablow. 1977. *The Myth of Africa.* New York: Library of Social Sciences.

Harvey, David. 1996. *Justice, Nature and the Geography of Difference.* Oxford: Blackwell.

Head, Dominic. 1998. 'The (im)possibility of ecocriticism' in Kerridge, R. and N. Sammells (eds). *Writing the Environment: Ecocriticism and Literature.* London: Zed Books. 27-39.

Kipling, Rudyard. 1986 [1894]. *The Jungle Book.* New York: Exeter.

— 1986 [1895]. *Second Jungle Book.* New York: Exeter.

Love, Glenn A. 2003. *Practical Ecocriticism: Literature, Biology, and the Environment.* Charlottesville: University of Virginia Press.

Martel, Yann. 2003 [2002]. *Life of Pi.* Edinburgh: Canongate Books.

Masson, Jeffrey and Susan McCarthy. 1996. *When Elephants Weep: The Emotional Lives of Animals*. London: Vintage.

Merchant, Carolyn. 1992. *Radical Ecology: The Search for a Livable World*. London: Routledge.

Mudimbe, V.Y. 1988. *The Invention of Africa: Gnosis, Philosophy, and the Order of Knowledge*. Bloomington: Indiana University Press.

Naess, Arne. 1995. 'The Third World, Wilderness, and Deep Ecology' in Sessions, G. (ed.) *Deep Ecology for the Twenty-First Century*. Boston: Shambala Books.

O'Brien, Susie. 2001. 'Articulating the World Between: Ecocriticism, Postcolonialism and Globalization' in *Canadian Literature* 170/171: 140-58.

Pepper, David. 1993. *Eco-Socialism: From Deep Ecology to Social Justice*. London: Routledge.

Quayson, Ato. 2000. *Postcolonialism: Theory, Practice, or Process?* Cambridge: Polity Press.

Regan, Tom. 1983. *The Case for Animal Rights*. Berkeley: University of California Press.

Singer, Peter. 1976 [1975]. *Animal Liberation: A New Ethics for Our Treatment of Animals*. London: Jonathan Cape.

Snyder, Gary. 1995. 'The Rediscovery of Turtle Island' in Sessions, G. (ed.) *Deep Ecology for the Twenty-First Century*. Boston: Shambala Books. 141-50.

Soper, Kate. 1995. *What is Nature?* Oxford: Blackwell.

Spiegel, Marjorie. 1988. *The Dreaded Comparison: Human and Animal Slavery*. New York: Mirror.

Tiffin, Helen. 2002. 'Postcolonialism, Animals and the Environment' in Ashcroft, W., G. Griffiths and H. Tiffin (eds). *The Empire Writes Back: Theory and Practice in Post-Colonial Literatures*, 2nd ed. London: Routledge. 213-16.

Vance, Linda. 1995. 'Beyond Just-So Stories: Narrative, Animals, and Ethics' in Adams, C. J. and J. Donovan (eds.) *Animals & Women: Feminist Theoretical Explorations*. Durham: Duke University Press. 163-91.

Westra, Laura. 1989. 'Ecology and Animals: Is There a Joint Ethics of Respect?' in *Environmental Ethics* 11(3): 215-30.

Wolfe, Cary. 1998. 'Old Orders for New: Ecology, Animal Rights and the Poverty of Humanism' in *Diacritics* 28(2): 21-40.

— (ed.) 2003. *Zoontologies: The Question of the Animal*. Minneapolis: University of Minnesota Press.

Young, Robert J.C. 1999. '"Dangerous and Wrong": Shell, Intervention and the Politics of Transnational Companies' in *Interventions* 1(3): 439-64.

Barry Macsweeney's Moorland Romance

Matthew Jarvis

Abstract

Barry MacSweeney's 1997 collection *The Book of Demons* contains two poetic
sequences, 'Pearl' and 'The Book of Demons'. In the latter sequence, MacSweeney
depicts an uncompromising destruction of the human subject by means of the
alcoholic demons which were eventually to kill MacSweeney himself. Although in
hell with the demons, MacSweeney is in heaven with 'Pearl', in a poetic exploration
of the moorland romance he experiences with his first love. A dramatic contrast is
thus established between the apparently urbanised world of demonic suffering
(complete with the poet "drunken to the last, flung / to the lost in the final Labour
council-run / public toilet on earth") and the moorland world of Pearl ("Pearl in the
Borage up to her waist. / Pearl in the wildmint. / Pearl in the wind-spilled water."). In
this essay Jarvis examines whether MacSweeney's use of moorland landscape is
merely a version of the postmodern nostalgia that Frederic Jameson outlines, or
whether it crucially provides the image by which MacSweeney poetically figures
nothing less than salvation itself.

The British poet Barry MacSweeney is perhaps most famous for his
collection *The Book of Demons*, which was published by Bloodaxe
Books in 1997, a little less than three years before he died.[1] However,
MacSweeney had been publishing since the late 1960s and had built
up a considerable body of work by the point of his death.[2] Early in his
career, he was famous for being nominated by his then-publishers,
Hutchinson, for Oxford University's Chair of Poetry, at the unusually

---

[1] *The Book of Demons* was a Poetry Book Society Recommendation and a winner of
the Paul Hamlyn Award in 1997. Barry MacSweeney died in May 2000 at the age of
51. For a brief introduction to MacSweeney, see 'The Barry MacSweeney Collection'.

[2] This is something that the recent Bloodaxe collection of MacSweeney's selected
poetry makes clear in its useful opening bibliography (MacSweeney 2003: 2).

young age of nineteen. In the event, he received three votes and, as
Nicholas Johnson (2000) says in his obituary for MacSweeney in *The
Independent*, his reputation "took half a lifetime [...] to recover".
Later, MacSweeney was also known for his struggles with alcohol, as
a number of the obituaries and retrospectives written about him
indicate.[3] Indeed, alcohol was crucial to MacSweeney's imagination
by the mid-1990s – something Andrew Crozier (2000) suggests when
he observes that, in *The Book of Demons*, MacSweeney "projects
himself as maimed and abject, a hapless yet percipient victim of the
demon drink".

Of the two sequences that make up *The Book of Demons* – 'Pearl'
(initially published as an independent volume in 1995) and 'The Book
of Demons' itself – Crozier's analysis is most applicable to the latter.
However, although 'The Book of Demons' manifestly offers some
parallels to MacSweeney's real-life struggles with alcoholism, the
poetic self-projection in this sequence is not autobiographical in a
simplistic sense. Rather, in its creation of a broken and suffering
central character who is relentlessly pursued by the (literalised)
demons of alcohol, MacSweeney's poetic was continuing an
engagement with what Gordon Burn describes as "the roster of flame-
outs and fuck-ups and holy losers he had been fixated on from his
youth" (2000: 2). In other words, 'The Book of Demons' can be seen
to demonstrate a persistence of what Andrew Crozier (2000) has
usefully identified as the "myth of exemplary failure" which fuelled
MacSweeney's "notion of the artist".

'The Book of Demons' is, then, substantially concerned with
depicting the alcoholic traumas of the speaker (the MacSweeney
persona) on whom the sequence centres. Throughout the text, the
speaker's brokenness – the key manifestation here of that "exemplary
failure" which Crozier notes – is presented in bluntly uncompromising
terms, as he is pursued and tormented by demons who are persistently
tempting him to drink. The first poem of the sequence, 'Ode to Beauty

---

[3] See, for example, Gordon Burn's feature on MacSweeney, the month after his death,
which was called 'Message in a Bottle' (Burn 2000). The theme of alcoholism runs
throughout Burn's account, and concludes by recalling that MacSweeney used to
"jokingly refer to himself" as "Clink Eastwood" (Burn 2000: 4). See also Dean
(2000), and Crozier (2000). Even Johnson (2000) refers to the issue obliquely, in his
reference to "the dissolution of [MacSweeney's] later years".

Strength and Joy and In Memory of the Demons' (1997: 37-38), establishes the 'demonic hordes' which surround the central character.[4] The demons themselves are presented as "reborn Stasi KGB neck-twisters/ and finger crushers", or are manifest as possibly vampiric "rustling bats". They speak the language of torture chambers ("from the mouths of [demons]/ words in Cyrillic Venusian torture chamber argot/ stream upwards"), and carry symbols of death ("Some carry zipper body bags,/ black and gleaming in the acid rain"). Significantly, in this latter description, the demons are metaphorically aligned with a potent symbol of potential ecological crisis in the reference to "acid rain". Indeed, later in the same poem, the sense of environmental danger is emphasised by the speaker's observation of "the fatal tidal reach" into which "you" may jump, having been tempted to suicide by the demons.[5] Within this context, the poem's earlier description of the same body of water as a "swollen tide" is also potentially negative. According to the *Oxford English Dictionary*, for a body of water *to swell* suggests a "rise above the ordinary level".[6] In other words, alongside "acid rain" and "fatal tidal reach", the "swollen tide" may also suggest something environmentally abnormal (at least from the point of view of human perception, in which a swelling tide may threaten the material patterns of human life). Furthermore, the movement from "acid rain", through "swollen tide", to "fatal tidal reach" suggests a distinctly developing sense, within the poem's symbolic structure, of the environment as a potentially lethal force. In short, part of the way in which the fears that surround alcoholic suffering are manifest at the start of 'The Book of Demons' is specifically to do with the non-human world – a world that is characterised by spectres of acidity and by the presence of lethal waters.

The pattern thus established in the opening poem – this connection between the brokenness of the central character and a broadly negative experience of landscape and environment – recurs elsewhere in the

---

[4] All quotations from both 'The Book of Demons' and 'Pearl' are taken from the Bloodaxe collection, *The Book of Demons* (MacSweeney 1997).

[5] The "you" in this part of the poem is effectively a projection of the suffering, central self of the sequence.

[6] See *OED*, Second Edition (1989), entry for "swell, *v*", definition 1b.

sequence. As the conclusion to 'Sweeno, Sweeno' puts it (1997: 92-93):

> Hands on knees and puffing hard I've had enough of this.
> Ankle-tapping, broken bones, demonic shirt-pulling, the
>
> beautiful game on the emerald field of dreams now turf
> churned, filthy, white line I shimmy down impossible to see.
>
> Chants, rants for Sweeno, zero hero. Come on ref, blow that whistle.
> Rockets, fires and flags on trouble-free terraces. Ferocity
>
> like mine. No-score draw. No extra time. No penalty shoot-out. No
> golden-goal finale, no golden boot. Down the tunnel into nightlight. Endgame.

In these lines, the central character of the sequence is on the brink of total ruin. "Living daily rim to mouth", as MacSweeney puts it elsewhere in the collection ('Buying Christmas Wrapping Paper on January 12' 1997: 41), brokenness is manifest here in footballing terms as a final walk down the tunnel into "nightlight" or as a terminal "Endgame". Yet the speaker is still trying to "shimmy" down the line; there are "Chants" for him from the terraces; he has "Ferocity" In short, there is something of the hero left in him. However, this is ultimately the heroism of what the poem identifies as the "zero hero" – the hero who is emptied out entirely, who faces blankness (the significance of the goalless "No-score draw"), and who knows that there will be no further extension to the game and thus no possibility of triumph ("No extra time. No penalty shoot-out"). In other words, in its evocation of a central character who is about to descend into nothingness (albeit shimmying down the line and being cheered from the terraces as he does so), this is very precisely the image of the "flame-out" or the "fuck-up" that Gordon Burn (2000: 2) has suggested was such an important, life-long fixation for MacSweeney. Moreover, as with the first poem of the sequence, the landscape in which such brokenness is manifest is significantly degraded or problematic. The football fan's iconic image of an "emerald field of dreams" has turned into a "filthy" place of churned turf, with what should be the crisply-painted white line now "impossible to see". Indeed, the "beautiful game" itself is also degraded, turned into a matter of sniping foul play in "Ankle-tapping" and "demonic shirt-pulling". Both the landscape and the human activities that are acted out upon it are consequently as broken as the speaker himself, with the poem's "zero hero" playing on, but waiting (even longing) for the referee's final, inevitable, blowing of the whistle.

The figuring of a landscape in which to place the "zero hero" of 'The Book of Demons' is thus a significant factor in the expression of that sense of brokenness which is such an important element within MacSweeney's poetic sensibility at this point. However, the landscape of alcoholic suffering is not merely characterised by its degradations and dangers; it is also a very particular *type* of landscape. As the speaker observes in the second poem of the sequence, "Hell is the pavement against my shit face" ('Free Pet with Every Cage'; 1997: 40). Of course, there is a grim pun here about being "shit-faced" (a slang reference to being "intoxicated with alcohol").[7] But what is more significant is that the location of suffering – here explicitly identified as hell – is envisaged in terms of the built environment. This is an association that recurs throughout 'The Book of Demons'. Thus, the drama of the opening poem takes place on a structure with a "parapet", from which the poem imagines the demon-tormented sufferer jumping in suicidal shame ('Ode to Beauty Strength and Joy and In Memory of the Demons'; 1997: 37). Similarly, in the poem 'Strap Down in Snowville', the speaker finds himself "drunken to the last, flung/ to the lost in the final Labour council-run/ public toilet on earth" (1997: 85). Indeed, in expressing the alcoholic sufferings of the central character, such identifications with the built environment are crucial to the metaphoric structure of the sequence as a whole. Thus, in the poem 'Demons Swarm Upon Our Man and Tell the World He's Lost', MacSweeney figures suffering in terms of the following place-based imagery (1997: 63):

I'm the storm-tossed tosser
on Earthquake Street, mindblown
dead on arrival sprawled on
Richter Scale Prospekt, found
crying wolf beside the troikas.

---

[7] See Spears (1981), entry for 'shit-faced'.

MacSweeney's alcoholic world of suffering, in other words, is a place of "streets" and "prospekts".[8] Similarly, elsewhere in the sequence, the central character is to be found "down Do-lalley Drive, Kerbcrawl Boulevard, Cirrhosis Street/ and Wrecked Head Road" ('Buying Christmas Wrapping Paper on January 12'; 1997: 41). He is in the vicinity of "Nilsville" ('Free Pet with Every Cage'; 1997: 39), and is seen on a "Bad bus one way" to the blanked-out nothingness of 'Snowville' ('Nothing are These Times'; 1997: 73). Unsurprisingly, 'Sweeno, Sweeno' incorporates a place called "Demon Town" (1997: 91), whilst the geography of 'Strap Down in Snowville' even includes a "Department Store of Sighs" (1997: 87). MacSweeney's landscape of suffering is crucially a collection of "villes" and "towns", "drives", "streets" and "stores". In other words, brokenness is inextricable from the imagination of that which has been built by human beings: the inorganic matter of the paved and the concreted; the fabricated locales of the town and the city. Of course, insofar as it includes locations that suggest broad emotional and physical states – "Cirrhosis Street", "Nilsville", and the "Department Store of Sighs" – the environment imagined in 'The Book of Demons' is not a specific place.[9] Instead, the inclusion of such names effectively creates a mythic arena of demonic torment, in which the human constructions of streets, towns, public toilets and department stores become archetypal sites of brokenness. In other words, 'The Book of Demons' suggests that the built, the urban, or the human-colonised is nothing less than the generic locus of suffering.[10]

---

[8] *OED*, Second Edition (1989), defines "Prospekt" thus: "In the Soviet Union: a long, wide street; an avenue, a boulevard. Esp. used of the great avenues of Leningrad, e.g. *Nevsky Prospekt*." Nevsky Prospekt is one of "three great avenues" in St. Petersburg (the name Leningrad was revoked in 1991) and "One of the world's great thoroughfares" ('Saint Petersburg', *Encyclopædia Britannica Online*).

[9] Even though specific places (such as Durham, Cambridge, Cork, and the Pennines) are mentioned in 'The Book of Demons', the inclusion of place-names drawn from broad emotional and physical states means that the sequence is not loco-specific in any straightforward way.

[10] The notion of landscape as 'colonised' by human activity is drawn from Douglas Coupland's novel *All Families are Psychotic* in which Coupland writes: "Wade tried to imagine Florida before the advent of man, but couldn't. The landscape seemed too thoroughly colonized – the trailers, factory outlets and cocktail shacks" (Coupland 2002: 69). The concept of 'colonised landscape' thus usefully summarises the sense of

Alongside this, however, MacSweeney's environmental aesthetics also link suffering and brokenness with an emphatic and complementary closing off of the organic. In 'Strap Down in Snowville', the speaker partly locates himself as follows (1997: 85):

> Who here needs a bardic throne on Christmas Eve
> in the tiled cubicle of magic marker messages – Proper
> Gay Sucks: Ring this number. No Jokers Please?

In a dark parody of the notion of a "bardic throne", these lines position the MacSweeney character in an emphatically *scatological* throne-room, surrounded not by words of bardic intensity but by sexual graffiti.[11] Such parodic associations again suggest that the built environment – here, the "tiled cubicle" with "urinal drain" and "bolted door" – is a distinctly problematic space within 'The Book of Demons'. Moreover, the connection between built environments and emotional trauma is sustained as the speaker observes "armies of rock-steady Goliath ants/ in bent Durrutti [sic] Columns proceed[ing] righteous/ [...] up the wall and into my eyes". However, at the start of the following stanza, the poem significantly complicates such identifications by indicating that "It is dark now along my swan meadow river and always dark". Suffering, in other words, is not simply a matter of being located within a built space (the "tiled cubicle"). It is also to do with the fact that an organic environment has now become inaccessible – an inaccessibility figured here in terms of the apparently unending darkness which has fallen over 'my swan meadow river'.

'Strap Down in Snowville' thus gestures towards the importance of the organic environment in MacSweeney's poetic. This is something that becomes especially apparent in 'Pearl', the first sequence in *The Book of Demons* and a work which forms a strong contrast to the topographical focus of the volume's title-sequence. In 'Pearl', then, MacSweeney recalls his childhood in the 1950s, concentrating specifically on time spent in the northern English hamlet of Sparty

---

landscape put to human use or human waste, and so helpfully covers such diverse notions as farmland, village, cityscape, or landfill.

[11] In slang, 'the lavatory' is also known as 'the throne'; see Spears (1981), entry for "throne", definition 2.

Lea.[12] The geographical arena of this poetry is the wild moorland of
the Northumberland Allen Valley, through which MacSweeney
wanders with his first love, Pearl, a mute girl he teaches to read and
write (1997: back-cover notes; Johnson 2000).

In contrast to the tone of crisis and suffering that dominates 'The
Book of Demons', the tone of 'Pearl' is recurrently ecstatic. This
ecstatic note emerges both from the youthful persona of the poet and
from the character of Pearl herself. Moreover – and crucially – the
physical arena for their ecstasy is persistently the organic world. The
seventh poem of the sequence, 'No Buses to Damascus', catches this
connection (1997: 17):

> We fell asleep at Blackbird Ford
> named by princes Bar and Paul of Sparty Lea.
> We splashed and swam and made the brown trout mad.
> Dawdled in our never-ending pleasure over
> earth-enfolded sheephorns
> by rivermist webs, half-hidden moss crowns.

The speaker's emotional state here is characterised by what he
exuberantly calls 'never-ending pleasure' – pleasure that is found,
significantly, not amongst "roads" and "villes" and "department
stores", but alongside the life of the river, or "Up a height or down the
dale" as the same poem goes on to put it. Other poems in 'Pearl' offer
similar perspectives. Thus, 'No Such Thing' observes a dog-rose in
the morning (1997: 15):

> How bright and sudden the dogrose,
> briefly touched by dew, flaming
> between the deep emerald and smoky blue.

At this point, MacSweeney's observation of the interplay between the
colours of flower, grass, and sky produces a rapt, poetic version of
natural history. However, what is crucial is not so much the
observation of the dog-rose itself as the comparison that the speaker
then draws between the dog-rose and Pearl's lips – lips that are, the
poem notes, entirely untouched by lipstick, and which thus constitute
a rejection of 'city chemist or salon'. Indeed, compounding this

---

[12] 'Lost Pearl' (MacSweeney 1997: 30) refers to 1998 as "forty years from now".

rejection of urban-derived or manufactured colours, MacSweeney makes it clear that the sense of colour shared by Pearl and the speaker is drawn from non-human sources: feldspar, peat, marigolds, cowslips. Crucially, then, both the speaker's sense of what is beautiful and the criteria of aesthetic judgement that he and Pearl employ are formed, not merely through reference to the non-human world, but by a striking rejection of urban or synthetic models. Indeed, although the mute Pearl may be dubbed an idiot by the outside world, the sequence makes it clear that she has no need for charity. In one of the poems which gives her a voice ('Pearl's Utter Brilliance'), Pearl describes her reaction to the Allen Valley, to being called an idiot, and to anyone who would pity her (1997: 13):

> We loved so much the lunar light
> on rawbone law or splashing in the marigold beds,
> our gazing faces broken in the stream.
> [...]
> Pity? Put it in the slurry with the rest of your woes.
> I am Pearl, queen of the dale.

The apparently non-colonised world of the Allen Valley is a place of ecstasy, in which troubles can, it seems, be swept aside by the sheer joy of "splashing in the marigold beds". Moreover, the landscape of 'Pearl' is also the location of MacSweeney's "angel boyhood" ('Strap Down in Snowville'; 1997: 87), and a place of romance.[13] As the speaker says in 'Mony Ryal Ray' (1997: 16):

> Skybrightness drove me
> to the cool of the lake
> to muscle the wind
> and wrestle the clouds
> and forever dream of Pearl.

It is out of this experience that the MacSweeney character proclaims, in a final-line coda to 'Sweet Jesus: Pearl's Prayer', "I cannot cease to dream and speak of Pearl" (1997: 12). The memory of young love is thus inextricable from notions of taking pleasure in the organic world of lake, wind, and clouds.

---

[13] For "angel boyhood", see also Burn (2000: 2).

However, in 'Pearl', the positive connotations of the organic world go further than this. MacSweeney's sequence is related to the medieval alliterative poem *Pearl*, which it parallels in a number of ways – one of the most significant similarities being the way in which the pearl maiden in both poems becomes the focal point for the discovery of heaven. Thus, in the medieval poem, the highly articulate lady of pearls guides the dreamer within the heavenly realm and lectures him on matters of spiritual importance (Andrew and Waldron 1987: 34-35). In MacSweeney's sequence, heaven also emerges out of Pearl's mouth – but in a somewhat different fashion. Thus, in the final three lines of 'No Buses to Damascus', the lustre of heaven – presented by the medieval *Pearl*-poet as a place shining with gold and jewels, in a vision drawn from the biblical book of Revelation (Andrew and Waldron 1987: 100, note to lines 973–1032) – finds itself manifest within the cleft palate and mute mouth of MacSweeney's first love (1997: 17): [14]

> The congenital fissure in the roof of her mouth
> laid down with priceless gems, beaten lustrous copper
> and barely hidden seams of gold.

In one sense, this association overturns ideas of disability in a radical way, by taking the precise point of suffering and turning it into something that is construed as especially beautiful. In other words, at this point, the politics of the human body move critically against normative ideas about what physical qualities are to be valorised. In addition, however, these lines figure the organic world of the Allen Valley not merely as a place of ecstasy, "angel boyhood", and romance; they also construe it as the place where MacSweeney sees heaven itself. In short, if MacSweeney is in hell with the demons – "Hell is the pavement against my shit face", as he puts it in 'Free Pet with Every Cage' (1997: 40) – then he is in paradise with Pearl.

It is in this contrast between the heavenly landscape of 'Pearl' and the hellish, colonised landscape of the demons that the landscape politics of *The Book of Demons* as a whole become most clearly apparent. On its own, the organic, non-colonised world that 'Pearl' envisions may seem to be merely a manifestation of nostalgia. Indeed,

---

[14] For Pearl's cleft palate, see 'Mony Ryal Ray' (1997: 16) and Johnson (2000).

it may even be construed as little more than the re-formation of some safe, eternal 1950s before MacSweeney's slide from "angel boyhood / to scarred bottledom" ('Strap Down in Snowville'; 1997: 87). However, setting one landscape against another, and from the perspective of "scarred bottledom", the organic world of 'Pearl' represents hope: it is the place of the unscarred; and it stands as the space in which a person may lose his or her possessing madness and become (in simple terms) good.

In 'The Book of Demons', the speaker of 'Free Pet With Every Cage' thus talks about recovery from alcoholic suffering in the following terms (1997: 40):

> The light of recovery is just a format.
> The light of recovery is just a lost fairy tale
> seeping with ferndamp
> in the bluebell vales of your childhood.
> The light of recovery is an ex-starre, furious with everlasting
> darkness.

In one sense, recovery is presented here as merely the formulaic dream ("format") of a "fairy tale" – a "fairy tale", moreover, that the speaker concedes to be "lost". However, unavailable though it may be in actuality, recovery as a concept is crucially understood by the suffering speaker in terms of "ferndamp" and "bluebell vales". In other words, the dream of recovery is the dream of the organic world. Likewise, in the difficult final image of this stanza, it seems that recovery is construed in terms of an "ex-starre" that is angered by its current state of darkness. What is envisioned here, in other words, is a condition in which the light of the star has been extinguished, and in which a veil has consequently been brought down over the non-human world – just as the speaker of 'Strap Down in Snowville' sees darkness fall over "my swan meadow river" (1997: 85). As a result, what this image ultimately implies is that recovery from alcohol can be understood in terms of the recovery of starlight. Indeed, it seems that even the city itself can be transformed if it is understood within the larger environmental context of the non-human. Thus, in the first poem of 'The Book of Demons', the urban becomes beautiful as it is placed alongside "the pure transmission of kissing you" (an experience in which "solar winds seethe in amber wonder"), and as it is set within the larger environmental vision of "novas and planets and starres" under which the material structures of the city exist ('Ode to Beauty Strength and Joy and In Memory of the Demons'; 1997: 38).

Given the apparently salvific qualities of the ex-urban and the non-human, it is consequently unsurprising that, in a later poem from 'The Book of Demons', the MacSweeney character turns explicitly to the rural arena of Sparty Lea as the place where he can see himself as unscarred – in a state, as he puts it, "before addiction overwhelmed me and / made me silent", "long before harm/ and its broods of violence" ('Up a Height and Raining'; 1997: 97). Moreover, as he imagines himself back in Sparty Lea, the speaker's environmental sense is significantly formed around signifiers that suggest the organic world, or that imply ex-urban space: breeze, stile, clouds, the moon. Indeed, in the same poem, MacSweeney makes it clear that the moon he sees is one that has been untouched by humanity – the moon "before men [...] stood upon it for the very first time". In other words, the speaker's sense of personal purity is bound up with the idea of places that are either completely free from human involvement or that are distinctly ex-urban. Thus, and perhaps most pertinently of all, in 'Pearl', the eponymous heroine, struggling with her cleft palate, declares ('Pearl's Poem of Joy and Treasure'; 1997: 31):

> Why am I ashamed of my permanent silence?
> In the brilliant heather, shin deep, I am
> a good lass, purring and foaming, friend of green breasted
> plover, keen listener to the wind in the wires; all
> the bees and beasts understand
> my milky fingers and palms.

In Pearl's terms, the organic world of the North Pennines thus offers the chance to be "good". It provides the arena of the unscarred self and displays the image of hope – however unlikely that hope may be. Salvation, it seems, is to be found in turning away from the world that is colonised by humanity.

The salvific turn in 'Pearl' is, however, also a turn to the past, as MacSweeney recollects a time before his alcoholic fall. Indeed, from the perspective of 'Up a Height and Raining' (in 'The Book of Demons'), Sparty Lea belongs to an almost mythic past, as the poem construes the state in which the speaker (the MacSweeney character) and Pearl lived as fundamentally prelapsarian. The speaker indicates that "We seized the sky and made it ours [...] Before we knew/ the moon was cold" (1997: 97). The past that we find in the 'Pearl' sequence – and, more broadly, in MacSweeney's memory of Pearl herself – is thus a past that takes place not only before the fall into alcohol, but also before the fall into knowledge. As a result, to the extent that the MacSweeney character looks to his time with Pearl as a state of former bliss or innocence ("long before harm// and its broods of violence" [1997: 97]), the moorland romance of 'Pearl' is emphatically nostalgic in the sense that it is crucially bound up with the "wistful memory [...] of an earlier time".[15]

However, although such nostalgia creates the vision of an unfallen human state, it is significant that this tendency does not extend into the creation of a parallel, pristine topography. In other words, MacSweeney does not move from the imagination of a prelapsarian human state to the construction of an equally prelapsarian landscape. Thus, although 'Pearl' undeniably presents the organic landscape of the Allen Valley as a place of potential salvation, the sequence engages bluntly with the historical sufferings of the landscape that is being recalled. In 'Pearl Suddenly Awake', for example, MacSweeney depicts an area in which the presence of deserted mines leads the speaker of the poem into explicit political statement (1997: 18):

> In my mind at the top of the valley,
> roar of lead ore poured crashing
> into the ghosts of now forsaken four-wheeled bogies
> distinctly off the rails. They –
> you call it government – are killing everything
> now. Hard hats abandoned in heather. Locked-up
> company huts
> useless to bird, beast or humankind.

Ironically, then, in the economic destitution that MacSweeney depicts here through the musings of Pearl, the place of personal salvation and innocence stands as a testament to communal fall. Indeed, in its critique of both government and the way in which government policy has material impacts on specific landscapes and the local communities within them, the Allen Valley of 'Pearl Suddenly Awake' crucially

---

[15] See *OED*, Second Edition (1989), entry for "nostalgia", definition 2.

represents the way in which landscapes function as nothing less than spaces on which political activity is inscribed.

MacSweeney's nostalgia, in other words, does not lead him into the creation of an uncritical, simulacral version of 1950s rural England – by which I mean, to draw on Fredric Jameson's discussion of postmodern nostalgia, a version of the 1950s that has been formed out of nothing more than archetypal models of 1950s style, "conveying pastness by the glossy qualities of the image" (Jameson 1991: 19). Of course, the sequence does contain signifiers of the 1950s. For example, in the poem 'Pearl and Barry Pick Rosehips for the Good of the Country' (1997: 26), the speaker recalls "picking rosehips [...] for NHS syrup quotas" (Johnson 2000). But 'Pearl' does not merely recall the stylistic iconography of the 1950s; nor does it evoke the past simply in order to create a retrospective simulation that eclipses the present (and all of its problems). Instead, MacSweeney's recollections present the topography of an ex-urban landscape, itself somewhat broken, in which the central character sees a revelation of heaven. The Allen Valley of MacSweeney's poetic memory thus functions as that "retrospective dimension indispensable to any vital reorientation of our collective future" – a quality which is, for Fredric Jameson (1991: 18), the very opposite of postmodern historicism. In other words, if there was to have been any hope for the poet-persona – or, if we believe the identification suggested by the two sequences in *The Book of Demons*, for MacSweeney himself – it lay in the rediscovery of that unfallen state of innocent comradeship with Pearl, in northern English wildness. In short, the Allen Valley of the 1950s is not, in itself, salvation: it is, after all, depicted politically in the sequence as a place of communal loss. Rather, for MacSweeney, it is the place in and through which salvation may be found.

In this sense, the environmental aesthetics of MacSweeney's poetic are clearly not ecocentric, because the landscape of 'Pearl' is a canvas on which human past is written for the sake of human future – a process which is, in effect, nothing less than a *metaphoric* colonisation of ex-urban, semi-wild, or wild space. Contrary to the thrust of much ecocriticism, however – which celebrates literatures that create a "self-effacement" of the human as "he or she becomes absorbed in a biocentric position of nonhierarchical interconnectedness" (Scigaj 1996: 15) – I want to suggest that the anthropocentric ethic of

MacSweeney's poetry is both defensible and useful. This is because such a position acknowledges that what both 'Pearl' and 'The Book of Demons' present as wild or 'natural' space can be ascribed value precisely as wild or 'natural' space – in all its relative lack of material development. In other words, such space is acknowledged as having value in the human economy even without (for example) re-opening the historic leadmines of the Allen Valley. In MacSweeney's poetry, wild or 'natural' space is seen to be valuable *just as it is*. To put it another way, allowing the metaphorical colonisation of such space by seeing it in terms of human economy – an emotional economy in 'Pearl' and 'The Book of Demons' – paradoxically protects it as wild space because of its subsequently acknowledged value.

Such a position is congruent with a 2002 report on the value of wild nature published in the journal *Science* (Balmford et al. 2002), whose authors conclude that, in a useful summary provided by Tim Radford (2002), "forests, wetlands and other natural ecosystems are worth far more to human economies than the farm or building land that could replace them". Or, in blunt economic terms, "to extend and effectively protect threatened areas of temperate and tropical forest, mangrove swamps, coral reefs and so on" will cost $45 billion each year; but the return value of such spaces – in terms of functions such as flood prevention, erosion control, carbon dioxide recycling, and insect propagation (to ensure crop pollination) – is at least $4,400 billion each year. Indeed, "wilderness converted to human use each year actually costs economies $250bn a year, every year" (Radford 2002). Thus, the authors of the report itself conclude that "our relentless conversion and degradation of remaining natural habitats is eroding overall human welfare for short-term private gain". Moreover, whilst acknowledging, in passing, the 'moral' element of "retaining as much as possible of what remains of wild nature", the main thrust of the report's conclusion acknowledges the "overwhelming *economic* [...] sense" of such retention (Balmford et al. 2002: 953; emphasis added). In short, even without resorting to ecocentric positions, wild or semi-wild space can be defended as valuable *just as it is*.[16] The

---

[16] In response to a question following a public lecture at the University of Wales, Aberystwyth, Andrew Dobson (2004) suggested that ecocentric positions were, in any case, near-impossible to argue in practice.

environmental aesthetics of Barry MacSweeney's moorland romance show contemporary British poetry functioning precisely as part of that defence.

Bibliography

Andrew, Malcolm, and R. A. Waldron (eds). 1987. *The Poems of the Pearl Manuscript: Pearl, Cleanness, Patience, Sir Gawain and the Green Knight.* Exeter: University of Exeter Press.

'The Barry MacSweeney Collection'. On line at: http://www.ncl.ac.uk/elll/research/literature/macsweeney/(consulted 11.08.2004).

Balmford, Andrew, et al. 2002. 'Economic Reasons for Conserving Wild Nature' in *Science* 297(5583): 950-53.

Buell, Lawrence. 2005. *The Future of Environmental Criticism: Environmental Crisis and Literary Imagination.* Oxford: Blackwell.

Burn, Gordon. 2000. 'Message in a Bottle' in *The Guardian* (1 June 2000). G2: 2-4.

Coupland, Douglas. 2002. *All Families are Psychotic.* London: Flamingo.

Crozier, Andrew. 2000. 'Barry MacSweeney' in *The Guardian* (18 May 2000): 24.

Dean, John. 2000. 'Losing the Battle Against Demons' in *The Northern Echo* (17 May 2000): 12.

Dobson, Andrew. 2004. 'Globalisation and the Environment: From Local Language to Global Grammar'. Public lecture (University of Wales, Aberystwyth, 27 April 2004).

Jameson, Fredric. 1991. *Postmodernism, or, the Cultural Logic of Late Capitalism.* London: Verso.

Johnson, Nicholas. 2000. 'Barry MacSweeney' in *The Independent* (13 May 2000). The Weekend Review: 7.

MacSweeney, Barry. 1997. *The Book of Demons.* Newcastle upon Tyne: Bloodaxe.

— 1995. *Pearl.* Cambridge: Equipage.

— 2003. *Wolf Tongue: Selected Poems 1965-2000.* Tarset: Bloodaxe.

Radford, Tim. 2002. 'World's Wealth Still Relies on Nature' in the *Guardian* (9 August 2002): 10. On line at: http://www.guardian.co.uk/uk_news/story/0,,771470,00.html. (consulted 11.08.2004).

'Saint Petersburg', *Encyclopædia Britannica Online.* On line at: http://search.eb.com/eb/article?eu=117462 (consulted 12.08.2004).

Scigaj, Leonard M. 1996. 'Contemporary Ecological and Environmental Poetry: Différance or Référance?' in *ISLE: Interdisciplinary Studies in Literature and Environment* 3(2): 1-25.

Spears, Richard A. 1981. *Slang and Euphemism: A Dictionary.* New York: Jonathan David.

Painting Landscape: Mediating Dislocation

Judith Tucker

Abstract

The thrust of this paper is to investigate how painting and 'landscape' might interrelate, how one can be the interface for the other, and what possibilities there are in the space that is created at this interface. The paper takes as its point of departure two encounters. One is with 'landscape' paintings, those of David Bomberg, and one with a piece of writing about 'landscape' painting, Griselda Pollock on Lydia Bauman. These serve as the foundation for a discussion, exploration, theorization and positioning of Tucker's own painting practice. Her recent work is about location and dislocation. It evokes travel, distance and being in place, and reflects the shift between direct experience and memory. The paintings become concretized evidence of fluid events, reflecting both the land and those processes involved in the making. The form of this essay has evolved out of a methodology parallel to Tucker's practice of painting: the issues have developed out of the painting/objects and the painting/processes, thus demonstrating how a very particular relationship with and understanding of 'landscape' might be imbricated in the creative process itself. This argument encompasses concerns that are both spatial and temporal: a consideration of Marianne Hirsch's notion of *postmemory* is pivotal. What emerges through the dialogue between these theoretical concerns and the materiality of both paint and landscape are the fertile possibilities inherent within the site of painting for both viewer and maker.

There is a transformation in the interpretation in the genre of landscape painting which relates directly to a growing interest in and use of the geographic metaphor and notions of place in a variety of disciplines. Inherent in these notions are issues of loss, un/belonging, dis/connection and home. It is these that particularly concern me. Lucy Lippard describes place in the following way:

> Place is latitudinal and longitudinal within the map of a person's life. It is temporal and spatial, personal and political. A layered location replete with

human histories and memories, place has width as well as depth. It is about connections, what surrounds it, what formed it, what happened there, what will happen there. (Lippard 1997: 7)

When I playfully replaced the word 'place' with the word 'painting' in this passage, I realised that I had hit upon a useful way of thinking about painting: as a "layered location replete with human histories and memories", combining past, present and future. Painting is about "connections": who made it? What will happen in the "place" of painting when it is viewed? I hope to indicate here in what sense my practice can be viewed as place. The piece that follows begins to become a texted equivalent to my studio practice, an interweaving of a reflexive account of my activities with considerations of related issues and references both visual and literary. It constitutes then, both some sort of genealogy, and, perhaps, mapping, of influences on my thinking, my practice and my thinking/practice.

There are those moments of synchronicity when an encounter with a painting, piece of writing or film resonates; in that relationship, in that place, something shifts and alters one's direction. At first the change might be imperceptible: one may not be consciously aware that anything has happened, it creeps in, it enables and will not go away. Only afterwards, sometimes years later, one looks back and thinks, 'that was where it stemmed from'. This has, of course, nothing to do with rational awareness; it is never expected. Often they are not paintings/writings that one would have thought would necessarily have such influence. The realisation might come as further experiences allow what might at that time have only been implicit to become explicit, and through recollection, those moments sometimes take on further personal significance. I wish to recount just two such moments out of many, one encounter with paintings and an encounter with a piece of writing about painting. Peter Fuller writes of his response to certain painters, such as Bonnard:

The painters I was able to appreciate last were those whose space seemed to me to be an attempt to fuse internal and external: this was of course something that I responded to affectively rather than intellectually. (Fuller 1980: 139)

The two encounters I have chosen to describe seem to me to occupy that fused space between internal and external.

1. Encounter no. 1: Tate Gallery 1988 in the David Bomberg Retrospective

I stood in front of a group of late David Bomberg landscapes. I felt as if I inhabited this place he had made forty or fifty years previously. I looked at those marks – some traces of struggle and awkwardness, others apparently effortless responses to what he had seen, bare canvas shining through in some parts, other areas thick, loaded with paint, sometimes one confident thin layer in harmony with the next of similar tonality, edges sharp and then unexpectedly smeared in, one colour dragged over another so that the two operated simultaneously upon the eye. I think for that moment I wanted to be him: his eye, mind, arm and hand all inextricably linked. What was it about the work that made me identify with him? Why did I feel compelled to paint landscape at the end of the twentieth century when there are so many other ways to represent? It was not that they were images of landscape; it was that they were painted landscapes. After seeing those works I have never used another subject matter.

For years afterwards I tried to make my paintings work, largely, I fear, in an inappropriate attempt to recreate something of what I had seen in Bomberg. I was trying, perhaps, to impersonate him, to make 'Bombergs', not landscapes. Recently, I have begun to clarify what the desires and intuitions are that I have hung on these landscapes I now create, what possibilities are available to me in making paintings about landscape at the beginning of the twenty-first century. Now, as I look at Bomberg's paintings again, I think of other matters: I imagine and project why this urban child of immigrants from the East End of London might have chosen to travel to 'wilderness' and paint it. I respond not only to the materiality of the pieces but also to a certain melancholy affect, and I imagine that I am able to sense both the audacity and the need which drove him to go to all those different locations and make his own places out of them.

1.1 Encounter no. 2: Yorkshire 1998

In 1998, when I had already been making painted images of landscape for ten years, I read a catalogue essay on the paintings of Lydia

Bauman by Griselda Pollock, 'Lydia Bauman: the Poetic Image in the Field of the Uncanny' (Pollock 1997: 25-37). Pollock describes the widespread, postmodern condition of uprootedness, arguing the necessity of theorising landscape painting in the light of this. She highlights the danger that the notion of the dislocated identity might too easily become a platitude of postmodern sociology, arguing that it is precisely through the singular testimonies which artists and writers might offer, that the more complex affects of this uprootedness might become available. Although my history is not the same as Lydia Bauman's, there is enough of a parallel to strike a chord. Two children of refugees choose to make paintings which image landscape, but not in the site of experience, although the processes involved and so, of course, the results are formally quite different. In spite of these differences in intent and in formal resolution, I saw the possibility of how consideration of an individual's personal history can open up ways of slotting into a bigger picture. I realised that I should begin with rethinking and looking at the nature of my current practice. Somehow I had always felt slightly uncomfortable about both the way in which, and the fact that, I had been imaging landscape from a distance. My studio based paintings often appeared as pale imitations of the studies I made directly in the landscape. I had been trying to make them appear as if I had made them on location and had felt defensive about the way I constructed them. I felt a sense of liberation when I realised that from then on I should start to make a virtue of this and would seek to find ways of demonstrating this through the material and fabrication of the paintings. Within Pollock's essay, I found some passages especially relevant; for example, the following definition of the imaginary space that a landscape painting might proffer:

> More than topography, its painted representations have offered poetic means to imagine our place in the world. The paradox of landscape is that it is both what is other to the human subject: land, place, nature, and yet, it is also the space for projection, and can become therefore, a sublimated self-portrait. (Pollock 1997: 25)

This notion of the sublimated self portrait in turn reminded me of Barry Lopez's words with which I was already familiar:

> To inquire into the intricacies of a distant landscape, then, is to provoke thoughts about one's own interior landscape, and the familiar landscape of memory [...] The land urges us to come to an understanding of ourselves.
> (Lopez 1986: 247)

I sought to come to some sort of understanding of myself through my painted relationship with land. I also found a useful and pertinent definition of painting which expressed that tension between the materiality of substance and its metaphor, as well as foregrounding the relationship between viewer and painting:

> In a word, painting oscillates between the emptiness of material substance, demanding a discrete understanding of its own properties and performance, and the metaphorical fullness of a material sign that stands for something other than itself which will engage the intellect or affectivity of an Other, the viewer who processes the signs and the form of their material existence. (Pollock 1997: 34)

Towards the end of the article, Pollock demonstrates how Bauman's paintings have worked on that viewer. This gave me a vocabulary to describe what had happened for me in front of other paintings, including the encounter with the Bombergs:

> Cloaked memories and a sense of loss infuse an art where the painted space promises presence, the presence of the art work in the present, while indexing us, its viewers to another, immemorial and motionless time, her past, and the time of the unconscious with its complete indifference to the chronology that allows any gesture we make in the present to resonate and echo. Thus the moment of the painting and the poetic image it can install is never caused by a fixed past. (Pollock 1997: 37)

For me, the most potent aspect of this quotation is the notion that in painting, and the viewing of painting, time could become conflated. Through its very materiality a painting has the potential to hold resonances and echoes of various pasts, the mutable pasts of both viewer and maker. I shall be returning to these ideas later.

2. From the Edges

This series of paintings was made in the studio after visits to the north Devon/Somerset coast. This has a dramatic geology, from blue lias fossilised cliffs at Kilve, to precipitous sandstone ramparts and scree slopes near Lynton. There are parallels between the way that, through the materiality of their strata and geology, cliffs might contain narratives and the way in which resonances and echoes might be evidenced through the materiality of and processes involved in painting. There, at the (always fluctuating) boundary of sea and land, the cliffs crumble and slip, while tide and weather daily reveal and conceal fragments of rocks and strata. These areas might be considered in some senses as 'wilderness', thus possibly places to be feared, but for me coastlines provide a possible route for escape, thus providing a sense of refuge and safety. Impermanence is crucial for my practice; the coasts I use as a catalyst for my work offer possibilities of passage, displacement, arrivals and departures, a sense of threshold, and possibilities of change. One of my concerns has been how to convey this sense of impermanence within a static image, and to this end I have produced work in series.

2.1 From the Edges no. 1: Distance from the Site of Experience

Of course, many artists make landscape imagery without necessarily referencing an actual encounter in a 'real' landscape or place. Never leaving their studios, their concerns might be with the nature of representation.[1] Those artists may well be concerned with divorcing themselves and their practice far from the 'landscape' they image, perhaps in an overt acknowledgement of an intense dislocation. What is important to me is that I am attempting to connect with or relate to something other than myself. Many other artists deliberately reference an encounter elsewhere. For example, the Cuban-American artist Ana Mendieta thinks of place through an embodied relation to land. As Anne Raine noted (1996: 228-49), critical to any reading of her work is the fact that we can never encounter her tactile interventions into the land directly. There are no sites to visit; we experience her encounters with the land 'second hand' through the series of photographs. This notion of experiencing at 'second hand' is most pertinent for my work, as will be seen. My own practice too, makes reference to a distant, embodied encounter in the landscape, albeit of a rather different sort.

---

[1] I am thinking here of, among many others, such artists as Peter Doig, Dan Hays, Masakatsu Kondo, Tania Kovats, Michael Raedecker and Carol Rhodes.

It has been an established part of my practice to make painted notes in small notebooks while seated in the landscape. These working notebooks, which I make myself from sheets of heavy watercolour paper, are long thin zigzag, concertina-like forms based on the format of some Japanese books.[2] They are made from robust, sturdy paper, strong enough to take heavy overworking and when folded up they are small, pocket-sized, easily hand-held and so can be looked at in a private moment. They contain miniaturised images of a grand rocky landscape. When drawing/painting in front of the motif, there is a way of experiencing, absolutely particular to the technology of painting. A painter's eye is not disembodied. Merleau-Ponty influentially uses the words of Valéry in his essay 'Eye and Mind':

> The painter 'takes his body with him,' says Valéry. Indeed we cannot imagine how a mind could paint. It is by lending his body to the world that the artist changes the world into paintings. (Merleau-Ponty 1993: 123)

The way I experience the landscape through drawing and painting is an active experience/relation, rather than a passive, reflexive one. It occurs through a panoply of bodily sensations.

Within the following passage from Marion Milner's *On Not Being Able To Paint*, it seems to me that she offers one possiblity of a rationale for painting landscape – mediating dislocation:

> So it became clear that if painting is concerned with the feelings conveyed by space then it must also be to do with problems of being a separate body in a world of other bodies which occupy different bits of space; in fact it must be deeply concerned with distance and separation and having and losing. (Milner 1950: 11-12)

When I am painting or drawing in the landscape I may feel completely immersed in, and connected to, the surroundings. Of course, this is an illusion of connectedness; the dislocation has already begun. At the moment of making the mark in the landscape painting, there is the hope of the possibility of a moment of connectedness and then a realisation that distancing is what actually happened. These "problems

---

[2] I used Two Rivers paper, which I discovered, after some years, is made in a small mill which manufactures handmade paper, near Watchet, coincidentally very close to the coast from which I was working.

of being a separate body in a world of other bodies", and then the attempt to mediate this experience through the activity of painting, indicates the relevance of a phenomenological approach. This approach is one that sits easily with a practitioner/maker who has never quite understood the whole mind/body binary.

On leaving the landscape, the drawings and paintings made on location become mementos and a sign that I was there. They act as maps and reminders of the journey that my eye and hand took when I was in the landscape. Work that is developed from them in the studio becomes a conduit between myself and the location. This paradox of deliberate distancing and the attempt to connect across that distance creates a tension. This tension then might itself be considered to become the subject of the work, thus providing an opportunity to consider the work in terms of belonging, longing, sensuality and desire.

My studio-based oil paintings stem from photographs of the folded sketchbooks which constitute a further gradation in the distancing from the location; new crevices and curves, new shadows and colours are developed from the folds in the paper notebooks. Whilst referencing the solid nature of the cliff structure, the structures created within the paintings appear delicate and fragile. Through their evolution, using the layers of paint, the harsh rock forms transmute into forms which do still reference landscape, but are also reminiscent of the intimate creases in skin. If, in my paintings, rocks might look like skin, outside might resemble inside. Through this echoing and investigation of the way in which natural forms repeat themselves from micro to macro, the mutual relation between self and environment is emphasised. A sensual quality is inherent not only in the forms and colouration, but in the tactility of the application of the paint. There are iridescent surfaces, metallic leaf and pigments, and this makes for shimmering, overlapping layers or skins of paint. Within each section there is a sense of fluidity and flow, dark watery sections with copper or silver leaf glinting and emerging through a viscous coagulating glaze, next to stippled, striated and scumbled areas. There is clear evidence of touch in vigorously drawn illusionistic forms, in the softer broken brush marks and in the smoothed, dragged and modulated surfaces. The liquidity of the materials adds to the fluid sense of spatial ambiguity. There are also vertical delineations in all the works, giving a splintered effect which gives an uneasy sense of reflection and mirroring. Through this fracturing I stop any illusion of deep pictorial space. Uneven, glossy, lustrous glazes become as broken skin, an outer layer covering something, but in that inadequate cover, perhaps revealing more than concealing. The decisions concerning what to reveal and conceal are critical to these pieces. This is a self-conscious reference to the folds in the notebooks and some illusionistic effect is evident. What is hidden behind the painted fold? A fold that can never be opened? What is visually absent, something not being there, becomes an integral part of these works. The painted folds might appear to conceal, but the accrued layers of paint actually cover what lies beneath. The sense of absence and distance is further invoked in a play with highly ambiguous pictorial space across these boundaries or demarcations, and with the physical edges of the paintings, preventing a monocular vision, so that the viewer is unpositioned. I have invented spaces into which a viewer might imaginatively project. At the same time as allowing the possibility of projection, the fragmented and fractured surface of the painting stops that possibility, pushing the viewer back into 'real' space, into an awareness of being in the gallery/room. The illusion of space is there, has been created, but has been subverted. There is a distancing process in place here, and unable to orientate herself, the viewer cannot 'enter' this space easily.

2.2 From the Edges no. 2: Places to go Places

In the following section I develop further some of what might become involved when a viewer encounters and then explores a landscape painting, and in this way I begin to address the relation of the material to the metaphoric. Thus far I have hinted at the phenomenological approach to being in the world which the activities of both making and viewing painting might allow. The choice of medium not only predicates the way in which I image the land, but also the way it might be viewed. Any viewer brings her own history to bear on what she is looking at, she might also become aware of the deictic quality of the marks that refer back to the body of the painter. Might it be possible that, in the viewing of paintings, past and present might become conflated? What is peculiar to the apparatus and technology of paint which other media and mediums might not have? Implicit in this is the question of what is involved in seeing through painting. Many painters, including myself, would consider that drawing and painting enable one to see 'properly', or at least more clearly. In the following two statements, Lippard, in discussing notions of landscape in relation to place, distinguishes between the visual and the sensual:

> A lived in landscape becomes a space which implies intimacy; a once lived in landscape can be a place if explored, or remain a landscape if simply observed. Sometimes a spontaneous attraction to place is really an emotional response to the landscape, which is place at a distance, visual rather than sensual, seen rather than felt in all its affective power. (Lippard 1997: 7)

Lippard explains later that while she derives a lot of pleasure from looking at landscape paintings, it is not as much as she gains from looking at the landscape itself. She considers that "[...] a painting, no matter how wonderful, is an object in itself, separate from the place it depicts. It frames and distances through the eyes of the artist" (Lippard 1997: 19-20). In one sense it is not part of my project to create an object completely 'separate' from the landscape which was the catalyst. Nor am I attempting to recreate the precise experience of being in the landscape Even if it were possible, would it be desirable? I consider my paintings to be 'connected/separate objects'. Although framing and distancing is critical to my work, so, too, is a sense of attempted connection, of 'having been there'. I consider that what is particular to painting as a practice (for example, time taken, layering, the evidence of the body which made the marks) is a way of mediating the external world which offers the possibility or bridge for some sort of possibility of synthesis between the internal and the external in Peter Fuller's sense.

The desolate coasts that I select in an apparently spontaneous way as my starting-points are unlived-in landscapes; they apparently lack intimacy, but through the making of my drawings and paintings on location I explore these landscapes in a sensual way and develop an emotional response to the landscape so that they become places. So what happens when a viewer explores the painted images of the landscape? Can the paintings become places themselves to be responded to in all their affective power? For the maker of these pieces, they do become places, and this making, perhaps, might be a homecoming.

According to Lippard, the painting which has been removed from the landscape, becomes a landscape/place which can only be "seen rather than felt in all its affective power." Certainly this remaking, a certain framing and distancing from the landscape through painting, might be considered apposite for my project. Naturally, the viewer cannot experience the landscape in the same way that I did. To look at a painting is considered, traditionally, a visual experience and the act of looking has a distancing effect. In that distance or space between viewer and object much can occur. However, if the viewer reconsiders the nature of the way she looks at the painting, engaging with it as a space/place with traces of the maker embedded in its fabrication, is it ever possible for seeing to become feeling?[3]

3. Past Lives

I am watching, as I have so many times before, a short video remastering of some ciné film from the sixties: jerky images of noiseless seagulls spiralling above a pier, blue misty clouds above mountains, a rough, dark pebbly beach visible against overexposed sea and sky. Erratic camera movements cut to the shimmering water surface, and I can just make out a distant sandbar caught in a shaft of sunlight, followed by more misty mountain views, faded, and yet at the same time somehow enlivened by the flickering of dust particles. Then some silent, light-damaged footage of children playing with their father in front of a large grey building. These are the only moving images of my early, coastal, childhood. Is it possible that I am trying to recreate my own first memories, nostalgically revisiting my own beginnings which took place by the coast with views of mountains, beaches and seas, before I moved to London as a small child? Of course, this may indeed be part of the narrative. I repeat a ritual of dislocation that goes back at least a generation. Of course, I can never know what it is to be a refugee, only what it is to be the child of a

---

[3] For a further development of this notion see Judith Tucker 2002: 77-81 and David Maclagan 2001: 37-45.

refugee, and to inherit the insecurities of the rootless and some sense of what permanent exclusion from the land of one's birth can mean.

My sisters and I grew up with legends of a vanished home: narratives of a grand flat in the Friedrichstrasse, and of Berlin in the thirties, the journey by train and boat that brought my mother and grandmother across the sea to Britain. There are these stories and a few precious artefacts, a few souvenirs of a disappeared world: a threadbare rug, some embroidered linen and an album of black and white photographs of places and people that are no longer there. Marianne Hirsch considers the different ways in which second-generation children construct notions of memory and the past, including how the trauma of refugeehood and exile is transferred to the next generation, and how that generation might be shaped more strongly by what happened to the preceding generation than what might have actually happened to them. She describes the various ways in which this memory of the world before the exile might be imparted to the children, who have not experienced this exile, and argues that what is imparted is "something akin to memory":

> Searching for a term that would convey its temporal and qualitative difference from survivor memory, I have chosen to call this secondary, or second-generation, memory 'postmemory'. (Hirsch 1998: 420)

Hirsch proposes an aesthetics of postmemory. In the following passage she also draws the comparison between art-making and wandering. I would like to consider how my own practice as a painter whose work is driven by landscape could fit into this notion:

> An aesthetics of postmemory, a diasporic aesthetics of temporal and spatial exile that needs simultaneously to rebuild and to mourn [...] What forms does their wandering take? What strategies do they invent to relocate themselves? What are the aesthetic shapes of postmemory? (Hirsch 1998: 423)

These notions of simultaneously rebuilding and mourning seem to be consistent with my practice. Although the paintings are not about a specific narrative, they concern the restlessness that stems from rootlessness, and in a way these re-presentations of images of land at the periphery are efforts to remember and recapture not a longing for home, but a longing for desire. My works are mediations of landscapes, and, as I have demonstrated, they are also mediations of a sense of absence and of longing. Of course, it is not my project, within this series of paintings, to deal quite so directly with these issues, but more obliquely, and within a poetic territory.[4] This might provide grounds for my returning to attempt some experience and connection on location and then returning to recreate/rebuild something parallel to this in the studio. These paintings might not be precisely postmemory but they are informed by it and analogous to it. In this instance the building blocks of my postmemory have not been things, not photographs and objects, but rather actions, some conscious, some unconscious, repeating separations, many preventing intimacy. In my studio, in the making itself, I begin to (re)create an indeterminate place for my imagination to inhabit. No viewers of my work have direct access to what I have experienced in the landscape. However, they can experience the painted place, and, then, they in turn have the possibility to create their own imagined place from this. Alison Rowley has considered the nature of the various places that might be created through an encounter with a painting. She considers both Bridget Riley's notion of painting as visual place-making described in formalist terms, and, through Bracha Lichtenberg Ettinger, the notion of the emergence of a psychic place:

> Bracha Lichtenberg Ettinger theorises the possible but always unforeseen, emergence of a psychic place, between artist and viewer, viewer and viewer, artist and artist, created by the processes of making and viewing a visual artwork, but experienced primarily as affective rather than visual. In this theory affect destabilises visuality, and transsubjectivity de-centres the modernist definition of art making and art viewing as fundamental sites for the realisation, conservation and reflection of a singular subjective existence. (Rowley 1999: 83)

This relational, transsubjective way – developed through the model of transference – of making and viewing a visual artwork, not only seems a development of the ideas I introduced earlier, but also incorporates a way in which the affective aspects of experience, such as postmemory, might be transmitted.

---

[4] My latest body of work, entitled 'Resort', deals more directly with these issues. This is part of a research project called 'Painting and Postmemory; re/visiting, re/visioning, re/placing?' made possible by an AHRC Fellowship in the Creative and Performing Arts.

4. Caesura

When choosing the title Caesura for this series of works I enjoyed the notion of using a word usually applied to poetry or music in relation to my paintings; it seemed to situate my activities in an appropriate field. The notion of a break, interruption, or pause, aptly seemed to represent my concerns. The paintings themselves are interruptions and in an interruption much can take place. The physical gap between the paintings becomes critical. The works may be seen as discreet pieces, but are also intended to be viewed in relation to one other. The white of the gallery wall provides not only a punctuation, but also a necessary foil for the complexities of the surfaces. Within the paintings the 'folds' operate as breaks in the compositions. These rifts, or unexpected ruptures in the work, then require 'new' beginnings. Although the adjacent sections might appear to use contrasting scales, spaces, or colour, they cannot help but be influenced by what has gone before or next to them, in the same way that a physical layer of paint is affected by the underlying one. The way in which each layer of paint might affect the next is not only analogous to the way that landscape is formed in geological strata, but is also apposite as an analogy for the way in which present generations of people are infected and coloured by the previous ones. This is evidenced on the canvas through what might appear to be distinct sections linking to each other across their borders, through seeping layers of glazes. There are other breaks implicit in the work: the break between the landscape and the studio, the gap between maker and viewer, and between viewer and painting. One might also consider the inter(dis)ruption inevitable in becoming a refugee, and the pause or gap inherent in the notion of transgenerational transmission. In these pauses or gaps 'in between', I seek to make a place for both viewer and maker. I feel that in general the site of painting, and in particular my landscape paintings, could be considered in multiple senses to be 'in between' – a place/space for transformation, of transition or 'transport stations'.[5] Images of coast are images of not land/not sea,

---

[5] I develop this notion in my PhD by studio practice of the same title as this article (Tucker 2002) in relation to the essay 'Art as the Transport Station of Trauma' in Bracha Lichtenberg Ettinger 2000: 97-118.

thresholds. Landscape painting 'happens' between here and there, between past and present. Painting is not movement and sight, but movement/sight; not thought and action, but thought/action; not seeing and feeling, but seeing/feeling; not material and affect, but material/affect. When painting, I am myself between subjectivities, not quite living between then and now, but then/now in the present, at home/not at home.

Judith Tucker *Caesura 2*

Bibliography

Cork, Richard. 1988. *David Bomberg*. London: Tate Gallery Publications.

Fuller, Peter. 1980. *Art and Psychoanalysis*. London: Writers and Readers Cooperative.

Hirsch, Marianne. 1998. 'Past Lives: Postmemories in Exile' in Suleiman, Susan (ed.) *Exile and Creativity*. Durham: Duke University Press. 418-446.

Lichtenberg Ettinger, Bracha. 2000. 'Art as the Transport Station of Trauma' in *Bracha Lichtenberg Ettinger Artworking 1985- 1999*. Ghent-Amsterdam: Ludion. 97-118.

Lippard, Lucy R. 1999. *On the Beaten Track: Tourism, Art, and Place*. New York: The New Press.

— 1997. *The Lure of the Local: Senses of Place in a Multicentered Society*. New York: The New Press.

Maclagan, David. 2001. 'Reframing Aesthetic Experience: iconographic and embodied responses to painting' in *Journal of Visual Art Practice* 1(1): 37-45.

Merleau-Ponty, Maurice. 1993 'Eye and Mind' in Johnson, Galen A (ed.) *The Merleau-Ponty Aesthetics Reader*. Illinois: Northwestern Press. 121-149.

Milner, Marion. 1957. *On Not Being Able To Paint*. London: Heinemann Educational Books.

Pollock, Griselda (ed.). 1996. *Generations and Geographies in the Visual Arts: Feminist Readings*. London: Routledge.

— 1997. 'Lydia Bauman: The Poetic Image in the Field of the Uncanny' in *Lydia Bauman, Landscapes*. Warsaw: Zacheta Gallery.

Raine, Anne. 1996. 'Embodied Geographies: Subjectivity and Materiality in the Work of Ana Mendieta' in Pollock, Griselda (ed.) *Generations and Geographies in the Visual Arts: Feminist Readings*. London: Routledge. 228-49.

Riley, Bridget. 1999. *The Eye's Mind*. London: Thames and Hudson.

Rowley, Alison. 1999. 'Introduction to Bracha Lichtenberg Ettinger's "Traumatic Wit(h)ness-Thing and Matrixial Co/inhabiting"' in *Parallax* 10 January-March: 83-87.

Tucker, Judith. 2002. *Painting Landscape: Mediating Dislocation*. Unpublished PhD thesis. University of Leeds.

Suleiman, Susan Ruben. 1998. *Exile and Creativity: Signposts, Travellers and Backwards Glances*. Durham: Duke University Press.

Modernity and the Politics of Place in Luis Trenker's *Der verlorene Sohn*

Guinevere Narraway

Abstract

Analyses of Luis Trenker's 1934 feature film *Der verlorene Sohn* (*The Prodigal Son*) ordinarily turn on the argument that this is a fascist or at least deeply reactionary text which endorses the blood and soil ideology, and the xenophobia, typical of the *Heimatfilm* (homeland film) of the Third Reich. In such critiques, reactionary politics are ascribed to a purported anti-modern attachment to place (the *Heimat*) and nature. However, it is argued that Trenker's love of his homeland – his topophilia – combined with his love of the camera – his technophilia – confound any such unambiguous reading of the film. It is in fact in the essence of *Der verlorene Sohn*'s most celebrated shot – a dissolve from the Dolomites to the high-rises of New York – that the film's ostensible celebration of the pre-modern *Heimat* (home, homeland) over the modernised *Fremde* (foreign parts or places) becomes problematic. This superimposition of shots reflects a love of the technology of the camera that infuses both the *Heimat* and the *Fremde*. If anything, the *Heimat* becomes, through the camera, a more technologised locale than the *Fremde*. While Trenker ultimately shoots a proto-Neorealist city symphony in New York, Tyrol is marked by even more stunning camera work and by montage sequences that prefigure Riefenstahl's work in *Olympia*. Arguably however, Trenker's representation of nature could be read as a reflection of the mind-set of his master, Arnold Fanck: that without man (and his machines), nature is not vital. The Baconian penetration of nature through the instrument of the camera finds its correlation in the domination of others. In *Der verlorene Sohn* this is manifested in the homogenous community of the *Heimat*, a community which does not tolerate otherness.

> The homeland at once provides meaning and forecloses thought. A space rooted in cyclical nature and therefore timeless, it is the site of the true and the genuine as well as an imposing obstacle to [...] "responsible, autonomous, rational practice".
>
> [...] Organic 'fact' as a primal given defies mind and reason. To submit to nature means bowing to its inexorable might.
> (Rentschler 1996a: 87)

It is an enduring scholarly argument that the *Heimat* (homeland/ home)[1] represented in the cinema of the Third Reich is a site which affords community, but precludes the possibility of rational thought and, therefore, democratic politics. The origin of this configuration of the *Heimat*, as Eric Rentschler argues above, lies in an over-determination of the significance of nature.

Trying to engage with filmic texts from the Third Reich from an eco-theoretical perspective, I have found positions like these confounding. Although I may agree on the fundamental political underpinnings of these texts, I often find myself at methodological odds with other scholars. Consequently I am left asking, how do I critique these metatextual discourses concerning nature, without slipping into the role of apologist for textual discourses which undermine social justice? This chapter is an attempt to do the former and avoid the latter by opening up textual, metatextual, and intertextual discourses concerning nature in the example of Luis Trenker's 1934 film *Der verlorene Sohn* (*The Prodigal Son*).

This film is the direct object of Rentschler's analysis above. It is, moreover, a perfect example for my argument because it is a generic hybrid of the *Bergfilm* (mountain film) and the *Heimatfilm* (homeland film), two genres which specifically foreground the relationship between the human community of the *Heimat* and the natural environment.[2]

---

[1] *Heimat* is one of several terms which I will not use in translation in this article because the English terms do not convey the full complexity of the German.

[2] The mountain film emerged in Germany in the 1920s. Flimsy narratives provided these films with an excuse for exciting and beautiful depictions of climbing and skiing. The *Heimatfilm* is a related genre, although it is more substantial. *Heimat* is one of several terms which I will not use in translation in this article. The *Heimatfilm* flourished during the Third Reich and continued to be a popular genre in the post-war German cinema of the 50s.

The Prodigal Son is arguably Trenker's best-known and most technically accomplished film. The film concerns the adventures of Tyrolean lumberjack Tonio Feuersinger who, in a mixture of *Wanderlust* and despair over the death of a friend and fellow climber, travels to New York to seek his fortune. In the depression-era United States he experiences unemployment and extreme poverty and is reduced to a subsistence existence sustained only through crime or the charity of others. Tonio's luck changes, however, when he overwhelms a savage boxer in the ring at Madison Square Garden. As luck would have it, the New York millionaire Mr Williams and his daughter Lilian are at the fight that same evening. Tonio had met the pair previously when they had visited his home village in the Tyrol. Lilian, in particular, is thrilled to renew the acquaintance and after a short time has elapsed she proposes to Tonio. On the verge of accepting the offer, Tonio sees, hanging on the wall of the Williams' apartment, a copy of the traditional Sun Mask worn at the festival of *Rauhnacht*.[3] Ineluctably drawn home to the Tyrol, he arrives just in time to participate in *Rauhnacht* and to reunite with his true love Barbl.

The dominant reading of the film – both among those who are apologists for Trenker as well as those who are his detractors – is as a paean to the *Heimat* and a condemnation of the *Fremde* (foreign parts/places). Rentschler argues that *The Prodigal Son* underhandedly generated loyalty to the *Heimat* by mobilising a curiosity about the *Fremde*: it indulged "the wish for another life so that audiences might recognize the danger abiding in non-German spaces [...]" (Rentschler 1996a: 81). In order to support this argument, Rentschler is compelled to read the German space that Trenker evokes as deeply conservative. Indeed, this may be so, but Rentschler looks, I believe, in all the wrong places. Most specifically, it is in images of the "immutable countenance" of nature that Rentschler finds the pre- and anti-modern counterposition of his liberal humanist construction of a liberating modernity. The political consequences of the hallowing of ahistorical nature, Rentschler argues, are the unquestioning acceptance of authoritarian rule.

---

[3] The *Rauhnächte*, because the English terms do not convey the full complexity of the German, are the twelve nights between Christmas Eve and Epiphany.

Arguments such as this are not uncommon in postwar critiques of both the mountain film and the related *Heimatfilm* genres. However, the unthinking slippage into traditional dichotomies of reason/nature and into the counterposition of "what is dictated by nature and what is humanly instigated" (Soper 1995: 37) on which many of these arguments are founded, leads critics to conflate too much (or rather, too much of a bad thing) under the heading 'nature'. That is, it seems that in abstracting *Blut und Boden* (blood and soil) ideology out to filmic representations of landscape and the natural environment, scholars invariably fall into traditional patterns of opposing modernity, rationality, and a liberal democratic politics to an undifferentiated and negative understanding of nature. Yet even taking an arguably typical blood and soil text, such as *The Prodigal Son*, as our example, we find nature as a potential nodal point for social justice issues and as a partner in discourse with (rather than in opposition to) modernity. In fact, I would suggest that the reactionary and racialist discourses in this film are not a result of anything immanent in nature itself. Rather, they are a product of the consumption and mechanical reproduction of nature.

In its counterposition of *Heimat* and *Fremde*, it is difficult to deny that *The Prodigal Son* ultimately celebrates rooted settlement over diasporic hybridity and endorses a form of bioregional existence over globalised identity. In itself this position is not inherently negative. Indeed as Andrew Milner argues in contrasting the work of Raymond Williams with that of Stuart Hall, rooted settlement offers an alternative identity independent of the hegemony of market relations and the operations of consumer capitalism:

> [...] the heart of the difference between Williams and the later Hall [...] is their quite different, even opposed, valuations of 'rooted settlement' as against 'diasporic hybridity'. It is a difference which leads, in turn, to quite different evaluations of 'socialism' as against 'liberalism', since the hybrid subjects who *"produce themselves anew and differently"* (Hall 1993: 362) are only able to do so, in practice, by way of "market and exchange relations". (Milner 2001, np)

Globalised identities are only available to those who have the capital (financial or cultural) to assume them (Milner 2001) and the liberal valorisation of diaspora over "native country or local attachment" overlooks the fact that homelessness, particularly when it is not a

choice, "is always a curse, not an ideal" (Hartman 1997: 158).
Moreover, as Geoffrey Hartman argues, in the valorisation of
globalised over localised identity, the global citizen requires a
crushing (and ultimately abstract) empathy for a universal suffering
too large to engage (Hartman 1997: 158). In contrast, the idea of
'home' with its focus on tangible experience is a useful strategy in
progressive environmental and social justice politics.

A strong sense of attachment to a local environment also entails the
possibility of social justice through "shared social identities" in
community (Milner 2002: 120). As Milner points out, this position is
evident, and prescient of both late twentieth-century environmentalism
and anti-globalisation, in the work of Williams. Milner observes that
Williams, in *The Country and the City*, "combined political sympathy
for Third World peasant revolution with a deeply ecological sense of
the connectedness of people and land" (Milner 2001). Indeed it was in
The Country and the City that Williams celebrated his own experience
of relationship to community and place when he wrote that he had
"had the luck [...] to repair and rebuild old drystone walls; to hedge
and ditch [...] and to see from skilled men how the jobs should be
done" (Williams 1973: 301-302).

Williams argues the political importance of care and continuity
again in *Towards 2000*:

> [...] it is often forgotten that the most widespread and most practical thinking
> about the future is rooted in human and local continuities. We can feel the
> continuity of life to a child or a grandchild. We can care for land, or plant trees,
> in ways that both assure and depend on an expectation of future fertility. We can
> build in ways that are meant to last for coming lives to be lived in them.
> (Williams 1983: 5)

Williams' use of the organicist image we find here predates *Towards
2000*. Already in *Culture and Society* he had claimed that a common
culture produced by creative and critical individuals in all walks of
life (Milner 2002) "rests on a metaphor: the tending of natural
growth" (Williams 1958: 335). For Williams, the socialist democratic
transformation involved in a common culture requires conscious
political participation of all its members. However, it is the diversity
of this collaboration that simultaneously and paradoxically involves an
unconscious element (Eagleton 2000: 119). Unlike a culture shaped

from the top down, a "common culture could never be wholly self-transparent precisely because of the range of active collaboration it engages" (2000: 120). Culture is thus consciously cultivated, but its ultimate outcome is unknowable because it grows organically.

When placed in the context of his wider oeuvre, one can see that Williams' metaphor of the organism is not only rhetorical, but is bound to a deeply ecopolitical consciousness. His programme of progressive politics conceives social justice simultaneously with an ethical and respectful approach to nature. This is, in fact, inherent in Williams' definition of the term 'culture' which incorporates "intellectual, spiritual and aesthetic development", "a particular way of life", and cultural production, and yet does not forget or abandon the origins of the word in agriculture (Williams 1988: 90). As Eagleton notes, Williams' definition of culture as structure of feeling is "interestingly close" to his definition of ecology: "the study of the interrelation of elements in a living system" (Eagleton 2000: 134). Place (and nature) therefore offer positive and progressive political possibilities through the web of locality, care, community, and work.

Trenker was known throughout his life for his love and promotion of his *Heimat*, the Tyrol,[4] and he was an accomplished mountain climber and skier. All of these factors contribute to what is fundamentally a topophilic representation of the Tyrol in *The Prodigal Son*. The *Heimat* that Trenker evokes in *The Prodigal Son* is characterised by a bioregional existence where people live off the land using low-impact technologies such as hand ploughs and axes. This is not the world of industrial farming and forestry. In contrast to the Weimar-era cities of the immediate past where man was perceived as under threat from the vampish New Woman, masculinity here in the *Heimat* is definitely not in crisis. Indeed, the entire fabric of society is healthy: the young respect the old and men respect women, and interwoven pagan and Christian rituals provide structure for social life. All of this takes place in a picturesque village situated under dramatic skies, against spectacular alpine backdrops and amidst tranquil fields of cows chewing cud.

---

[4] Trenker also used his love of his *Heimat* opportunistically during the Third Reich in order to manoeuvre "like an acrobat between the National Socialists and the Italian Fascists to his own benefit" (Birgel 2000: 38).

This utopian image fits critics' predominant description of the *Heimatfilm* as a genre informed above all by blood and soil ideologies where pre- and anti-industrial idylls of life on the land stood in "absurd contradistinction" to reality (Wolf Donner cited in Beindorf 2001: 22).[5]

This popularly held idea that in the *Heimatfilm* of the Third Reich, *Heimat* and modernity are diametric opposites, is, however, deeply problematic. On the contrary, the supposedly backward-looking genre is structured by the overlap of discourses of *Heimat* and those of modernity:

> To suggest, as many have, that the *Heimatfilm* is quintessentially an escapist genre, is to overlook the fact that the escape routinely contains elements of the world from which viewers were allegedly escaping. In particular, if *Heimat* in the *Heimatfilm* is simply conceived as an escape from modernity, this does not account for the fact that the modern is not 'outside' of *Heimat*, it is part of it. (von Moltke 2002: 24)

In the 1920s and 1930s, the *Heimatfilm* and the mountain film promoted and successfully generated regional tourism (Nenno 2003: 63-64),[6] and it is here, in the commodification of *Heimat*, that on one level modernity meets nationalist discourse in *The Prodigal Son*.

Images such as Trenker's of rural idylls and spectacular mountain-scapes fed the spectator's desire to flee the alienation and industrialisation of modernity. However the "ontological homeless-ness" generated by the experience of modernity is a condition of tourism "where the *Heimat* functions [...] as that lost origin which is sought in the alien world" (Frow 1991: 135). Thus, paradoxically, modernity does not only produce homelessness but it also, and resultantly, covertly *reproduces* itself within the *Heimat* as the tourism which facilitates the search for origin and produces a simulation of that home. Moreover, the natural environment to which the tourist attempts to flee is a literal product of industrialised civilisation:

---

[5] My translation. All translations are mine unless otherwise indicated.

[6] The mountain film died out in the 40s, but in the case of the *Heimatfilm* this association with tourism endured into the 50s.

[a]n industry has been established to manufacture deliverance from the industrial world; travel beyond the world of commodities has itself become a commodity. (Enzensberger 1996: 129).

The enframing and packaging of the *Heimat* in cinema encourages the modern tourist to consider "the landscape a consumer good, an item to be desired and visually devoured" (Nenno 2003: 68). In *The Prodigal Son,* tourists Lilian and her father are the viewer's stand-ins as they take guided tours in the mountains and buy the 'authenticity' of the *Heimat* in a replication of the *Rauhnacht* Sun Mask.

The mountain film exemplifies the consequences of the industrial logic of "the romantic ideology of tourism" according to which the search for "the 'elemental,' the 'pristine'" destroys precisely that once the search is complete (Enzensberger 1996: 126). The genre derived its authenticity not only from its inaccessible, 'pristine' location but also from the experience of its inaccessibility. It was indeed the cinematic manufacture of this latter aspect of the mountain film that allowed the viewer-tourist to touch the untouchable (and made them long to go there).

Trenker learnt his craft from the architect of the mountain film genre (and the ski film sub-genre), Arnold Fanck, and Fanck's legacy endures in *The Prodigal Son.* Fanck's work was characterised by pioneering cinematography, and the technical proficiency and innovation of his representation of the alpine landscape is often noted. Among other things, he exploits the chiaroscuro effect created by shadows cast through a haze powder snow or by torchlight on the ice inside a crevasse; he uses long shots of formation skiing to create abstract patterns on the canvas of snow; he captures the elegance of skiers' movements in slow motion; and he employs a diversity of perspectives from low-angle shots taken from cameras mounted on moving skis to aerial shots taken from planes.[7]

Fanck's spectacular landscape photography and the dynamism resulting from the sheer formal diversity of his footage and from his hectic assemblage of this material using his 'free montage' style creates an often exhilarating experience for the viewer. Christian Rapp notes that the mountain film's lack of plot and its obsessive focus on

---

[7] Significantly, Fanck's use of the 'unchained camera' predated its use in the Street Film – the genre where it is usually considered to have originated.

cinematography produced a genre that for contemporary critics appeared to be beyond discourse. The viewing subject dissolved in "nameless beauty" (Rapp 1997: 16-17). Weimar critic Siegfried Kracauer effuses that whoever saw the mountain films

> [...] will remember the glittering white of glaciers against a sky dark in contrast, the magnificent play of clouds forming mountains above the mountains, the ice stalactites hanging down from roofs and windowsills of some small chalet, and, inside crevasses, weird ice structures awakened to iridescent life by the torchlights of a nocturnal rescue party. (Kracauer 1947: 111)

That such a harsh critic of the mountain film as Kracauer should be able to describe the mountain film so lyrically speaks volumes about the power with which the genre evokes a sense of place (Rentschler 1996b: 694).

However, this is only a simulation of an unmediated experience of the beautiful and the sublime. This "pre-modern wonder and enchantment" is restored by a modern means, the cinematic apparatus. (Rentschler 1996b: 698-9). What lies behind these breathless experiences is ultimately 'technical know-how':

> With Fanck's filming of nature it is easy to forget the meaning of technology in his films. It is precisely this solid, crafted aspect of his work and the thematisation of technology which is essential to his role of precursor of the *Neue Sachlichkeit*. Technical know-how is evident in every image. Fanck's experience as a photographer working with natural light sources, and as an officer in the newsreel service utilising slow-motion shots, converged in films like *Das Wunder des Schneeschuhs*. [...] He was one of the first cameramen to employ the Ernemmann slow-motion techniques, and he was the first to work with extremely long focal length. (Brandlmeier 1984: Lg.4 E4)[8]

Camera work and editing in this genre are thus the most powerful non-representational signs of what is ultimately the film's utopian sensibility (Dyer 1985: 223). That is, they induce potent feelings of the experience of utopia – a utopia the *Heimat* represents. Fanck's work leads us to believe that we are experiencing nature in an unmediated fashion. However Fanck 'sutures' us into his films – despite his innovative cinematography – much as Hollywood cinema

---

[8] Elsaesser's translation (2000: 392).

does and this masks the mediation of our experience by technology. [9] Fanck does not effectively 'bare the device' – that is, he does not make the viewer aware of the filmic process. Rather, his films conceal the possibility that our utopian experience of nature in the *Heimat* is, in fact, a euphoric experience of cinematic technology.

The dynamism in camerawork and editing in Fanck's work resonates in *The Prodigal Son*. However, in the case of Trenker's diurnal and nocturnal ski sequences, the somatic elation of Fanck's films is not as effectively reproduced because close-ups of Trenker himself intermittently interrupt this experience. That is, the close-up of a human face has a negative impact on the film's utopian sensibility, as does Trenker's confounding need to have a plot trajectory – something with which Fanck is barely concerned.

Indeed, Trenker's depiction of the *Heimat* becomes more captivating in the moments when the film is less representational and the characters more irrelevant. It is, in fact, these non-narrative moments that persist in the viewer's mind after watching the film. One example is a montage sequence early in the film of falling logs creating dazzling fountain-like displays in a mountain lake. Another more significant section is the climb that precipitates Trenker's departure for New York. As the climbers gradually ascend the mountain, the textures, surfaces, geometry and whiteness of the mountain constantly draw the viewer's attention from the human figures. [10]

The ecstatic moments in Fanck's films are also those where the figurative and the narrative recede and people and landscape form abstraction:

---

[9] Nenno also comments on this: "Fanck's innovative mobilization of cameras, the extreme physical exertions of both actors and crew, and his experimental montage techniques suture the spectator into the action, creating the illusion of participation" (Nenno 2003: 69). My point here however is that *despite* the innovative nature of Fanck's camerawork, which *should* interrupt suture – in the way that experimental film aims to – Fanck nevertheless achieves suture.

[10] Kracauer observes that Fanck's films did progressively include more substantial plots. However, he maintains that "the fictional element [...] did not interfere with an abundance of documentary shots of the silent world of high altitudes" (Kracauer 1947: 110-111). There is more of a struggle between plot and spectacle in *The Prodigal Son*, but in the two sequences I mention here, spectacle certainly wins out.

diagonal division of the screen, traces, curves and signs in the snow, *Jugendstil* ornaments, circular cut-outs of images, little points emerging on the horizon, which rush up to the camera and then disappear out of the picture, in giant close-up. (Brandlmeier 1984: Lg 4, E1)[11]

These examples point to the genre's relationship to modernist filmmaking, which, as one critic for *Der Deutsche Film* argued, originated in the alpine landscape itself (Hoffmann 2001: 181).[12] It is, however, not the landscape that is at issue, but what Thomas Brandlmeier characterises as 'nature-choreography' (1984: Lg.4 E3).

Brandlmeier argues that Fanck's approach anticipated the symphonic film and, more generally, the cinema of the *Neue Sachlichkeit* (New Objectivity) (1984: Lg.4 E3). Avant-garde director Walter Ruttmann was the progenitor of the former genre and a major proponent of the *Kulturfilm* (culture films) of the New Objectivity.[13] Ruttmann's work – and that of contemporaries such as Walter Frentz and Willy Zielke – manifests a fascination both with technological artefacts and with experimental approaches to rendering them. However his obsession with form too often led to vacuity that could be filled with any political intent. As Kracauer argues of the *Kulturfilm* in general, "[r]eality is portrayed not so as to make facts yield their implications, but to drown all implications in an ocean of facts" (1947: 165-166).

An archetypal example in this case is Ruttmann's 1940 film *Deutsche Panzer* (*German Tanks*). Here instruments of war, from the drawing board to the completed tank, are abstracted out to formal shapes and patterns with little real engagement with their function and much more with their form, and with the formal approach to rendering them. Ruttmann's figurative work, in fact, appears to echo his origins

---

[11] Elsaesser's translation (2000: 391).

[12] Of course, the association between the mountain film and 1920s and 30s modernist filmmaking in Germany can most clearly be found in the work of Leni Riefenstahl. In her propaganda films *Olympia* and *Triumph of the Will*, human forms become abstract or ornamental. The origin of her style is a result both of her apprenticeship to Fanck and of the participation of avant-garde cinematographers and filmmakers in producing these films.

[13] The *Kulturfilm* is a documentary form.

in the absolute film, ultimately producing surface at the expense of meaning.[14]

Like the machines of this modernist machine aesthetic, so nature in 'nature-choreography' is emptied of intrinsic meaning and is at the directors' disposal. Nature as construct is taken to its literal extreme. Nowhere is this more clearly expressed than in Fanck's – and Trenker's – seemingly relaxed attitude to manufacture dramatic narrative and visual effect by blowing up sections of mountainside in order to set off avalanches.

For Fanck, nature remained "mute and unexpressive unless captured by a camera" (Rentschler 1996b: 698). Béla Balázs seems to agree, arguing that it was through its encounter with, and opposition to, man and, more importantly, because it was "seen through the eyes of man", that nature was enlivened and "attained a countenance" in Fanck's films (Balázs 1992: 4-5). Thus the gaze of the protagonist and that of the camera – and consequently the gaze of the spectator – frequently coincide. Through this gaze, nature as lack is annexed by the human.

The manufacture of nature and place remained largely hidden and implicit in Fanck's work. By contrast, in *The Prodigal Son*, it is the modern metropolis – the apparent opposite of the alpine *Heimat* – that exposes the modernity of the *Heimat* itself.

The central section of *The Prodigal Son* takes place in New York and, on the surface, a correlation between *Heimat* and *Fremde* is suggested. As many scholars note, the establishing shot of New York, a gradual dissolve from the Dolomites to the New York skyline, implies an affinity between the two places. The correspondence between the two persists throughout the New York section with Tonio continually set against the monumental Manhattan skyline much as he is framed in the *Heimat* by the mountains and their dramatic skies. The sheer ice and rock of the mountains of the *Heimat* become the stone, steel and glass surfaces of the city. The sublime of the cityscape provokes a parallel (topophilic) aesthetic response to the sublime of the mountainscape (White 1994: 141).

The skyscraper as mountain is also suggested in the production manager's report to the paper *Der Film* in 1934. In discussing shooting

---

[14] The absolute film was a completely abstract, non-representational form.

a sequence high on a skyscraper construction site, he inadvertently aligns the cityscape with the mountainscape by reproducing complaints usually made about location shooting for the mountain film (Lyssa 1934: n.p.).

Narratively, this sequence on the construction site offers at least one moment in the film when the seemingly straightforward mapping of rooted/rootless onto *Heimat/Fremde* is interrupted and which suggests again a relationship between *Heimat* and *Fremde*: the sense of community among the construction workers parallels the bond among forestry workers, mountain climbers or skiers that we only otherwise see in the *Heimat*.

However, as Rentschler argues, the narrative and editing logic of the city section fundamentally expresses Tonio's dislocation and alienation in New York through unmotivated cuts between spatially unrelated locations: "[...] the overall editing pattern of the Manhattan sequence shows Toni confused and floundering, wandering aimlessly in space" (Rentschler 1984: 608-609). This is certainly true. Tonio, however, is a tourist. From this perspective, the choice of locations arguably reads a little like a tourist itinerary and the editing logic could equally express the experience of a foreign city for any traveller who visits one sight after another without any real comprehension of their spatial interrelationship. Perhaps, then, the choice of locations (as well as the proto-neorealist quality of the cinematography) in the Manhattan section has as much to do with the narrative of hardship in the *Fremde* as with Trenker's desire to document his extratextual enjoyment of New York.[15]

The series of locations and spectacular vistas and constructions that motivate visual consumption in the city are complemented by night-time sequences where electric advertising creates another landscape of consumption, one which, as Janet Ward argues, had been the most spectacular aspect of the modern metropolis:

> the great era of electric advertising helped make the major urban centers of the 1920s [...] into something far more than the sum of their buildings. Manhattan in particular inspired Weimar producers of architecture: Mendelsohn, for example, in his transatlantic photobook homage, America (1926), waxes in an ecstatic

---

[15] Trenker's enthusiasm for New York is evident in his account of shooting this section of the film (1979: 294-301).

commentary on the "light circus" of the New York metropolis with its "texts of flames," its "rocket fires of moving electric advertisements diving up and down, disappearing and exploding over the thousands of cars and the merry rush of people". (Ward 2001: 110-111)

Consumption is also offered in the windows of the butcher shops and eateries through which Tonio longingly looks. With no job and no money however, Tonio cannot afford the products in the store window. Downtrodden, he experiences the alienation of modernity that makes him long for the *Heimat*. He plays out the modern tourist's yearning for home.

While there are clear markers of market relations and production on the surface of the city, the commodification and objectification of nature in the *Heimat*, produced as it is by the cinematic apparatus, must also inevitably be present on the 'surface':

> [...] modernity's store window and silver screen share perhaps not so much a calm process of seeing and deciding, as enthrallment: both consumer and filmgoer are captivated by the image behind the transparent pane – ultimately driven to suspend disbelief enough to feel a need for the product [...] (Ward 2001: 221)

Ultimately New York – the epitome of modern space – is the explicit coalescence of constructed place and of spectacular advertisement. It is the mirror image of nature in the *Heimat* as a cinematically constructed product.

Considering the intertextual and textual discourses in *The Prodigal Son*, it is not necessarily inevitable that 'nature' and 'modernity', and their related constellations of ideas, necessarily occupy distinct, discreet, and opposing spheres in the film. Neither is it clear that the film, in its oscillation between a picture-postcard approach to the *Heimat* and a formalist one, manifests a reactionary over-identification with, or over-determination of, nature. These ideas are underpinned by a limited conception of the interrelationship of the human with nature, one which overlooks both what is beneficial in this interrelationship and what is detrimental in abandoning it.

In his work, Raymond Williams suggests that nature is a locus for a sense of place and shared identity, and that in the practice of rooted settlement a space for a politically radical relationship to the earth and others is possible:

It is by working and living together, with some real place and common interests to identify with, and as free as may be from external ideological definitions, whether divisive or universalist, that real social identities are formed. (Williams 1983: 196)

In theory these politics of place could be realised in the *Heimat*.[16] However it is a truism that the *Heimat* of Germany under National Socialism was burdened with 'external ideological definitions'. The ideology that tends to be read into *The Prodigal Son* is that of blood and soil racialist nationalism and anti-modernism. I would suggest however that *Heimat* in the film is both different from and more than this. It is a literal product of modernity that paradoxically promises an escape from modern ills. This film's spectacular and euphoric cinematography as well as its picture-postcard evocation of the rural idyll, conceal market relations and instrumentalism that conceivably sell the blood and soil *Heimat* and certainly, as much as the fascist nationalism of blood and soil ideology, make no space for a democratic, inclusive, and ecological connectedness of people and land.

Bibliography

Balázs, Béla. 1992. 'Der Fall Dr. Fanck' in *Film und Kritik* 1: 4-7.

Beindorf, Claudia. 2001. *Terror des Idylls. Die kulturelle Konstruktion von Gemeinschaften in Heimatfilm und Landsbygdsfilm 1930-1960*. Baden-Baden: Nomos.

Birgel, Franz A. 2000. 'Luis Trenker: A Rebel in the Third Reich? *Der Rebell, Der verlorene Sohn, Der Kaiser von Kalifornien, Condottieri*, and *Der Feuerteufel*' in Reimer, C. Robert (ed.) *Cultural History through a National Socialist Lens: Essays on the Cinema of the Third Reich*. Rochester, New York: Camden House. 37-64.

Brandlmeier, Thomas. 1984. 'Arnold Fanck' in Bock, H. M. (ed.) *Cinegraph. Lexikon zum deutschsprachigen Film*. Munich: edition text + kritik.

Dyer, Richard. 1985. 'Entertainment and Utopia' in Nichols, Bill (ed.) *Movies and Methods: An Anthology. Vol. 2*. Berkeley and London: University of California Press. 220-232.

Eagleton, Terry. 2000. *The Idea of Culture*. Oxford: Blackwell.

---

[16] The inclusive possibilities, envisaged by Williams, of living together locally are realised to some degree in the much maligned post-war *Heimatfilm* (King 2003).

Elsaesser, Thomas. 2000. *Weimar Cinema and After: Germany's Historical Imaginary*. London: Routledge.

Enzensberger, Hans Magnus. 1996. 'A Theory of Tourism' in *New German Critique*, Special Issue on Literature, 68 (Spring-Summer): 117-135.

Frow, John. 1991. 'Tourism and the Semiotics of Nostalgia' in *October* 57 (Summer): 123-151.

Garrard, Greg. 2004. *Ecocriticism*. London and New York: Routledge.

Hartman, Geoffrey H. 1997. *The Fateful Question of Culture*. New York: Columbia University Press.

Hoffmann, Kay. 2001. 'Rhythmus, Rhythmus, Rhythmus! Avantgarde & Moderne im Faschismus' in von Keitz, Ursula and Kay Hoffmann (eds). *Die Einübung des dokumentarischen Blicks. Fiction Film und Non Fiction Film zwischen Wahrheitsanspruch und expressiver Sachlichkeit 1895-1945*. Marburg: Schüren. 169-191.

King, Alasdair. 2003. 'Placing Green Is the Heath (1951): Spatial Politics and Emergent West German Identity' in Halle, Randall and Margaret McCarthy (eds). *Light Motives: German Popular Film in Perspective*. Detroit: Wayne State University Press. 130-147.

Kracauer, Siegfried. 1947. *From Caligari to Hitler*. Princeton: Princeton University Press.

Lyssa, Fred. 1934. 'Filmreise nach New York. Beobachtungen und Erlebnisse' in *Der Film* 39.

Milner, Andrew. 2001. 'Theorise This! Globalising Theory and the Politics of Identity.' Unpublished lecture notes. Monash University, Melbourne.

— 2002. *Re-Imagining Cultural Studies: The Promise of Cultural Materialism*. London: Thousand Oaks.

Nenno, Nancy P. 2003. '"Postcards from the Edge": Education to Tourism in the German Mountain Film' in Halle, Randall and Margaret McCarthy (eds). *Light Motives: German Popular Film in Perspective*. Detroit: Wayne State University Press. 61-84.

Rapp, Christian. 1997. *Höhenrausch: Der deutsche Bergfilm*. Vienna: Sonderzahl.

Rentschler, Eric. 1984. 'How American Is It? The U.S. as Image and Imaginary in German Film', *The German Quarterly* 57(4): 603-620.

— 1996a. *The Ministry of Illusion: Nazi Cinema and its Afterlife*. Cambridge: Harvard University Press.

— 1996b. 'Mountains and Modernity: Relocating the Bergfilm' in Ginsberg, Terri and Kirsten Moana Thompson (eds). *Perspectives on German Cinema*. New York: G. K. Hall. 693-713.

Soper, Kate. 1995. *What is Nature? Culture, Politics and the non-Human*. Oxford: Blackwell.

Trenker, Luis. 1979. *Alles gut gegangen. Geschichten aus meinem Leben. Neuauflage*. [New ed.] München: C. Bertelsmann.

Von Moltke, Johannes. 2002. 'Evergreens: The Heimat Genre' in Bergfelder, Tim Erica Carter, and Deniz Göktürk (eds). *The German Cinema Book*. London: BFI. 18-28.

Ward, Janet. 2001. *Weimar Surfaces: Urban Visual Culture in 1920s Germany.* Berkeley, Los Angeles and London: University of California Press.

White, Iain Boyd. 1994. 'The Sublime' in Hartley, Keith et al. (eds). *The Romantic Spirit in German Art 1790-1990.* London: South Bank Centre.

Williams, Raymond. 1963. *Culture and Society 1780-1950.* Harmondsworth: Penguin.

— 1973. *The Country and the City.* New York: Oxford University Press.

— 1983. *Towards 2000.* London: Chatto and Windus.

— 1988. *Keywords: A vocabulary of culture and society.* London: Fontana.

Heidegger and Merleau-Ponty: Ecopoetics and the Problem of Humanism

Louise Westling

Abstract

Addressing problems of humanism and hierarchy in Heidegger's concept of dwelling, this essay will attempt to show how Merleau-Ponty , in dialogue Heidegger, restores humans to their place within the living world of Brute or Wild Being that transcends us. Rather than seeing humans as the only beings capable of *Dasein*, the only ones for whom Being comes into presence as Heidegger does, Merleau-Ponty asserts the plenitude of Being active within the whole flesh of the world. For him, 'dwelling' would be an intertwining within an historical unfolding congruent with biological evolution and the insights of modern physics. Creativity is then the unfolding, ever novel form of Being which includes earth and its denizens, as well as the cosmos. A post-humanist ecological ethics can be shaped from Heidegger's ideas of the 'saving grace' possible in human caring, but adapted according to Merleau-Ponty's perspective, to participate within the larger community of kindred beings in our biosphere, who also may be understood as having agency and sentience.

Jonathan Bate's final chapter in *The Song of the Earth* offers Martin Heidegger's late philosophy as an ecopoetics. Heidegger describes poetry – and thus literature more generally – as the presencing of Being that overrides dualism and idealism, grounds human beings, and allows them to save the earth (2000: 262). Other writers such as Australian poet Martin Harrison and philosopher Michael Zimmerman have also found Heidegger a central thinker for the emerging ecological consciousness. Zimmerman explains that Heidegger shows how poetry "embodies nature as ontological difference, thereby granting things their own self-defining outline" (1994: 130-131). But Heidegger's involvement with National Socialism and reactionary German modernism have led Zimmerman to question the degree to which his philosophy offers an adequate understanding of the human place in the world and poetry's ecological possibilities (1990: xvi-xxi; 1994: 121). Bate also raises the question of Heidegger's political past but sidesteps its consequences by recourse to a poem of Paul Celan (2000: 263-273). I propose that a reactionary Humanism led Heidegger to retreat from the consideration of humans as animal members of the biotic community, and thus to reject the consequences of evolutionary thought. Maurice Merleau-Ponty, in productive dialogue with Heidegger's thought, developed an embodied ontology that similarly relies upon interrogative epistemology and recourse to poetic language. However, Merleau-Ponty's writings imply a very different political orientation – not a hierarchical one like Heidegger's, that places humans (and only an elite group of humans) in a superior position at an abyssal remove from all other life, but instead a lateral relationship with the animal and plant communities in which humans have co-evolved. Thus Merleau-Ponty's embodied phenomenology offers an alternative, genuinely ecological view of the human situation and poetry's function.

Both Heidegger and Merleau-Ponty are heirs of Edmund Husserl's phenomenology. Husserl began to recognize one hundred years ago the bankruptcy of the Cartesian and Kantian heritage of Humanism. Three overlapping generations are represented here: Husserl who lived from 1859 to 1938 and was Heidegger's mentor and friend; Heidegger born in 1889 and living until 1976; and Merleau-Ponty born in 1908 but living only until 1961. Their work opened a new direction for Western philosophy, and it provides a crucial grounding for ecological thought and for ecocriticism. Husserl called for a return to the body and concentration upon immediate lived experience, but he never could abandon the concept of transcendent mind (idealism). Heidegger and Merleau-Ponty developed Husserl's picture of humans as dynamically engaged in an unfolding temporal reality, and both claim the language of poetry as the proper language for interrogating that situation. As Charles Taylor says, "one might claim some preeminence for Heidegger, in that he got there first. In the case of Merleau-Ponty, the breakthrough is plainly built on Heidegger's work" (1993: 317). But for all his profound radicalism, Heidegger remained bound within a deeply Eurocentric frame of reference and grounded his philosophy upon a cultural nostalgia for classical Greece which gives it originary status. This tendency is part of what led some of his critics in the 1930s to find idealism hovering in the background of his work. He was anti-Darwinist, antagonistic to science, and a believer in a virtually sacred human superiority and separateness among living creatures. Although Merleau-Ponty continued to think in dialogue with both Husserl's and Heidegger's work throughout his life, he broke away from that kind of hierarchical view. He insisted on taking embodiment seriously, while Heidegger evaded doing so, and that made all the difference. Merleau-Ponty's work is engaged and congruent with twentieth-century science. He assumed that humans co-evolved with all other life forms, and he embraced a profound human kinship with animals which Heidegger found appalling. Brute or Wild Being was for Merleau-Ponty the very ground of human life as he explained in his final, posthumously-published book: "This environment of brute existence and essence is not something mysterious: we never quit it, we have no other environment" (1968: 116-117).

In order to understand this perspective, we should review the general context for Heidegger's and Merleau-Ponty's work, look more closely at the appeal of Heidegger's philosophy for ecocriticism and at some key problems in Heidegger's definition of the human. We should consider positions Merleau-Ponty shares with Heidegger, and finally examine how Merleau-Ponty moved in a new direction that fulfilled Husserl's intention of turning to the body and dissolving the illusion of its separation from mind. Such a refutation of traditional subject/object, spirit/matter, mind/body dualisms reinstates human beings within the living community and explains their intertwining with animal and vegetable kindred.

In an essay called 'The Philosophy of Existence,' Merleau-Ponty described the philosophical milieu in which his generation developed, clarifying that important period for us today. He explained that during the 1920s, the period of his generation's formal education in France, Bergson's influence was waning while a neo-Kantian idealism dominated philosophical training. But during the 1930s he and his contemporaries discovered Husserl, Jaspers, Heidegger, and Gabriel Marcel – the philosophers of existence who emphasized "a completely different theme, that of *incarnation*" (1992: 132). Instead of considering the body as an object, as Western philosophy had done since the Greeks, these philosophers began to realize that we are given our experiences through our flesh, and therefore we need to examine "this sensible and carnal presence of the world" (1992: 132). The new philosophy of existence initiated by Husserl was not only a theme, Merleau-Ponty explained, but really a new style of philosophizing that explored mysteries rather than attempting to analyse clearly defined problems. In this new mode, the philosopher "is not spectator in relation to the problem, but is rather caught up in the matter, which for him defines the mystery" (1992: 133).

Heidegger's attention to Being became the dominant focus among 'the philosophers of existence'. The concept of human dwelling on the earth was central to his articulation of a distinctively human relation to Being, *Dasein*. In 1951 he asked, "What is the state of dwelling in our precarious age?" (1975: 161). In a group of lectures composed around this time he sought in the figures of myth and poetry some "saving power" that would lead to a new way of understanding humanity's position in an age of technology. He was concerned with many of the questions that trouble us today, such as modern humanity's sense of homelessness, the quality of our being in relation to earth and sky, the need for humans to care for the world and respect its spaces, denizens, and things. He lamented the collapsing of distances caused by airplane travel, the draining out and flattening of experience by television, and the loss of rootedness in earthly life brought by space travel (Guignon 1993: 55). As we have seen, many environmental philosophers and critics of literature have found this thinking suggestive of hopeful grounds for a new, environmentally responsible consciousness. "For Heidegger," Jonathan Bate explains,

> language is the house of being; it is through language that unconcealment [of Being] takes place for human beings. By disclosing the being of entities in language, the poet lets them be. That is the special, the sacred role of the poet. (2000: 258).

And poetic dwelling is the distinctive way humankind inhabits the earth.

Heidegger's confidence in poetry as giving access to full Being is indeed heartening in an era of diminishing respect for literature and the other arts. It accords with the way many think about the power of environmentally focussed writing to lead to fuller ecological consciousness. But a closer look at his essays from the late 1940s and early 1950s, such as the 'Letter on Humanism' (1947), 'Building, Dwelling, Thinking' (1951), and 'The Question Concerning Technology' (1953), where the concept of careful dwelling is set out, reveals a troubling humanistic elitism (1977). Heidegger grants sentience and agency *only* to humans. For him, humans are not animals. Rather, they are closer to the 'divine' than they are to other animals in the fourfold 'unity' of divinities, mortals, earth, and sky. For Heidegger, man dwells poetically, but "dwelling" also means building and thinking, shaping the things that create meaningful locations in space. Only men and women (and only *some* of them) can "dwell", can be the beings for whom Being comes into presence. That is because *Dasein* is by definition only possible for humans: it results from a kind of self-consciousness made possible by language. As he explained in the 'Letter on Humanism,' "What man is – or, as it is called in the traditional language of metaphysics, the 'essence' of man – lies in his ek-sistence" (1977: 205). This means that

> man occurs essentially in such a way that he is the 'there' [*das*, '*Da*'], that is, the lighting of Being. The 'Being' of the *Da*, and only it, has the fundamental character of 'ek-sistence', that is, of an ecstatic inherence in the truth of Being (1977: 205).

Heidegger resists placing humans fully within the living community, in an anti-Darwinian recoiling from an acknowledgment of our kinship with animals and plants. This human exceptionalism is also an implicit denial of embodiment, for it is our bodies that most obviously link us with the other animals:

> Of all the beings that are, presumably the most difficult to think about are living creatures, because on the one hand they are in a certain way most closely related to us, and on the other are at the same time separated from our ek-sistent essence by an abyss. However, it might also seem as though the essence of divinity is closer to us than what is foreign in other living creatures, closer, namely, in an essential distance which however distant is nonetheless more familiar to our ek-sistent essence than is our appalling and scarcely conceivable bodily kinship with the beast. Such reflections cast a strange light upon the current and therefore always still premature designation of man as *animal rationale*. Because plants and animals are lodged in their respective environments but are never placed freely in the lighting of Being which alone is "world", they lack language. But in being denied language they are not thereby suspended worldlessly in their

environment. Still, in this word "environment" converges all that is puzzling about living creatures. In its essence language is not the utterance of an organism; nor it is the expression of a living thing. Nor can it ever be thought in an essentially correct way in terms of its symbolic character, perhaps not even in terms of the character of signification. Language is the lighting-concealing advent of Being itself. (1977: 206)

The problem of bodily kinship with animals leads Heidegger to seek refuge in a kind of neo-Platonic spiritual realm of Being which reveals itself in human language, which is not the utterance of an organism or living thing. But even that does not seem an adequate distinction for him. The question continues to trouble him so that he sets even the human body apart from the animal realm, stating in a later work, "The human body is something essentially other than an animal organism" (1977: 204). What might seem parallel limbs and abilities in other animals are not so. For Heidegger, the human hand is a unique marker of the human. Apes may have organs that can grasp, but they do not have hands, because only a being who can speak and thus think, can have hands and achieve works of handicraft (1968:16).

Given this essentially separate status which seems to reinstate the traditional mind/body dualism, Heidegger's view of human destiny suggests the kind of dominance assumed in traditional Humanism. It is clearly implied in his distinctive concept of "dwelling," set forth in 'Building, Dwelling, Thinking'. Human dwelling means acting upon the world, as Heidegger explains in a complicated argument based on German etymology. Delving into the Old High German backgrounds of the verb *bauen*, 'to build', he determines that its archaic meaning was derived from *bin*, 'to be' and synonymous with the concept of dwelling, 'to remain, to stay in place'. Thus:

The way in which you are and I am, the manner in which we humans *are* on the earth, is *buan*, dwelling. To be a human being means to be on the earth as a mortal. It means to dwell. The old word *bauen*, which says that man *is* insofar as he *dwells*, this word *bauen*, however, *also* means at the same time to cherish and protect, to preserve and care for, specifically to till the soil, to cultivate the vine. Such building only takes care – it tends the growth that ripens into its fruit of its own accord. Building in the sense of preserving and nurturing is not making anything. [But he goes on to include the constructing of things such as ships and houses, also as "comprised within genuine building"]. (1977: 325)

From a practical ecological perspective, this position fails to acknowledge the historical evolution of agriculture as involving the manipulation of wild plants to make them serve human purposes, and the tilling of the soil which disrupts the normal diversity of microorganisms and patterns of water retention and plant diversity. Although attractive in its positive sense of human interrelationship with plants and the soil, this argument also suffers from being grounded in the linguistic contingency of one particular European community.

In a passage describing the function of a bridge as exemplary of building, we see very clearly how in Heidegger's view, dwelling means building human structures that give meaning to place. He writes about the bridge as if from outside the scene, playing what Donna Haraway calls "the god trick," of seeing from everywhere and nowhere, not from any situation within the world. This is a framed image, picturesque in the bad sense:

> The bridge swings over the stream "with ease and power". It does not just connect banks that are already there. The banks emerge as banks only as the bridge crosses the stream. The bridge designedly causes them to lie across from each other [...] The bridge *gathers* the earth as landscape around the stream. Thus it guides and attends the stream through the meadows [...] Even where the bridge covers the stream, it hold its flow up to the sky by taking it for a moment under the vaulted gateway and then setting it free once more [...] The bridge *gathers* to itself in *its own* way earth and sky, divinities and mortals [...] Thus the bridge does not first come to a location to stand in it; rather, a location comes into existence only by virtue of the bridge. (1977: 330-332)

For Heidegger, therefore, building is a human intervention in Nature, a shaping dwelling that gives meaning to place, gathering the "fourfold unity" of Being and caring for the world. This dwelling does not really seem to occur within the normal state of nature, but instead to intervene somehow from outside it.

Such a view reasserts the Humanist elevation of humans to a semi-divine status essentially distinct from the rest of creation. This is the kind of *hubris*, or arrogance, that David Ehrenfeld has blamed for the present environmental crisis. While there is no doubt that humans have an enormous impact upon the global environment, and corresponding responsibilities for restraining or mitigating that impact Heidegger's claims of human uniqueness are problematic in the light of evolutionary biology, cognitive neuroscience, and the last century's work in physics. When, exactly, did humans diverge from their co-evolved living kin and become capable of *Dasein*? With Lucy, or the newest fossil finds in South Africa? With *homo habilis*? At the time of the cave paintings in Combray, or those at Lascaux? Or during the Neolithic period when they began to manipulate plant and animal reproduction and build megaliths like Stonehenge and Newgrange? Or with the first written languages of Sumer and China? For that matter, when does an individual human person become capable of *Dasein*? At three or so, when language is acquired? At ten, the traditional Catholic age of reason? At university when reading Heidegger or Proust? Is the capacity for *Dasein* located in the cerebral cortex only? How is it related to the limbic system? What happens to it when brain lesions result from wounds, and particular mental capacities are lost? How is *Dasein* related to the relativity and uncertainty of our knowledge of Nature, which became apparent as twentieth-century physics developed?

Let us leave these questions hovering, and turn to Maurice Merleau-Ponty. As previously stated, Merleau-Ponty shared many of the emphases of Heidegger's approach to Being. Some of the most important of these are:

1. Anti-dualistic, anti-Cartesian efforts which are common among twentieth-century philosophers and owe much to Husserl's understanding that Cartesian science had reached a dead end.

2. The importance of horizons, growing out of the fact of each person's situatedness in place and time, so that there is no possibility of a God-like survey. Instead, our horizons are always changing as our position does, and thus we are limited to temporary and partial perspectives.

3. Letting things be – openness to Being and things in themselves without efforts to control.

4. Emphasis on questioning – philosophy as interrogation.

5. Emphasis on poetic language as the most appropriate to knowing, to philosophy.

In spite of these similarities of emphasis, Merleau-Ponty avoided Heidegger's humanistic elitism by embracing the body and erasing the heritage of dualism. Merleau-Ponty centrally engaged Husserl's call to return to things themselves. He explained in *Phenomenology of Perception* that to do this "is to return to that world which precedes knowledge, of which knowledge always *speaks* [...]" In relation to that world, any attempt at objective knowledge "is an abstract and derivative sign-language, as is geography in relation to the countryside in which we have learnt beforehand what a forest, a prairie, or a river is" (1962: ix). We encounter that world as bodies; indeed, he claims, "we are our body" (1962: 206). Meaning is dynamic, participatory bodily attunement to the world in the particular situations where we find ourselves at any given moment: "The points in space do not stand out as objective positions in relation to the objective position occupied by our body; they mark, in our vicinity, the varying range of our aims and our gestures. To get used to a hat, a car, or a stick, is to be transplanted into them, or conversely, to incorporate them into the bulk of our body" (1962: 143). This interconnection of bodies with the world is profound:

> The subject of sensation is neither a thinker who takes note of a quality, nor an inert setting which is affected or changed by it, it is a power which is born into, and simultaneously with, a certain existential environment, or is synchronized with it. The relations of sentient to sensible are comparable with those of the sleeper to his slumber: sleep comes when a certain voluntary attitude suddenly receives from outside the confirmation for which it was waiting. (1962: 211)

Things and qualities radiate around themselves "a certain mode of existence" and cast a spell over us because "the sentient subject does not posit them as objects, but enters into a sympathetic relation with them, makes them his own and finds in them his momentary law" (1962: 214). According to this view, there is no clear distinction between subject and object, or mind and body, or each of us and the things around us. By implication there is no such separation between humans and Nature.

The acknowledgment of this kind of embodiment requires a radical reorientation of common assumptions about what it means to be human. *Phenomenology of Perception* is a painstakingly careful exploration of this reorientation, one that relies heavily on Gestalt psychology and cognitive neuroscience of the 1930s and early 1940s, especially studies of the effects on cognition of brain lesions caused by accidents and wounds of various sorts. The work of cognitive neuroscientists since Merleau-Ponty's death in 1961, particularly in the past couple of decades when brain imaging has become more and

more sophisticated, fully supports the embodied description of mind
that Merleau-Ponty set forth in that 1947 book. An ambitious recent
philosophical study that brings such assumptions up to date and links
them with the past several decades of cognitive neuroscience is
George Lakoff and Mark Johnson's *Philosophy in the Flesh* (1999).

Merleau-Ponty went on to develop the ontological consequences of
embodiment and the interrelation of subject and world in the book he
was writing when he suddenly died. It was published posthumously as
The Visible and the Invisible, remaining in the rough and fragmentary
form he left behind. Even so, this draft manuscript and the appendix of
Working Notes clearly define a radical new view of the human place,
our bodies intertwining with the flesh of the world in a plenitude of
emergent being. As he had already demonstrated in *Phenomenology of
Perception*, Merleau-Ponty insists that knowledge is situated. He calls
for an abandonment of the search for essences, acknowledgment of
ambiguity, and a radical openness to the wildness of being. In his
view, culture is variably and specifically situated within an
environment of wildness:

> In short, there is no essence, no idea, that does not adhere to a domain of history
> and of geography. Not that it is *confined* there and inaccessible for the others, but
> because, like that of nature, the space or time of culture is not surveyable from
> above, and because the communication from one constituted culture to another
> occurs through the wild region wherein they all have originated [...] We never
> have before us pure individuals, indivisible glaciers of beings, nor essences
> without place and without date. Not that they exist elsewhere, beyond our grasp,
> but because we are experiences, that is, thoughts that feel behind themselves the
> weight of the space, the time, the very Being they think, and which therefore do
> not hold under their gaze a serial space and time nor the pure idea of series, but
> have about themselves a time and a space that exist by piling up, by proliferation,
> by encroachment, by promiscuity – a perpetual pregnancy, perpetual parturition,
> generativity and generality, brute essence and brute existence, which are the
> nodes and antinodes of the same ontological vibration. (1968: 115)

To define this relationship, he used the term *Chiasm*, from the Greek
letter **X**, suggesting crossing over. He also used the French word
entrelacs, which in English means 'intertwining'. This concept
extends the notion of embodiment to include the entire world:
"Everything said about the sensed [and sentient] body pertains to the
whole of the sensible of which it is a part, and to the world". If this is
so, he asks, "Where are we to put the limit between the body and the

world, since the world is flesh?" (1968: 138). But what is this flesh? It is not matter,

> is not mind, is not substance. To designate it, we should need the old term 'element,' in the sense it was used to speak of water, air, earth, and fire, that is, in the sense of a *general thing*, midway between the spatio-temporal individual and the idea, a sort of incarnate principle that brings a style of being wherever there is a fragment of being. The flesh is in this sense an 'element' of Being (1968: 139).

Within the flesh of the world our bodies participate in constant dynamic reciprocity and reversibility, both touching and touched:

> Now why would this generality, which constitutes the unity of my body, not open it to other bodies? The handshake too is reversible; I can feel myself touched as well and at the same time as touching [...] Why would not the synergy exist among different organisms, if it is possible within each? Their landscapes interweave, their actions and their passions fit together exactly: this is possible as soon as we no longer make belongingness to one same "consciousness" the primordial definition of sensibility, and as soon as we rather understand it as the return of the visible upon itself, a carnal adherence of the sentient to the sensed and of the sensed to the sentient. (1968: 142)

This is a coiling over of the visible and the sensible upon the seeing and sensing body.

Similarly, there is a reversibility, an intertwining, and a coiling over of the visible and the invisible which explains the bond between the flesh and the idea,

> between the visible and the interior armature which it manifests and which it conceals. No one has gone further than Proust in fixing the relations between the visible and the invisible, in describing an idea that is not the contrary of the sensible, that is its lining and its depth. (1968: 149)

Here, Merleau-Ponty indicates the crucial role of language – and for our purposes, it is important to note that it is especially poetic language in the widest sense – in helping us grasp the intertwining of the visible and the invisible doubleness of the flesh of the world. Where Heidegger claimed that language was not "the utterance of an organism or the expression of a living thing" (1977: 206), for Merleau-Ponty, it is corporeal, intertwined with the flesh of the world. In *Phenomenology of Perception* he had spoken of its physical, gestural[,] qualities that are especially apparent in poetry, and he said that "the words, vowels and phonemes are so many ways of 'singing' the world [...]" (1962: 187):

> Like the flesh of the visible, speech is a total part of the significations, like it, speech is a relation to Being through a being, and like it, it is narcissistic, eroticized, endowed with a natural magic that attracts the other significations into its web, as the body feels the world in feeling itself [...] If speech, which is but a region of the intelligible world, can be also its refuge, this is because speech prolongs into the invisible, extends unto the semantic operations, the belongingness of the body to being and the corporeal relevance of every being [...] (1968: 118)

In a world in which, for Merleau-Ponty, "the whole landscape is overrun with words", philosophy must see itself as restoring a power to signify. It must seek "a birth of meaning, or a wild meaning". And in a sense, as Valéry said, "language is everything, since it is the voice of no one, since it is the very voice of the things, the waves, and the forests" (1968: 155). Joseph Margolis explains that such a view opposes Heidegger's notion of

> the *Kehre* by which pure structureless noumenal Being 'speaks' in its own 'language' to certain gifted human mediums. Merleau-Ponty means here to assign thought and speech – *as it determinately obtains in our perceived world* – to the entire 'body' of the 'world's' flesh (1992: 253).

Garth Gillan goes even further, to say that for Merleau-Ponty, "[the] Being of language is that of the flesh," called forth by "the surfeit of meaning in the sensible world". The experience of language is that of "a truth lived in the thick and embroiling relations we have with others", and is thus groping, emotionally turbulent, giving our contact with ideas through language a savage quality (1973: 56-57).

Although Merleau-Ponty never quite came to the point of acknowledging animal sentience, he was moving in that direction (Abram 1988: 101-120). In *Nature*, notes from his courses at the Collège de France during the last three years of his life, he gets very close indeed, and these were the same years when he was writing *The Visible and the Invisible*. In *Nature*, Merleau-Ponty quotes Konrad Lorenz as saying that no one familiar with animals would deny consciousness to them, but he himself merely asks if that is so, up to what point it is so? (2003: 199). Though he continues to see humans as different from the other animals, Merleau-Ponty describes a lateral, not a hierarchical relationship (2003: 268), and makes a long, careful survey of the philosophical significance of evolution (as well as quantum physics and developmental biology) to show that we never lose the parenting/kinship out of which we developed. In *The Visible and the Invisible*, his Working Notes speak of the "man-animal intertwining" and "the order of brute or wild being which, ontologically, is primary" (1968: 200). Indeed, "even the cultural rests on the polymorphism of the wild Being" (1968: 253). These gnomic comments bring to mind Gary Snyder's more recent assertion of basic human wildness and embodiment in essays like 'The Etiquette of Freedom', where he describes wild, instinctive reactions like "the involuntary, quick turn of the head at a shout [... or] the heart-in-the-throat in a moment of danger"(1990: 16). Merleau-Ponty's notions of intertwining and the coiling up of the world upon itself within an environment of Brute or Wild Being require the kind of kinship and continuum of sentience increasingly assumed in ecological thought.

As Heidegger says, humans should care for the earth, and poetry – or literature more broadly – is a central human way of dwelling. But Heidegger's notion that humans are the shepherds of Being (1977: 221) is too darkly shadowed by the instructions of Yahweh to Adam in the Genesis story. Because, for Heidegger, humans have exclusive access to language and the presencing of Being, the human species remains, for him, much as it was for Pico della Mirandola and all the early Humanists – closer to divinity than other living creatures, in a privileged position in a hierarchy of authority and agency. As the planet grows warmer and species extinction gathers speed, it is all too obvious where the presumptions of human superiority and domination are leading. Following Gary Snyder, I would challenge that traditional view, by acknowledging full human membership in the wild community of life. Poetry and culture would then be understood as Merleau-Ponty defined them – part of embodied being and the human intertwining within the flesh of the world.

Bibliography

Abram, David. 1988. 'Merleau-Ponty and the Voice of the Earth' in *Environmental Ethics* 10: 101-120.
Bate, Jonathan. 2000. *The Song of the Earth.* Cambridge: Harvard University Press.
Biehl, Janet and Peter Staudenmaier. 1995. *Ecofascism: Lessons from the German Experience.* San Francisco: A.K.
Ehrenfeld, David. 1978. *The Arrogance of Humanism.* New York: Oxford.
Euripides. 1978. *The Bakkhai* (tr. R. Bagg). Amherst: University of Massachusetts.
Farías, Victor. 1989. *Heidegger and Nazism.*(tr. P. Burrell and G.R. Ricci). Philadelphia: Temple.
Gillan, Garth. 1973. 'In the Folds of the Flesh' in Garth, Gillan (ed.) *The Horizons of the Flesh: Critical Perspectives on the Thought of Merleau-Ponty.* Carbondale: Southern Illinois University. 1-77.
Guignon, Charles B. (ed.). 1993. *The Cambridge Companion to Heidegger.* New York: Cambridge University Press.
Haraway, Donna. 1991. 'Situated Knowledges: The Science Question in Feminism and the Privilege of Partial Perspective.' *Simians, Cyborgs, and Women.* New York: Routledge. 183-201.
Heidegger, Martin. 1977. *Basic Writings.* (ed. D. F. Krell). San Francisco: Harper.
— 1968. *What Is Called Thinking?* (tr. Harper and Row Publishers, Inc.). New York: Harper.
— 1975. *Poetry, Language, Thought.* (tr. A. Hofstadter). New York: Harper.
Lakoff, George, and Mark Johnson. 1999. *Philosophy in the Flesh.* New York: Basic Books.
Liddell, H. G. and Robert Scott. 1987. *An Intermediate Greek-English Lexicon.* Oxford: Oxford University Press.
Margolis, Joseph. 1992. 'Merleau-Ponty and Postmodernism' in Busch, T. W. and S. Gallagher (eds). *Merleau-Ponty, Hermeneutics, and Postmodernism.* Albany: State University of New York. 241-256.
Merleau-Ponty, Maurice. 1962. *Phenomenology of Perception.* London: Routledge.
— 1964. *Signs.* (tr. R.C. McCleary). Evanston: Northwestern University.
— 1968. *The Visible and the Invisible.* (ed. Claude Lefort; tr. Alphonso Lingus) Evanston: Northwestern University.
— 1992. *Texts and Dialogues/Maurice Merleau-Ponty.* (ed. and with Intro. by H. J. Silverman and J. Barry, Jr.). New Jersey : Humanities.
— 2003. *Nature: Course Notes from the Collège de France.* (tr. R. Vallier. Compiled and with notes by D. Séglard). Evanston: Northwest University.
Neske, Günter and Emil Kettering. 1990. *Martin Heidegger and National Socialism.* (tr. L. Harries, with an Introduction by K. Harries). New York: Paragon House.

Plumwood, Val. 1996. 'Nature, Self, and Gender: Feminism, Environmental Philosophy, and the Critique of Rationalism,' in Warren, Karen (ed.) *Ecological Feminist Philosophies.* Bloomington: Indiana University. 155-180.

Shepard, Paul. 1982. *Nature and Madness.* San Francisco: Sierra Club.

Snyder, Gary. 1990. *The Practice of the Wild.* New York: North Point.

Sophocles. 1977. *The Oedipus Cycle.* (tr. D. Fitts and R. Fitzgerald). New York: Harcourt.

Taylor, Charles. 1993. 'Engaged Agency and Background in Heidegger' in Guignon, C. B. (ed.) *The Cambridge Companion to Heidegger.* New York: Cambridge University. 317-336.

Zimmerman, Michael. 1990. *Heidegger's Confrontation with Modernity.* Bloomington: Indiana University.

— 1994. *Contesting Earth's Future.* Berkeley: University of California.

Notes on Contributors

Fiona Becket is Senior Lecturer in English Literature at the University of Leeds. She is author of *D. H. Lawrence: The Thinker as Poet* (Macmillan, 1997) and *The Complete Critical Guide to D. H. Lawrence* (Routledge, 2002) and is currently completing a book on literature and the environment.

Hannes Bergthaller is an assistant professor at National Taipei University of Technology and an adjunct lecturer at Tamkang University, both in Taiwan, where he teaches English and American literature. His book *Populäre Ökologie: Zu Literatur und Geschichte der modernen Umweltbewegung in den USA* (*Popular Ecology: On the Literature and History of the Modern Environmental Movement in the U.S.*) was published in 2007.

Greg Garrard is Lecturer in English at Bath Spa University College and Chair of the Association for Studies in Literature and Environment in the UK. Author of *Ecocriticism* (Routledge, 2004), he has written on Heidegger, Heaney, Wordsworth, Thoreau, Lawrence and pastoral literature.

Terry Gifford is Visiting Professor at the University of Chichester, UK and Profesor Honorario, University of Alicante, Spain. He is the author of *Reconnecting With John Muir: Essays in Post-Pastoral Practice* (University of Georgia Press, 2006), *Pastoral* (Routledge, 1999) and *Green Voices: Understanding Contemporary Nature Poetry* (Manchester University Press, 1995).

Axel Goodbody is Reader in German Studies in the Department of European Studies and Modern Languages at the University of Bath. His research is concerned with twentieth-century German literature and film, ecocritical theory and cultures of memory. He was President of the European Association for the Study of Literature, Nature and Culture from 2004 to 2006.

Graham Huggan is Chair of Commonwealth and Postcolonial Literatures in the School of English at the University of Leeds, and founding co-director of the university's cross-disciplinary Institute for Colonial and Postcolonial Studies (ICPS). He is the author of, among others, of *Territorial Disputes* (U Toronto P, 1994), Peter Carey (Oxford UP, 1996), *Tourists with Typewriters* (U Michigan P, 1998, with Patrick Holland), and *The Postcolonial Exotic* (Routledge, 2001). Forthcoming work includes books on Australian literature (for Oxford UP), contemporary travel/travel writing (for U Michigan P), and postcolonial literatures, animals and the environment (for Routledge, with Helen Tiffin).

Matthew Jarvis is now a full-time father in Aberystwyth. In spare moments he is a freelance writer and critic, and is currently working on a book for the University of Wales Press called *Welsh Environments in Contemporary Poetry*.

Guinevere Narraway is a Research Associate at Goldsmiths, University of London. She received her PhD from Monash University, Melbourne in 2007. Her thesis, entitled 'Making Nature: Visions of Mastery in Third Reich Cinema,' undertakes an examination of the reason/nature dualism in film under National Socialism.

John Parham teaches media theory and research methods at Thames Valley University, London. He has published on pedagogy and environmental value, edited *The Environmental Tradition in English Literature* (Ashgate, 2002), and is writing a book on Gerard Manley Hopkins and 'humanist ecocriticism', also for Rodopi's 'Nature, Culture and Literature' series.

Val Plumwood is Australian Research Council Fellow at the Australian National University, Canberra and author of *Feminism and the Mastery of Nature* (Routledge, 1993) and *Environmental Culture: The Ecological Crisis of Reason* (Routledge, 2002). She has lived in her forest house outside Braidwood, NSW, since 1974.

Gillian Rudd is a Senior Lecturer in the School of English at The University of Liverpool. She has recently published *Greenery: Ecocritical Readings of Late Medieval English Texts* (Manchester University Press, 2007) and is currently writing a series of essays on the natural world in medieval literature, focusing particularly on clouds and flowers.

Judith Rugg is Reader in Fine Art Theory at the University College for the Creative Arts, Canterbury. Her other publications include: 'Maternal Loss, Transitional Space and the Uncanny in Alison Marchant's *Kingsland Road, London-East'* in *Textile Journal of Cloth and Culture* (Summer, 2005) and 'Sophie Calle's *Appointment* at The Freud Museum, London: Intervention or Irony?' in *New Practices, New Pedagogies*, Malcolm Miles, ed. (Routledge, 2005).

Judith Tucker is a painter and lecturer in the School of Design at the University of Leeds. From 2003- 6 she was AHRC Research Fellow in the Creative and Performing Arts at Leeds. She is co-convenor of LAND2, a research network of artists associated with Higher Education who are concerned with radical approaches to landscape with a particular focus on memory, place and identity. She exhibits regularly both in the UK and elsewhere in Europe.

Louise Westling is Professor of English and Environmental Studies at the University of Oregon. She is author of *The Green Breast of the New World: Landscape and Gender in American Fiction* (University of Georgia Press, 1996). Recent essays include 'Literature, the Environment, and the Question of the Posthuman' and 'Darwin in Arcadia: Brute Being and the Human Animal Dance from Gilgamesh to Virginia Woolf'.

Index

Lightning Source UK Ltd.
Milton Keynes UK
UKOW051643280312
189773UK00001B/365/A